ITALY
Today
THE BEAUTIFUL COOKBOOK

Contemporary recipes reflecting simple, fresh Italian cooking

Radish, Apple and Provolone Cheese Salad (recipe page 103)

ITALY
Today
THE BEAUTIFUL COOKBOOK

Contemporary recipes reflecting simple, fresh Italian cooking

RECIPES BY
LORENZA DE' MEDICI

TEXT BY
FRED PLOTKIN

FOOD PHOTOGRAPHY BY
PETER JOHNSON

FOOD STYLED BY
JANICE BAKER

SCENIC PHOTOGRAPHY BY
STEVEN ROTHFELD

CollinsPublishers
A Division of HarperCollinsPublishers

First published in the USA in 1997
by Collins Publishers
10 East 53rd Street, New York, NY 10022
http://www.harpercollins.com

Produced by Weldon Owen Inc.
814 Montgomery Street, San Francisco, CA 94133
Chairman: Kevin Weldon
President: John Owen
Publisher: Wendely Harvey
Associate Publisher: Tori Ritchie
Editor: Hannah Rahill
Copyeditor: Sharon Silva
Proofreaders: Desne Border, Ken DellaPenta, Sharilyn Hovind
Indexer: Ken DellaPenta
Recipe Translator: John Meis
Pre-Production: Stephanie Sherman
Designer: Tom Morgan, Blue Design
Assistant Designer: Brenda Rae Eno
Design Assistant: Eleanor Reagh
Illustrations: Marlene McLoughlin
Map Illustrations: Kenn Backhaus
Calligraphy: Kathy McNicholas
Scenic Photographer: Steven Rothfeld
Food Photographer: Peter Johnson
Food Stylist: Janice Baker
Photographer Assistants: Mil Truscott, Robert White
Food Stylist Assistants: Cara Hobday, Liz Nolan, Amanda Biffin

Library of Congress Cataloging-in-Publication Data
De' Medici Stucchi, Lorenza, 1926–
Italy today the beautiful cookbook / recipes by Lorenza de'
Medici ; text by Fred Plotkin ; food photography by Peter
Johnson ; styled by Janice Baker ; scenic photography by
Steven Rothfeld.
         p.   cm.
      Includes index.
      ISBN 0-00-225053-5
      1. Cookery, Italian. 2. Italy—Description and
      travel.
      I. Plotkin, Fred. II. Title.
      TX723.D4277   1997   96-27506
      641.5945—dc20   CIP

Printed in China
A Weldon Owen Production

Endpapers: Olive groves line a terraced hillside near Greve in Chianti in Tuscany.

Pages 2–3: The medieval towers of San Gimignano have made this hilltown one of Tuscany's most popular destinations.

Right: A Venetian gondoliere takes a break from navigating the canals.

Pages 8–9: Clockwise from top: Braided Bread with Cumin Seeds (recipe page 214); Cheese Bread Crown (recipe page 218); Rosemary Breadsticks (recipe page 221); Crackers with Sesame Seeds (recipe page 218)

Pages 10–11: With the cathedral of Pisa in shadow, the legendary tower seems to tilt into the sun.

Pages 14–15: Along the coast of Liguria, five charming towns are linked by a single footpath. Called Cinqueterre, their hillsides are covered with fragrant herbs and lush vineyards, as seen here near Riomaggiore.

Left to right: Pecorino Cheese and Fava Bean Salad (recipe page 43); Tomato and Mozzarella Salad with Arugula (recipe page 99);
Yellow Peppers and Fennel with Cumin Seeds (recipe page 99)

Contents

The quiet grandeur of an old-growth olive grove bears testament to the importance of this fruit in the Italian diet.

Introduction

COOKING AND EATING IN ITALY TODAY

Today, the food of Italy is still one of the world's most popular and most imitated. While dishes from other countries may periodically come into vogue, people everywhere continue to eat and cook in the Italian manner. Why is this so?

La cucina italiana thrives because its practitioners understand and respect each ingredient they use. This has always been the case and it remains so today. While cooks in other countries may attempt to blend or transform ingredients, Italians believe that their job is to exalt each individual flavor and fragrance in a dish. They do this by striving to understand the innate properties of an ingredient: is it better raw or cooked, young or aged, by itself or in combination with other flavors, boiled, braised, baked, broiled or fried?

The genius of Italian cookery is that it can be as simple or elaborate as one wishes, as long as it pleases the eater with its colors, textures, aromas and gratifying taste. Invariably, a sense of *allegria,* of lighthearted happiness, comes with eating an Italian meal.

Yet some people consider Italian dishes too heavy or too time-consuming to prepare, and therefore out of step with modern life. In fact, Italian food adapts readily to the way we live now, with the added advantages of great flavor and healthfulness that other kinds of cooking cannot provide. And this is what *Italy Today the Beautiful Cookbook* is all about.

Because the pace of Italian life is accelerating, Italian cooks have begun looking for ways to present traditional flavors more quickly and easily. This does not mean fast food, but rather recipes that use ingredients that are familiar, comfortable and welcome. In other words, there is something old and something new about the food of Italy today: Italians are essentially cooking as they always have, but they are eating in new ways.

In the past, all but poor families would sit down to a meal comprised of a first course *(il primo),* then a second course *(il secondo)* and a vegetable side dish *(il contorno),* followed by a piece of fruit and perhaps a wedge of cheese. Portions would be generous but not overbearing. The traditional beverages were mineral water and local wine. In some cases, an appetizer *(antipasto)* launched the repast and a pastry or pudding *(il dolce)* capped it. In most cases, the appearance of an espresso *(il caffè)* signaled the end of the meal.

Poorer families also sat down together, but typically ate one-course meals of pasta, polenta or rice dressed with locally grown vegetables or whatever inexpensive pieces of meat or fish could be obtained. Bread and a modest wine completed the meal. Coffee was a luxury. The food and portions of less-well-off families came to be thought of abroad as typical Italian dining because those people were the ones who emigrated in search of a better standard of living.

A produce vendor and his friend greet each other warmly in the streets of Bologna, reputed by many to be Italy's finest eating town.

Radical economic, social and agricultural shifts have wrought changes in the way Italians eat. The country is said to have the world's fifth-largest economy (after the United States, Japan, Germany and France, and ahead of Great Britain), due primarily to the initiative, industriousness and creativity of the Italian people as the nation rose from the ashes of World War II. In Italy today, hunger is an issue that affects few citizens, and most people have the luxury of choosing when and what to eat. They also have access to some of the most divine ingredients a cook could want.

Using herbs, superb olive oils, balsamic and other vinegars, the finest fish and seafood, cheeses, vegetables and fruits, along with judicious amounts of meat and poultry, the modern Italian is able to routinely eat food that is healthful and exquisitely delicious. That is as it always has been. Therefore, the recipes in this book, both classics and new innovations, respect the *profumi e sapori*—the fragrances and flavors—of these high-quality ingredients.

On a wall in the Villa dei Misteri in Pompeii, an elegant, colorful fresco is evidence of the sophisticated culture that was buried beneath ashes and lava when Vesuvius erupted in A.D. 79.

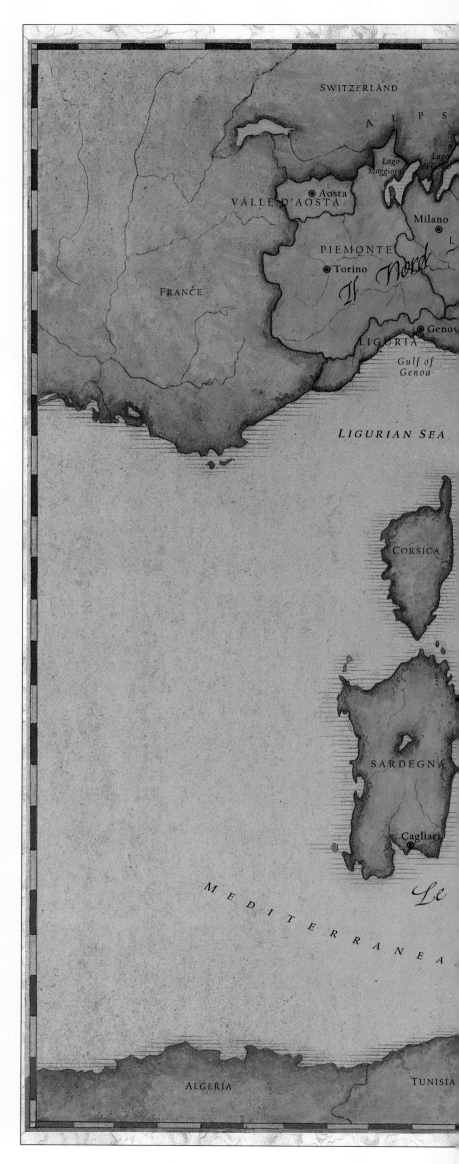

*A view of the expansive Umbrian countryside is glimpsed from behind
a centuries-old tower in the hilltown of Assisi.*

Just a few of Florence's many landmarks are telescoped in one corner of the Piazza della Signoria: a replica of Michelangelo's David, *statues of Hercules and Neptune, the rugged stones of the Palazzo Vecchio, and the tip of Brunelleschi's magnificent Duomo.*

But how and when is this food eaten today? In Italy, it is no longer a given that a family sits down together for a leisurely lunch or dinner. Lunch used to be the traditional family meal, but this is now only the case in rural areas, small towns and parts of the urban south. Italians travel farther to work than they used to, and lunch hours in northern and central Italy are shorter, as the nation has aligned itself with more international trends of commerce. Schoolchildren often grab an Italian version of fast food—a pizza or a *panino* (sandwich)—because their mothers may now be working. So the chief meal in most of Italy today is eaten in the evening, and families are no longer governed by a rigorous sequence of courses from *il primo* to *la frutta*.

Although most Italians have never grappled with obesity, the weight consciousness that has obsessed other nations has arrived. Low-fat foods are now prized in Italy, with one major difference: the vegetables, fruits, pasta and rice that have long been the pillars of the nation's diet are the very foods that diet-conscious people are encouraged to eat. Thus, Italians have not had to make major adjustments in what they consume.

Furthermore, while historically Italians ate mostly what was available to them in their immediate area and, as a result, a strong regionality defined overall Italian cooking, that is somewhat less true today. The

pesto of Liguria is served everywhere from Lombardy to Basilicata. And some dishes blend flavors of many areas—the Gorgonzola of the north topping the pizza of the south, for example—into one very Italian, but not specifically regional, dish. Therefore, not every recipe in this book has a regional designation.

The key change in Italian cooking is that people now eat what they want, when they want, selecting freely from all parts of the traditional standard meal. In some regions, especially Piedmont, Liguria, Emilia-Romagna and Apulia, antipasti have always figured prominently. Nowadays, rather than having them only at the start of a meal, many Italians combine two or three antipasti, to be preceded or followed, perhaps, by a bowl of pasta, rice or soup. It is also increasingly common to make a meal of a bowl of salad greens combined with a simple piece of fish or meat and maybe some sliced fruit. In other words, there is more of a mix-and-match, but one informed by the knowledge most Italians have about how foods go together. Interchangeability is a key to many of the recipes in this book, and the chapters are organized to emphasize that. You should combine flavors, textures and dishes that suit your taste to make the meal of your choice.

This Italian willingness to experiment may seem new, but it is one of the oldest traditions in the nation's kitchen. Many key ingredients in *la cucina italiana* are not native to the peninsula, but were introduced throughout the centuries: rice, corn, many grape varieties, tomatoes, spinach, beans, potatoes, eggplants (aubergines), sweet peppers (capsicums), chilies, codfish, salmon, chicken, turkey, oranges, almonds, sugar, coffee and numerous spices. These foods were all adopted, and made more glorious in the process.

This spirit of innovation has not slackened. When a new ingredient (curry powder, for instance) arrives in Italy, it is usually subjected to traditional Italian cooking

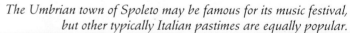

The Umbrian town of Spoleto may be famous for its music festival, but other typically Italian pastimes are equally popular.

In Rome, and throughout Italy, efficient transportation is a must. The trusty motor scooter remains one of the most popular options.

methods designed to bring out its flavor and to see if it fits into Italian dishes. Italians have also become more open to new cooking methods. When roasted garlic became the rage in North America, Italians found ways to employ its distinct flavor and texture on pizzas and in pasta sauces.

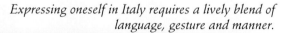

Expressing oneself in Italy requires a lively blend of language, gesture and manner.

It is possible to bemoan this evolution in Italian eating and regard the abandoning of certain old ways as an irretrievable loss. Indeed most industrial societies have seen their eating habits evolve, but not with the grace and refinement that have occurred in Italy. While much of the rest of the world has discarded important old values, Italy reinvents them.

For Italians, eating is still a social event, albeit a more spontaneous one than in the past. Friends, relatives or coworkers decide to eat at a moment that is suitable to them and then eat exactly what they fancy. They can spend more money on a one-course meal or a sublime slice of cheese and a perfect piece of fruit than they would on a traditional repast, so they insist that the quality of everything be first-rate. The ordinary half liter of wine of two decades ago may now be cast aside during daytime hours, to be replaced by a glass of outstanding wine that will enhance the flavors of the foods being eaten. A meal will still be closed with a perfect cup of espresso and perhaps a glass of grappa or limoncello, and that sense of *allegria* will still invariably cast its warm glow over the happy diner.

The food of Italy today awaits you, as wonderful as ever and much more accessible. Here, then, are all the flavors, colors and images that you will want to visit and revisit in your mind's eye and palate, in your kitchen and in your dreams.

At right: Verona by moonlight, seen from the base of the Torre dei Lamberti.

Il Nord-Ovest

GABBIANO

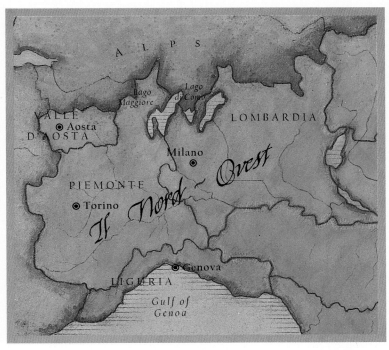

Il Nord-Ovest

LIGURIA, PIEMONTE,
VALLE D'AOSTA, LOMBARDIA

Without a doubt, northwestern Italy is at the cutting edge of recent changes in Italian cooking. This is not surprising, as the area has led Italy in countless ways since the nation was unified in the 1860s. The movement for national unity was guided by royalists in Piedmont, republicans from Liguria and patriots and businessmen from Lombardy. Turin became the united Italy's first capital, and although that role was later ceded to Rome, Piedmont's chief city retains its grandeur. For most of its history, Genoa has been Italy's major seaport, gathering more wealth even if Venice gathered more glory. And Milan, in Lombardy, is the undisputed financial capital of Italy and one of Europe's wealthiest cities.

Northwestern Italy's cities have glorious histories dating back to antiquity. Liguria was a leading trade center of the ancient world and maintained its primacy for centuries. Christopher Columbus, a son of Genoa, sailed to the Americas and changed history. Aside from all of their other accomplishments, the members of Columbian expeditions brought many foods back to the Old World, including tomatoes, corn, zucchini (courgettes), pumpkin, white and green beans, potatoes, sweet peppers (capsicums), chilies, turkey and cacao. The food of Italy would be very different without these ingredients.

Milan has been the trading capital of Italy since the Middle Ages, and other Lombardian and Piedmontese

Previous pages: People and pigeons vie for space in the Piazza del Duomo, the spiritual and social heart of Milan. At left: Wooden boats bob in the waters of Lake Maggiore, which borders Lombardy and Piedmont.

towns have established preeminence in certain industries, such as the silk of Como, the textiles of Biella and the armaments of Brescia. Pavia, which was the capital of the Italian peninsula in the early Middle Ages, created a law school in the ninth century that later became the nucleus for one of the country's top universities. Cremona has always been the international center of violin making and gave birth to Claudio Monteverdi, the first great composer of opera.

Although Turin was a glorious nineteenth-century capital that was the seat of the House of Savoy, in the twentieth century it became the center of the Italian automotive industry, attracting engineers and manual laborers from throughout Italy. It went from being a city of refined graciousness to a metropolis of diverse cultural and gastronomic influences. During the industrial revolution of the late nineteenth century through the so-called Italian economic miracle that lasted until the early 1970s, the triangle formed by Genoa, Milan and Turin was the epicenter of the Italian economy. This was the first place in Italy to shun the leisurely lunch and the first to adopt the business dinner, both of which meant an end to families gathering at the table twice a day. The manual laborer ate from a lunch box or in the company cafeteria, while the executive dined in restaurants but kept an eye on the clock. Not surprisingly, this is the area of Italy where American-style fast food has made its most successful incursions.

Below: Despite the frantic pace in the Northwest, the custom of frequenting a caffè has not been abandoned. At right: A Mediterranean tableau of brightly painted façades, ironwork balconies and wooden shutters characterizes the buildings of Santa Margherita Ligure (Liguria).

In recent years, the Veneto region to the east has become at least as economically dynamic as the northwest, but the Veneto has long had a tradition of delicious "faster" foods such as a wedge of precooked polenta topped with cheese, fish or vegetables. By contrast, the classic dishes of Liguria, Piedmont, the Valle d'Aosta and Lombardy required slower, more methodical preparation, so that in recent years they have been discarded and replaced with a new type of cooking that continues to prize flavor but also pays attention to quicker techniques. This change has been abetted by innovations in *elettrodomestici,* the ingenious kitchen appliances created by the engineers of Milan and Turin that have replaced manual labor in many northwest Italian kitchens, effectively cutting preparation times.

Technological advances have also had an impact on the agriculture of the area. Historically, the region has produced outstanding raw materials, and technology has for the most part been put to good use in increasing yields without affecting quality. The province of Cremona, which produces some of Italy's finest beef, milk and cheese, has the highest agriculture yields in the nation. The valley of Italy's longest river, the Po, extends from Piedmont through Lombardy and into the Veneto and Emilia-Romagna. The western part of the valley boasts the largest cultivation of rice in Europe, so this starch is the most popular first course for most of the area, except in Liguria, where pasta is always preferred. Liguria and southern Piedmont produce some of the most delicious fruits and vegetables in Italy, and Liguria has a bounty of herbs—particularly basil—without rival in terms of fragrance and flavor. Ligurian olive oil is often called the world's best, too. Ligurian basil and oil combine to make pesto, arguably the finest of all pasta sauces. In Liguria, pesto is also added to minestrone, a rich vegetable soup. In this book, you'll find it put to new use as a flavoring in a cold rice salad.

Piedmont is blessed with the glorious white truffles of Alba to shave over pasta or rice. This flavor is further exalted by the region's red wines, including Barolo and Barbaresco, whose only rivals are those of Tuscany, Burgundy, Bordeaux and California. Piedmont also has superb hazelnuts (filberts) and Italy's finest chocolate, and citizens of Turin proudly tell you that their hometown was the birthplace of the chocolate bar.

The chief agricultural products of Lombardy are beef, milk, butter, cheese and rice, all of top quality. Southern Lombardy includes a section of the delimited zone in which Parmigiano-Reggiano cheese may be produced. Other local cheeses include Bitto, mascarpone, Taleggio and stracchino. Although Gorgonzola, one of the world's great blue cheeses, was born in the Lombardy town of that name, most of it is now produced in Novara in Piedmont.

Lombardy's great contribution to modern Italian eating, and one that should not be undervalued, is the *panino.* The translation is "sandwich," which does not fully communicate the sense of the Italian word. At lunch hour in Milan, a *paninoteca* will have a line of office workers snaking out the door, waiting to order a *panino* made with superb bread filled with the best ingredients northern Italy has to offer. A sandwich might contain a

An arcade in Milan's Galleria Vittorio Emanuele, the world's first shopping mall, leads to the Duomo and its famous fountain.

fresh herb frittata, roast veal with sliced truffle, or perhaps Gorgonzola and pears. The genius of this "meal" is that it takes classic food combinations that may normally appear on a plate and puts them between slices of bread. There is no recipe required; let your imagination be your guide. While the *panino* is a revolutionary change in the way people eat, having stripped away social interaction and the time necessary to appreciate food fully, it also indicates that many Italians will not sacrifice excellent ingredients even as they accelerate the pace of their lives.

The Valle d'Aosta remains an anomaly in northwestern Italy. Bordering on France and Switzerland, it is the nation's smallest region in terms of terrain and population (115,000 citizens in a nation of 57 million) and, except for some iron mining, makes all of its money from tourism and agriculture. It is the roof of Europe, embracing Monte Bianco (Mont Blanc), Cervinia (the Matterhorn) and the continent's highest vineyards (2,800 feet/900 m above sea level). The region is fully bilingual, although in rural areas French predominates, while Italian is the language of the towns. Its capital, Aosta, is of Roman origin (the name was Augusta Praetoria). The neat efficiency typical of Alpine areas is encountered throughout, and the friendly citizens welcome visitors with attractive ski resorts and national parks along with hearty food.

The food traditions of the Valle d'Aosta draw from surrounding areas, although the ingredients are largely of local origin. *Mocetta* is meat cured like prosciutto, but instead of pork, the Valdostani use chamois, mountain goat, ibex or veal. Prosciutto is flavored with fourteen mountain herbs, resulting in a taste remarkably different from the hams of other Italian regions. Rather than having first courses based on pasta, rice or cornmeal, the locals favor soups made with such ingredients as chestnuts, walnuts, rice, bread, cinnamon and Fontina cheese. This last, made each day with cow's milk from the region's farms, is a nutty-tasting versatile cheese that is good young or aged and has superb melting properties. Fontina is the heart and soul of *fonduta* (fondue), which can be delicious and warming on a cold winter's night.

The major change in eating that one finds in most of northwestern Italy (except in the Valle d'Aosta) is the abandonment of the traditional structure of an Italian meal. People here are less likely than ever to sit down to an appetizer, first course, second course and dessert, and are more inclined to pause to eat the foods they are interested in trying. In the process they are revolutionizing their approach to dining. The flavors may be fundamentally the same, but the way they are assembled is different. This is not unlike the work of Pablo Picasso (whose ancestors were Ligurian), who could paint someone's portrait but create an entirely new configuration.

So if, in Piedmont, a particular vegetable from an antipasto goes well with a small portion of meat and a piece of cheese that may have once been eaten separately, these foods are likely to find their way onto the same plate and be served with a glass of splendid wine that complements the diverse flavors. Or in Lombardy, where it was once traditional to use only saffron and Parmigiano-Reggiano cheese in risotto, chefs now combine all sorts of ingredients with rice, with results that sometimes set new taste standards that are then imitated around the world.

This tradition of creation through experimentation is the essence of the mentality of northwestern Italy, and the reason the area is on the cutting edge of Italian cooking.

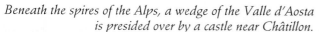

Beneath the spires of the Alps, a wedge of the Valle d'Aosta is presided over by a castle near Châtillon.

Antipasti e Primi

Sweet peppers (capsicums) are offered for sale at the central market in Padua. They add vivid color and lush flavor to numerous antipasti and primi.

Antipasti e Primi

APPETIZERS AND FIRST COURSES

Once upon a time, the *antipasto* and the *primo* were polar opposites in their significance in Italian eating. The antipasto was the delicacy enjoyed before the actual meal, even though it was consumed at the table. It was something special that would titillate the palate and represented an extension of generosity on the part of the host. In other words, the antipasto was intended to make an impression that went beyond flavor into the realm of psychology. Only in Piedmont and Apulia, and to a lesser extent Liguria and Emilia-Romagna, did the appetizer have a role in a typical meal. In the first three regions, the appetizer was largely vegetable based, while in the last it was composed of cured meats.

By contrast, the primo was often the star of the meal. This was the pasta, risotto, polenta or soup that would provide much of the caloric and nutritional content of the repast and was the dish that received the most attention both in the kitchen and at the table. Even when a second course was planned, it was the primo that offered the soul gratification, and the *secondo* was designed to contrast with it.

The greatest revolution in modern Italian eating is that the antipasto has made significant strides in its role in the Italian meal. While it has not usurped the primo (and probably never will), it has now presented a strong challenge to the secondo. The nature of the antipasto has changed, however, from a mouth pleaser to a smaller version of many secondi with adaptations to modern taste.

While pasta has been made in almost every shape imaginable, colors are a whole new palette for pasta makers today.

Previous pages: Clockwise from left: Risotto with Spinach (recipe page 62); Rice and Beans with Basil (recipe page 66); Grilled Polenta with Radicchio (recipe page 53)

will never go out of style, many cooks now seek more dramatic flavors that both enhance the ubiquitous pasta or rice and play off the antipasto. So a vegetable-based antipasto may lead to a meat-based pasta sauce, and vice versa. An herb used in an antipasto may reappear as the dominant note in a risotto or pasta sauce. If fish is an element in the antipasto, shellfish might be employed in the primo.

Primi dressed with seasonal porcini are now among the most popular preparations in Italy. Diners in other countries can make acceptable adaptations of these dishes at any time by using imported Italian dried mushrooms. Vegetable sauces, light and quickly made, often replace long-simmered toppings on pasta. These flavors are a perfect follow-up to nearly any antipasto that precedes them.

More and more Italians are eating meals composed only of an antipasto and a primo, especially at lunch. In this brave new world of Italian eating, is the secondo threatened with extinction? Hardly. The difference is that as the balance has shifted to the antipasto, the secondi have become lighter, but no less flavorful.

At a restaurant in the small Tuscan town of Montefollonico, the art of making homemade ravioli is preserved.

In Reggio-Emilia, a cheese maker shows the interior of a perfectly aged Parmigiano-Reggiano. Spade-shaped knives are used to pry loose chunks of the cheese.

It is now possible, for example, to have an antipasto of goose or duck breast cooked, perhaps, with balsamic vinegar or fruit and served with carefully selected greens, a dish that may once have come in a larger portion as a secondo. Similarly, a frittata that typically followed a bowl of soup or spaghetti may now appear first, this time containing herbs, cheese, mushrooms or even leftover pasta. In customary fashion, it will be served at room temperature and sliced into wedges.

If a vegetable-based antipasto is still preferred, it may no longer simply be sliced seasonal vegetables or those cured in oil or vinegar. Rather, it might be vegetables prepared in a tart, mold or salad, or stuffed and baked. Antipasti that combine meat or fish and vegetables are also increasingly popular. Starches, including beans or cold boiled potatoes, are popular foils for fish and seafood, requiring only to be tossed with fresh lemon juice and superb extra-virgin olive oil. And many recipes can serve dual purposes, either as a vegetable antipasto or as a *contorno* (side dish).

In response to the overall rise in status of the antipasto, many primi have become more elaborate. This does not imply bigger portions, but rather a desire to dress pasta or rice with fancier ingredients. While a perfectly prepared dish of spaghetti with tomato sauce

SPAGHETTI AL TONNO

Spaghetti with Tuna

If you remember to keep these basic ingredients on hand, this dish can be prepared in no time at all for unexpected guests. Romans add reconstituted dried porcini mushrooms to this classic central Italian recipe. You can vary it by adding tomatoes.

¾ cup (6 fl oz/180 ml) extra-virgin olive oil
2 large yellow onions, chopped
10 oz (300 g) ripe plum (Roma) tomatoes, peeled and
   chopped, or canned tomatoes, chopped, with their juice
   (optional)
1 can (8 oz/240 g) olive oil–packed tuna, drained and
   broken into small pieces

½ cup (4 fl oz/120 ml) dry white wine
leaves from 1 bunch fresh flat-leaf (Italian) parsley, chopped
2 lb (1 kg) spaghetti

In a large, deep saucepan over medium heat, warm the oil. Add the onions and cook, stirring, until translucent, about 3 minutes. Add the tomatoes, if desired, and tuna, stir well and pour in the white wine. Cook over medium heat, stirring occasionally, for about 10 minutes. Remove from the heat and sprinkle with the parsley.

Meanwhile, bring a large pot filled with salted water to a boil. Add the pasta, stir well and cook until al dente. Scoop out a ladleful of the pasta water and reserve.

Drain the pasta and pour it into the saucepan with the tuna. Add the ladleful of pasta water, mix well and warm over low heat for no more than a couple of minutes. Transfer to a warmed bowl and serve immediately.

SERVES 10

pinch of red pepper flakes
⅓ cup (2½ fl oz/80 ml) extra-virgin olive oil
¼ cup (2 fl oz/60 ml) heavy (double) cream
2 lb (1 kg) orecchiette or other small dried pasta shape
½ cup (2 oz/60 g) grated Parmesan cheese
½ cup (2 oz/60 g) grated Romano cheese
salt

✑ Bring a large saucepan filled with salted water to a boil. Add the broccoli rabe and cook until tender, about 10 minutes. Drain well and set aside.

✑ In a large, deep saucepan over medium heat, warm the garlic and the pepper flakes in the oil. When the garlic begins to take on color, after about 3 minutes, add the broccoli rabe and cook over medium heat, stirring occasionally, until well browned, about 10 minutes.

✑ Reduce the heat to very low and slowly add half of the cream, mixing well. Cook for another 3 minutes, stirring occasionally.

✑ Meanwhile, bring a large pot filled with salted water to a boil. Add the pasta, stir well and cook until al dente. Scoop out a ladleful of the pasta water and reserve.

✑ Drain the pasta and pour it into the saucepan that holds the broccoli rabe. Add the ladleful of pasta water, the remaining cream and the grated cheeses. Taste and adjust with salt. Warm over low heat, mixing gently, until the sauce blends thoroughly with the pasta, just a couple of minutes. Transfer to a warmed bowl and serve immediately.

SERVES 10

Sicilia

CONCHIGLIE CON SALSA DI COZZE E POMODORI

Conchiglie with Mussel and Tomato Sauce

This is a classic sauce of the Mediterranean. Mussels are among the most flavorful fruits of the sea and well worth the patience required to clean them.

¼ cup (2 fl oz/60 ml) extra-virgin olive oil
2 cloves garlic, smashed
2 lb (1 kg) ripe plum (Roma) tomatoes, peeled and chopped
salt and freshly ground pepper
4 lb (2 kg) mussels, scrubbed and debearded
1¼ lb (600 g) conchiglie or other small dried pasta shape

✑ In a saucepan over medium heat, warm the oil. Add the garlic and cook, stirring occasionally, until it begins to take on color, about 3 minutes. Discard the garlic and add the tomatoes. Cover and cook over medium heat, stirring occasionally, until the sauce thickens, about 30 minutes. Season to taste with salt and pepper.

✑ Meanwhile, place the mussels with the water clinging to them in a large frying pan, cover and cook over high heat until the shells open, about 3 minutes. Remove from the heat. Extract the mussels from the shells, discarding any that did not open. Discard the shells. If the mussels are small, leave them whole; if they are large, chop into pieces.

✑ Meanwhile, bring a large pot of salted water to a boil. Add the pasta, stir well and cook until al dente.

✑ Meanwhile, add the mussels to the sauce and cook over low heat for a couple of minutes to blend the flavors. Drain the pasta and transfer to a warmed bowl. Dress with the sauce, toss well and serve immediately.

SERVES 6

Clockwise from top: Conchiglie with Mussel and Tomato Sauce; Orecchiette with Broccoli Rabe; Spaghetti with Tuna

Campania

ORECCHIETTE CON I RAPINI

Orecchiette with Broccoli Rabe

Although this dish is typical of the region of Apulia, it is also popular in Naples. In southern Italy it is made with the tender local vegetable known as friarielli, *as shown in the photograph. Broccoli rabe* (rapini) *works just as well. Apulian cooks often make orecchiette, small ear-shaped pasta, at home and serve them fresh.*

2 lb (1 kg) broccoli rabe, tough stems removed
2 cloves garlic, chopped

Campania

VERDURE ALL'ACCIUGATA
Vegetables with Anchovy Sauce

A Neapolitan variation on the Tuscan appetizer known as pinzimonio, this dish, composed of vegetables, toast, pecorino cheese and a pleasantly pungent dipping sauce, makes an excellent beginning to a summer luncheon. Sometimes I serve it as a main course, surrounded with slices of hard-cooked egg. The cheese can be served in strips or left whole and cut into chunks with a cheese knife at the table.

4 olive oil–packed anchovy fillets, drained
1 cup (8 fl oz/240 ml) extra-virgin olive oil
4 cloves garlic, chopped
1 tablespoon chopped fresh basil
1 tablespoon chopped fresh flat-leaf (Italian) parsley
1 tablespoon drained capers, chopped
1 tablespoon red wine vinegar
1 red bell pepper (capsicum), seeded
1 yellow bell pepper (capsicum), seeded
1 cucumber, peeled
6 slices coarse country bread, toasted
10 oz (300 g) pecorino cheese
2 ripe tomatoes
1 fennel bulb
1 bunch celery
6 green (spring) onions (optional)

In a bowl, using a fork, mash the anchovy fillets with 1 tablespoon of the olive oil. Add the garlic, basil, parsley, capers, vinegar and the remaining oil and mix well. Cut the bell peppers, cucumber, bread slices and, if desired, cheese into narrow strips. Cut the tomatoes into wedges. Cut off the fennel tops and discard or reserve for another use; cut the bulb lengthwise into slices. Separate the stalks from the celery bunch and cut into long pieces. If using green onions, trim but leave whole.

Arrange the cut vegetables on a large platter, alternating them with the green onions, if using, and the toast and cheese. Place the bowl of sauce alongside for dipping the vegetables and other ingredients.

SERVES 6

Toscana

MINESTRA DI CARCIOFI E POMODORI
Artichoke and Tomato Soup

The best artichokes for this soup are the very small, young ones known as morellini, so tender you can eat them raw, but they are difficult to find outside of Italy. Look for the smallest artichokes available. If you use large artichokes, the tough outer leaves and the "beard" near the core must be removed.

juice of 1 lemon
6 artichokes (see note)
6 tablespoons (3 fl oz/90 ml) extra-virgin olive oil
3 cloves garlic, chopped
1 bay leaf
10 oz (300 g) ripe plum (Roma) tomatoes, peeled and chopped, or canned tomatoes, chopped, with their juice
6 cups (48 fl oz/1.5 l) light vegetable stock (see recipe for light meat or chicken stock on page 40)
salt and freshly ground pepper
1 tablespoon fresh thyme leaves

Fill a bowl with cold water and add the lemon juice. Cut off the top one-third of each artichoke, cut off the stem even with the bottoms and then cut or snap off the tough outer leaves. Using a sharp spoon, dig out the chokes and discard. As each artichoke is trimmed, place it in the lemon water to prevent discoloring. When they have all been trimmed, drain, dry and thinly slice crosswise.

In a soup pot over medium heat, warm the oil. Add the garlic and cook, stirring, until translucent, about 3 minutes. Add the artichokes and bay leaf and cook for a few minutes. Add the tomatoes and stock, mix well, reduce the heat to low, cover and cook until the artichokes are tender and the flavors have blended, about 30 minutes longer.

Remove and discard the bay leaf and season to taste with salt and pepper. Transfer to a warmed tureen, sprinkle with the thyme and serve immediately.

SERVES 6

Artichoke and Tomato Soup

Veneto

Risotto con Funghi Secchi

Risotto with Dried Mushrooms

Dried porcini mushrooms give risotto a robust flavor. This dish is appealing served surrounded by veal rolls stuffed with sage and ham (recipe on page 184). To make this a vegetarian risotto, substitute vegetable stock for the meat stock, using the directions included in the recipe for light meat stock.

1 oz (30 g) dried porcini mushrooms
6 cups (48 fl oz/1.5 l) light meat stock (recipe below)
3 tablespoons unsalted butter
3 tablespoons extra-virgin olive oil
2 cloves garlic, chopped
3⅓ cups (1¼ lb/600 g) Arborio rice
½ cup (4 fl oz/120 ml) dry white wine
6 tablespoons (1½ oz/45 g) grated Parmesan cheese
2 tablespoons finely chopped fresh flat-leaf (Italian)
    parsley
salt and freshly ground pepper

In a small bowl, soak the mushrooms in warm water to cover for 30 minutes. Drain the mushrooms and strain the water through a fine-mesh sieve lined with cheesecloth (muslin). Set aside. Squeeze out any excess moisture from the mushrooms. Chop coarsely and set aside.

Pour the stock into a saucepan, bring to a boil and adjust the heat to maintain a low boil.

In a saucepan over medium heat, warm the butter and oil. Add the garlic and cook, stirring, until translucent, about 3 minutes. Add the rice and cook, stirring frequently, until the rice is warm and coated with the butter and oil, about 3 minutes. Add the mushrooms and their filtered water and cook over medium heat, gradually adding the wine and allowing it to evaporate before adding more. Add 1 or 2 ladlefuls of the stock, enough just to cover the rice, and cook, stirring frequently but not constantly. As the liquid is absorbed, add a little more of the simmering stock, again stirring frequently. Continue to add the stock in this manner, making sure the rice is always covered with a veil of liquid. After about 15 minutes from the moment the stock is first added, the rice should be tender but firm and the risotto should flow but not be runny.

Add the Parmesan cheese and parsley and mix well. Season to taste with salt and pepper. Allow the risotto to rest for 2 minutes, then serve immediately.

SERVES 6

Lombardia

Zuppa di Pane e Lattuga

Bread Soup with Lettuce

Typically, a bread soup from Lombardy would consist of bread and cabbage or just bread and broth. Lettuce is a recent addition. If you want to thin this soup, add a little milk just before serving. It can be prepared with vegetable stock, if you prefer; follow the directions included in the recipe for light chicken stock.

1¼ lb (600 g) butter (Boston) lettuce (2 or 3 heads)
6 tablespoons (3 fl oz/90 ml) extra-virgin olive oil
4 cloves garlic, chopped
6 cups (48 fl oz/1.5 l) light chicken stock (recipe at right)

salt and freshly ground pepper
10 oz (300 g) coarse country bread, sliced and lightly toasted

Core the lettuce heads and cut the leaves into thin strips. In a soup pot over medium heat, warm the oil. Add the garlic and cook, stirring, until translucent, about 3 minutes. Add the lettuce, cover and cook until wilted, about 2 minutes. Add the stock, bring to a boil and boil for about 10 minutes to blend the flavors. Season to taste with salt and pepper.

Place the bread in a soup tureen or divide it among individual bowls. Pour the lettuce and stock over the bread and serve immediately.

SERVES 6

Brodo Leggero di Carne o Pollo

Light Meat or Chicken Stock

Italian stock is very light, but flavorful. When light stock is called for in various recipes in this book, this is the stock required. A light vegetable

Clockwise from left: Bread Soup with Lettuce; Risotto with Dried Mushrooms; Light Meat or Chicken Stock; Rice, Potato and Parsley Soup

stock can be made from this recipe by omitting the chicken or beef and adding more vegetables. Adding a tomato will give the stock slightly more color. You could also use other herbs such as thyme, basil or sage.

1 beef brisket or whole chicken, about 2 lb (1 kg)
2 celery stalks, sliced
1 small yellow onion, sliced
2 carrots, sliced
1 zucchini (courgette), sliced
handful of fresh flat-leaf (Italian) parsley
1 bay leaf
1 teaspoon peppercorns
3 qt (3 l) cold water
salt and freshly ground pepper

☞ Place the beef or chicken in a deep pot with all of the vegetables, the parsley, bay leaf and peppercorns. Add the water and bring to a boil. Reduce the heat, skim off any foam that forms on the surface, cover with the lid ajar and simmer gently until the liquid has been reduced by half, about 2 hours.
☞ Strain the stock, let cool to room temperature and refrigerate to solidify the fat on the surface.
☞ Lift off the fat and reheat the stock. Season to taste with salt and pepper. Pour into soup cups and serve, or use in recipes as directed. Any leftover stock should be frozen in ice-cube trays and the cubes stored in plastic bags for ease of use.

MAKES ABOUT 6 CUPS (48 FL OZ/1.5 L); SERVES 6

ℒ o m b a r d i a

MINESTRA DI RISO, PATATE E PREZZEMOLO

Rice, Potato and Parsley Soup

Typically Lombardian, this satisfying soup is perfect for last-minute guests because it goes together quickly and is pleasing to the eye. For an unexpected touch, I substitute fresh cilantro (fresh coriander) for the parsley.

¼ cup (2 oz/60 g) unsalted butter
3 boiling potatoes, peeled and thinly sliced
1⅔ cups (10 oz/300 g) white rice
6 cups (48 fl oz/1.5 l) light meat stock (recipe at left)
2 tablespoons finely chopped fresh flat-leaf (Italian) parsley
salt

☞ In a deep saucepan over low heat, melt the butter. Add the potatoes and cook, stirring frequently, until half-cooked, about 5 minutes. Add the rice and stir well for a couple of minutes to coat with the butter. Pour in the stock and bring to a boil. Cook until the rice is tender yet firm to the bite, about 16 minutes.
☞ Mix in the parsley and season to taste with salt. Ladle into warmed bowls and serve immediately.

SERVES 6

CROSTONI DI MOZZARELLA
Grilled Bread with Mozzarella

The ingredients of this simple recipe are staples of the region of Campania, the countryside around Naples. These crostoni make an easy-to-prepare first course or perfect antipasto. Or they can be transformed into a main dish simply by placing a fried egg on top.

4 ripe tomatoes, peeled and seeded
salt
6 slices coarse country bread, each ½ in (1 cm) thick
10 oz (300 g) mozzarella cheese, thinly sliced
6 olive oil–packed anchovy fillets, drained and roughly chopped
6 tablespoons (3 fl oz/90 ml) extra-virgin olive oil
1½ teaspoons chopped fresh oregano
freshly ground pepper

Dice the tomatoes and place in a colander set over a bowl. Sprinkle with salt and set aside to drain for about 30 minutes.

Preheat a broiler (griller). Place the bread slices on a broiler pan (tray) and broil (grill), turning once, until lightly golden on both sides, just a few minutes. Remove from the broiler. Cover each bread slice with mozzarella, top with anchovy pieces and then a layer of tomatoes. Return to the broiler until the cheese begins to melt, about 5 minutes.

Arrange the crostoni on a platter, drizzle evenly with the oil and sprinkle with the oregano and pepper to taste. Serve very hot.

SERVES 6

INSALATA DI PECORINO CON LE FAVE
Pecorino Cheese and Fava Bean Salad

This very Tuscan dish, a specialty of the restaurant at Badia a Coltibuono, is composed of a saladlike mixture served over grilled bread. Offer it as an appetizer or a first course. It can be enjoyed for only two months of the year in Italy, May and June, when vegetable stalls are overflowing with tender young fava beans that can be eaten straight from the pod. Older, larger beans have to be peeled and do not work for this dish.

3 lb (1.5 kg) young, tender fava (broad) beans
6 slices coarse country bread, each ½ in (1 cm) thick
1 clove garlic
10 oz (300 g) slightly aged pecorino cheese, diced
salt and freshly ground pepper
½ cup (4 fl oz/120 ml) extra-virgin olive oil

Preheat a broiler (griller).

Shell the fava beans. Place in a bowl and set aside. Place the bread slices on a broiler pan (tray) and broil (grill), turning once, until lightly golden on both sides, just a few minutes. Remove from the broiler and when cool enough to handle, rub one side of each bread slice with the garlic clove. Place the slices, garlic side up, on individual plates.

Add the cheese to the favas and toss. Season to taste with salt and pepper. Cover the bread slices with the fava mixture, dividing it evenly. Drizzle the oil over the tops and serve.

SERVES 6

Left to right: Grilled Bread with Mozzarella; Pecorino Cheese and Fava Bean Salad

Campania

Linguine con Peperoni e Origano
Linguine with Peppers and Oregano

Peppers and pasta are a satisfying combination evocative of the south. For a last-minute sauce, use jarred peppers packed in olive oil. Look for them in any Italian food store. Traditionally, cheese is not added to this pasta.

4 yellow or red bell peppers (capsicums)
1¼ lb (600 g) linguine
½ cup (4 fl oz/120 ml) extra-virgin olive oil
1 tablespoon dried oregano
salt and freshly ground pepper

✍ Preheat an oven to 350°F (180°C).
✍ Cut the bell peppers in half lengthwise and discard the stems, seeds and ribs. Place skin down on a baking sheet (tray) and bake until tender, about 40 minutes. Remove from the oven and place in a paper bag. Close tightly and let steam for about 10 minutes to loosen the skin. Using your fingers, peel off the skin and cut the bell peppers into long, narrow strips.
✍ Bring a large pot of salted water to a boil. Add the pasta, stir well and cook until al dente. Drain and transfer to a warmed bowl. Add the oil, oregano, bell peppers and salt and pepper to taste and toss well. Serve immediately.

SERVES 6

Risotto al Pepe Verde
Risotto with Green Peppercorns

Green peppercorns have recently found their place in the Italian kitchen. They combine perfectly with a traditional risotto. Remember that risotto should be all'onda, or "wavy," that is, still moist, and it must be served and eaten as soon as it is ready. Vegetable stock can be substituted for the meat stock; follow the directions included in the light meat stock recipe.

8 cups (64 fl oz/2 l) light meat stock (recipe on page 40)
½ cup (4 oz/120 g) unsalted butter
1 white onion, chopped
3⅓ cups (1¼ lb/600 g) Arborio rice
½ cup (4 fl oz/120 ml) dry white wine
3 tablespoons green peppercorns
½ cup (2 oz/60 g) grated Parmesan cheese
salt

✍ Pour the stock into a saucepan, bring to a boil and adjust the heat to maintain a low boil.
✍ In another saucepan over low heat, melt half of the butter. Add the onion and cook, stirring frequently, until translucent, about 3 minutes. Add the rice, raise the heat to medium and cook, stirring frequently, until the rice is warm and coated with the butter, about 3 minutes. Pour in the wine

Clockwise from top: Little Bread and Mushroom Gnocchi; Linguine with Peppers and Oregano; Risotto with Green Peppercorns

and cook the mixture until the wine has evaporated. Add 1 or 2 ladlefuls of the stock, enough just to cover the rice, and cook, stirring frequently but not constantly.
✍ As the liquid is absorbed, add a little more of the simmering stock, again stirring frequently. Continue to add the stock in this manner, making sure the rice is always covered with a veil of liquid. About 10 minutes after the first addition of stock, stir in the green peppercorns. Continue to add the stock and stir the rice until the rice is tender but firm and the risotto flows but is not runny. This should take about 15 minutes from the moment the stock is first added.
✍ Remove from the heat and stir in the Parmesan cheese and the remaining butter. Season to taste with salt and cover the pan. Allow the risotto to rest for 2 minutes, then serve immediately.

SERVES 6

Veneto

Gnocchetti di Pane e Funghi Secchi
Little Bread and Mushroom Gnocchi

In the mountains of the northern Veneto, wild mushrooms grow abundantly. Much of the crop is dried for use year-round. It is essential to use at least two-day-old coarse country bread or the gnocchi dough will not hold together properly. Potatoes can be substituted for the bread: boil 2 pounds (1 kg) until tender, drain, peel and pass through a ricer.

3 eggs
1 lb (480 g) coarse dried bread crumbs
½ cup (4 fl oz/120 ml) milk
salt and freshly ground pepper
2 oz (60 g) dried porcini mushrooms
1 tablespoon extra-virgin olive oil
1 small yellow onion, chopped
1 cup (4 oz/120 g) all-purpose (plain) flour
6 tablespoons (3 oz/90 g) unsalted butter
grated Parmesan cheese (optional)

✍ In a bowl, whisk the eggs for 1 minute to blend fully. Add the bread crumbs and the milk and season to taste with salt and pepper. Set aside for about 30 minutes to allow the crumbs to absorb the liquid.
✍ Soak the mushrooms in warm water to cover until soft, about 30 minutes. Drain, squeeze dry and chop finely.
✍ In a saucepan over low heat, warm the oil. Add the onion and cook, stirring, until translucent, about 3 minutes. Add the mushrooms, cover and allow the flavors to blend for about 10 minutes, stirring occasionally. Remove from the heat and let cool.
✍ Transfer the mushrooms to a deep bowl. Add the bread-egg mixture and ¾ cup (3 oz/90 g) of the flour. Using your hands, mix well. Flour your hands and a work surface with the remaining flour. Form the mixture into balls ¾ in (2 cm) in diameter. As the gnocchi are formed, arrange in a single layer on a floured surface.
✍ Bring a large pot filled with salted water to a boil. Working in batches, add the gnocchi and boil until they float. Using a slotted spoon, lift out the gnocchi, allowing them to drain over the pot. Place on a warmed platter.
✍ Melt the butter in a small saucepan and pour it over the gnocchi. Serve immediately. Pass Parmesan cheese at the table, if desired.

SERVES 6

Coppe di Pompelmo ai Gamberetti

Grapefruit Halves Filled with Shrimp

On summer days when I have guests visiting at Badia a Coltibuono, I often serve this easy dish. I prepare it ahead of time and keep it in the refrigerator for a couple of hours. About half an hour before serving, I bring it out so that it will return to room temperature. It makes a good antipasto or primo.

10 oz (300 g) shrimp (prawns), peeled and deveined
3 grapefruits
1 orange
1 egg yolk
½ cup (4 fl oz/120 ml) extra-virgin olive oil
salt
6 tablespoons (3 fl oz/90 ml) heavy (double) cream
½ fennel bulb, cut into matchstick-sized pieces
freshly ground pepper
6 lettuce leaves

Bring a saucepan filled with water to a boil. Add the shrimp and boil until they turn pink and begin to curl, just a few minutes. Drain and set aside to cool.

porated and a mayonnaise has formed. Season to taste with salt and stir in the orange juice. Then add the cream, fennel and pepper to taste and stir well.

Line each grapefruit cup with a lettuce leaf. Divide the shrimp evenly among the cups and dress with the fennel mayonnaise. Decorate with the reserved orange zest and serve at room temperature.

SERVES 6

Toscana

POMODORI AL TONNO
Tomatoes Filled with Tuna

Traditionally, tomatoes are filled with a tuna and mayonnaise blend, then served as a cold antipasto. This lighter version features capers, parsley and onion and a little oil instead. Serve these tomatoes on a bed of finely chopped lettuce, if you like.

6 large, ripe tomatoes
2 cans (6½ oz/200 g each) olive oil–packed tuna, drained
1 tablespoon drained capers, finely chopped
1 tablespoon fresh flat-leaf (Italian) parsley, chopped
1 small yellow onion, chopped
2 tablespoons extra-virgin olive oil
6 Gaeta or other Mediterranean-style small black olives

Cut a slice off the top of each tomato. Using a spoon, gently scrape out the pulp; be careful not to pierce the sides. Set aside 1 tablespoon of the pulp and reserve the remainder for another use.

Pass the tuna through a food mill placed over a bowl. Add the capers, parsley, onion, oil and the 1 tablespoon tomato pulp to the bowl and mix well.

Spoon the tuna mixture into the hollowed-out tomatoes, dividing it evenly, and place the tomatoes on individual plates. Place an olive on top of each tomato and serve at room temperature.

SERVES 6

INSALATA DI UVA
Grape Salad

This first course suits an elegant dinner at harvesttime, the first days of autumn when the air is still warm. It is also delicious as a main dish for a luncheon, served in more abundant portions. It can be accompanied by slices of prosciutto.

10 oz (300 g) red grapes
10 oz (300 g) white grapes
3 oz (90 g) well-drained small white onions pickled in vinegar
6 oz (180 g) Fontina cheese, cut into matchstick-sized pieces
salt
1 tablespoon Worcestershire sauce
¼ cup (2 fl oz/60 ml) extra-virgin olive oil
freshly ground pepper

Remove the stems from all the grapes; leave the skins and seeds intact, if desired. In a salad bowl, combine the grapes, onions and cheese.

In a cup, mix salt to taste with the Worcestershire sauce, then add the oil and the pepper to taste. Stir well and pour over the salad. Toss gently and serve at room temperature.

SERVES 6

Clockwise from top: Tomatoes Filled with Tuna; Grape Salad; Grapefruit Halves Filled with Shrimp

Cut each grapefruit in half horizontally and, using a spoon, carefully scrape out the pulp to form 6 cups. Set the cups aside. (Reserve the pulp for another use.)

Remove the zest from the orange in narrow strips. Bring a small saucepan filled with water to a boil, add the orange zest and boil for 3 minutes. Drain and set aside to dry. Squeeze the orange pulp and measure out 3 tablespoons juice. Set aside.

In a bowl, using a wooden spoon, beat the egg yolk until blended. Then slowly add the oil, first just a drop at a time, while beating constantly. Once the mixture has begun to emulsify, add the remaining oil in a slow, steady stream, continuing to beat constantly until all the oil has been incor-

Top to bottom: Tagliolini with Small Peas and Fava Beans;
Pasta with Eggplant and Mascarpone

PASTA CON MELANZANE E MASCARPONE

Pasta with Eggplant and Mascarpone

Here, the cuisines of northern and southern Italy are combined,
with the pairing of mascarpone, a classic cheese of Lombardy, and
melanzane—eggplants—characteristic vegetables of the south.

2 eggplants (aubergines), about 1 lb (480 g) total weight
6 tablespoons (3 fl oz/90 ml) extra-virgin olive oil
salt
1 teaspoon freshly ground pepper
1¼ lb (600 g) penne (quills) or other dried pasta shape
½ lb (240 g) mascarpone cheese
½ cup (2 oz/60 g) grated Parmesan cheese

Cut the eggplants into ½-in (1-cm) cubes. Place in a saucepan with the oil and season with salt to taste and the pepper. Cover and cook over very low heat, stirring occasionally, until the eggplant cubes are tender, about 45 minutes.

Bring a large pot filled with salted water to a boil. Add the pasta, stir well and cook until al dente.

While the pasta is cooking, in a saucepan, dilute the mascarpone with ½ cup (4 fl oz/120 ml) of the pasta water. Place over low heat to warm gently; take care that it does not boil.

Drain the pasta and place in a warmed bowl. Top with the mascarpone and the eggplant and toss to mix; serve immediately. Pass the Parmesan cheese at the table.

SERVES 6

TAGLIOLINI CON PISELLINI E FAVE

Tagliolini with Small Peas and Fava Beans

Offer this pasta as a first course followed by fish or meat. It also
stands well on its own as a main dish for a spring luncheon.

6 tablespoons (3 oz/90 g) unsalted butter
1 white onion, finely chopped
1 lb (480 g) young, tender peas, shelled (1 cup/5 oz/
    150 g shelled)
1 lb (480 g) fava (broad) beans, shelled (1 cup/5 oz/
    150 g shelled)
salt
1¼ lb (600 g) fresh tagliolini (see fresh pasta, page 246)
⅔ cup (3 oz/90 g) grated Parmesan cheese

In a deep saucepan over low heat, melt 2 tablespoons of the butter. Add the onion and cook, stirring, until translucent, about 3 minutes. Add the peas and fava beans and continue to cook, stirring, until the vegetables are tender, about 5 minutes. Season to taste with salt.

Meanwhile, bring a large pot filled with salted water to a boil. Add the pasta, stir well and cook until al dente.

Drain the pasta and pour into a warmed bowl. Add the peas and beans and the remaining butter and sprinkle with the Parmesan. Toss well and serve immediately.

SERVES 6

Sardegna

Minestra di Lenticchie al Finocchio

Lentil Soup with Fennel

Lentils are popular throughout the Mediterranean; in Sardinia, wild fennel abounds. The two flavors are combined very success-fully in this soup. I use the common green lentil for this Sardinian soup, but red lentils or other varieties will do just as well. For the best results, cook the lentils over low heat for as long as necessary to obtain a creamy consistency.

1⅔ cups (10 oz/300 g) dried lentils, picked over and rinsed
8 cups (64 fl oz/2 l) water
¼ lb (120 g) pancetta, chopped
1 tablespoon extra-virgin olive oil
1 tablespoon tomato paste
½ cup (4 fl oz/120 ml) dry white wine
1 tablespoon fennel seeds
salt and freshly ground pepper

In a saucepan, combine the lentils and water and bring to a boil. Reduce the heat to very low, cover and cook until very tender, 1–1½ hours.

In a small saucepan over medium heat, cook the pancetta in the oil until the fat is rendered, about 6 minutes. Add the tomato paste, white wine and fennel seeds and stir well. Reduce the heat to low and cook, stirring occasionally, for another 5 minutes.

Add the pancetta mixture to the lentils, cover and cook over low heat for about 5 minutes to blend the flavors. Season to taste with salt and pepper. Ladle into warmed bowls and serve very hot.

SERVES 6

Stracciatella alla Maggiorana

Egg Soup with Marjoram

The light soup known as stracciatella *is very popular throughout Italy. The traditional recipe is Roman, and the ingredients never vary in the capital. In other parts of Italy, however, cooks freely invent their own versions. I find this one particularly pleasing.*

4 eggs
1 cup (4 oz/120 g) grated Parmesan cheese
grated zest of 1 lemon
¼ teaspoon freshly grated nutmeg
6 cups (48 fl oz/1.5 l) light chicken stock (recipe on page 40)
1 tablespoon fresh marjoram leaves
salt and freshly ground pepper

In a bowl, beat the eggs with a fork until blended. Add the Parmesan cheese, lemon zest, nutmeg and ½ cup (4 fl oz/120 ml) of the stock.

Pour the remaining stock into a saucepan and bring to a boil. Pour in the egg mixture while stirring constantly with a fork and remove from the heat as soon as the mixture returns to the boil.

Add the marjoram and season to taste with salt and pepper. Ladle into warmed bowls and serve immediately.

SERVES 6

Top to bottom: Lentil Soup with Fennel; Egg Soup with Marjoram

Clockwise from top: Spaghetti with Anchovies, Eggplant and Thyme;
Rice with Porcini Mushrooms and Peas; Vermicelli with Zucchini

SPAGHETTI ALLE ACCIUGHE, MELANZANE E TIMO

Spaghetti with Anchovies, Eggplant and Thyme

Anchovies are salty and strong in flavor, so when it comes time to adjust this dish for salt, be judicious. If you wish, place a bowl of toasted bread crumbs on the table for guests to sprinkle over the pasta.

⅓ cup (2½ fl oz/80 ml) extra-virgin olive oil
1 clove garlic, chopped
½ yellow onion, chopped
3 slender (Asian) eggplants (aubergines), about 10 oz (300 g) total weight, unpeeled, cut into small pieces
6 olive oil–packed anchovy fillets, drained
pinch of red pepper flakes
2 tablespoons dried thyme
salt
1¼ lb (600 g) spaghetti

In a large, deep saucepan over medium heat, warm the oil. Add the garlic and onion and cook, stirring, until translucent, about 3 minutes. Add the eggplants, anchovies, pepper flakes and thyme. Cook, stirring continuously, until the eggplants are tender, about 10 minutes. Season to taste with salt.

Meanwhile, bring a large pot filled with salted water to a boil. Add the pasta, stir well and cook until al dente. Scoop out about ⅓ cup (2½ fl oz/80 ml) of the pasta water and set aside.

Drain the pasta and pour it into the saucepan holding the sauce. Add the reserved pasta water. Cook over medium heat for 2 minutes, stirring continuously. Transfer to a warmed bowl and serve.

SERVES 6

RISO AI FUNGHI PORCINI E PISELLI

Rice with Porcini Mushrooms and Peas

Rice is combined with peas and other vegetables in endless ways in the Veneto. For this dish, use only the freshest mushrooms. Button mushrooms can be used in place of the porcini. For a vegetarian rendition, use vegetable stock (see directions included with light meat stock).

2⅓ cups (13 oz/400 g) long-grain white rice
½ cup (4 fl oz/120 ml) extra-virgin olive oil
1 yellow onion, left whole, plus 1 tablespoon finely chopped yellow onion
5 whole cloves
4 cups (32 fl oz/1 l) light meat stock (recipe on page 40)
2 tablespoons unsalted butter
13 oz (400 g) fresh porcini mushrooms, stemmed and sliced (see note)
2 cups (10 oz/300 g) peas (2 lb/1 kg unshelled)
salt and freshly ground pepper

Preheat an oven to 400°F (200°C).
In a flameproof baking dish, combine the rice and oil.

Stud the whole onion with the cloves and add to the dish. Mix well and place over medium heat. Cook, stirring, for 3 minutes. Add the stock and bring to a boil. Cover and transfer to the oven. Bake until the stock is completely absorbed and the rice is tender yet firm to the bite, about 15 minutes.

About 10 minutes before the rice is ready, in a saucepan over medium heat, melt the butter. Add the 1 tablespoon chopped onion and cook, stirring, until translucent, about 3 minutes. Add the mushrooms and peas and season to taste with salt and pepper. Raise the heat to high and cook for 5 minutes, stirring frequently. Remove from the heat and keep warm.

Remove the rice from the oven and discard the clove-studded onion. Add the peas and mushrooms and season to taste with pepper.

Mix well and serve in a warmed bowl.

SERVES 6

VERMICELLI CON LE ZUCCHINE

Vermicelli with Zucchini

One of the most popular of all Neapolitan pasta dishes, this simple recipe must achieve a perfect blend of all its various flavors to be successful. Also, if you are not careful, the pasta will stick together when it is dressed with the sauce. To prevent this, allow some cooking water to cling to the drained pasta.

1 cup (8 fl oz/240 ml) extra-virgin olive oil
1 lb (480 g) small zucchini (courgettes), diced
handful of fresh mint leaves, chopped
1 oz (30 g) pancetta, diced
1¼ lb (600 g) vermicelli or bucatini
1 egg yolk, lightly beaten
1 tablespoon unsalted butter
handful of fresh basil leaves, torn
¼ cup (1 oz/30 g) grated Parmesan cheese
salt and freshly ground pepper

Pour the oil into a large frying pan over medium-high heat and heat to 340°F (170°C). When the oil is ready, add the zucchini and fry, turning occasionally, until golden, about 10 minutes. Using a slotted spoon, transfer the zucchini to a bowl. Add the mint leaves to the bowl and mix well.

Remove about two-thirds of the oil from the pan and discard. Leave the remainder in the pan. Add the pancetta to the pan and fry over medium heat until golden and crisp, just a few minutes. Using the slotted spoon, transfer the pancetta to the bowl and mix with the zucchini. Reserve the oil in the pan.

Bring a large pot filled with salted water to a boil. Add the pasta, stir well and cook until al dente. Scoop out a ladleful of pasta water and set aside.

Drain the pasta and transfer it to the frying pan holding the oil. Add the zucchini and the reserved pasta water and place over very low heat. Stirring gently, heat for no more than a couple of minutes.

Turn off the heat and add the egg yolk, butter, basil, Parmesan cheese and salt and pepper to taste. Mix quickly but thoroughly to distribute the ingredients evenly. Transfer to a warmed bowl and serve immediately.

SERVES 6

Spaghetti with Spicy Tomato Sauce

Campania

SPAGHETTI ALLA PUTTANESCA

Spaghetti with Spicy Tomato Sauce

Said to have originated on the island of Ischia in the Bay of Naples, this sauce is now made all over Italy. The name literally means "the harlot's spaghetti," an allusion to its zesty, lusty flavors.

3 cloves garlic
6 tablespoons (3 fl oz/90 ml) extra-virgin olive oil
1 lb (480 g) ripe plum (Roma) tomatoes, peeled, seeded and diced, or canned tomatoes, chopped
3 tablespoons drained capers
⅔ cup (3 oz/90 g) Gaeta or other Mediterranean-style small black olives, pitted
pinch of red pepper flakes
1 teaspoon chopped fresh oregano
3 oz (90 g) salt-packed anchovies, rinsed, filleted and chopped
leaves from 1 large bunch fresh flat-leaf (Italian) parsley, finely chopped
salt
1¼ lb (600 g) spaghetti or linguine

52

In a saucepan over medium heat, warm the whole garlic cloves in the oil. When they begin to color, add the tomatoes, capers, olives, pepper flakes and oregano. Cook, stirring occasionally, until slightly thickened, about 10 minutes. Add the anchovies and parsley, mix well and leave for a couple more minutes over the heat. Taste and adjust with salt.

Meanwhile, bring a large pot filled with salted water to a boil. Add the pasta, stir well and cook until al dente. Drain the pasta and place in a warmed bowl. Pour the sauce over the top, toss to mix thoroughly and serve immediately.

SERVES 6

Smoked Cheese Frittata

Campania

FILOSCIO

Smoked Cheese Frittata

This is the traditional Neapolitan frittata, which, like all frittatas, is highly versatile. It can be sliced as an appetizer, or it can be served as a first course, as the main course of a light meal or as a change from the usual breakfast eggs.

6 eggs
⅓ cup (2½ fl oz/80 ml) milk
leaves from 1 bunch fresh flat-leaf (Italian) parsley, chopped
salt and freshly ground pepper
½ lb (240 g) mozzarella cheese, diced
½ lb (240 g) smoked provola cheese, diced
2 tablespoons extra-virgin olive oil

In a bowl, lightly whisk together the eggs, milk and parsley until blended. Season to taste with salt and pepper and divide into 6 equal portions. In another bowl, mix together the 2 cheeses and then divide into 6 equal portions.

In a deep nonstick frying pan over medium heat, warm 1 tablespoon of the oil. When the oil is hot, pour in the first portion of the egg mixture. When it begins to set, add 1 portion of the cheeses and stir gently until set. Pour another portion of the egg over the top to form a second layer. When it begins to set, add another portion of cheese. Continue in this way with the remaining 4 portions of egg mixture and of cheese, taking care to shake the pan from time to time so that the eggs do not stick.

When the frittata is set, invert it browned side up onto a flat pan lid or plate. Add the remaining 1 tablespoon oil to the pan and, when hot, slide in the frittata browned side up. Cook over low heat until the second side is golden, just a few minutes. Slide onto a warmed round platter and serve.

SERVES 6

Veneto

POLENTA ALLA GRIGLIA

Grilled Polenta with Radicchio

In the Veneto, this dish is prepared when there is leftover polenta. Cooks there use the radicchio from Treviso, which has long, dark red leaves, but any radicchio is satisfactory. Instead of grilling, you can lightly brush the polenta slices with olive oil and cook them in a 400°F (200°C) oven for about 30 minutes.

6 cups (48 fl oz/1.5 l) water
salt

2 cups (10 oz/300 g) polenta (coarse-grained cornmeal)
4 tablespoons (2 fl oz/60 ml) extra-virgin olive oil
1¼ lb (600 g) radicchio (red chicory), preferably Treviso variety
freshly ground pepper

In a deep saucepan, bring the water to a boil and add salt to taste. Then add the polenta in a slow, steady stream, whisking constantly to prevent lumps from forming. Reduce the heat to low, cover and cook, stirring occasionally with a wooden spoon, until the polenta thickens and pulls away from the sides of the pan, about 30 minutes.

Pour the polenta into a shallow rectangular 2-qt (2-l) mold moistened with water and set aside to cool completely. Invert onto a cutting board and cut into long strips about 1 in (2.5 cm) wide.

Preheat a broiler (griller) or prepare a fire in a charcoal grill. If using a broiler, grease a large flameproof frying pan with 1 tablespoon of the oil.

Cut each radicchio head lengthwise into quarters. Brush the polenta strips on both sides with most of the remaining oil, place in the pan and slip into the broiler about 6 in (15 cm) from the heat. If using a charcoal grill, brush the polenta strips with the oil and place on the grill rack about 6 in (15 cm) above the fire. Broil or grill until golden, about 10 minutes. Turn over, add the radicchio quarters and brush them with the remaining oil. Broil (grill) the polenta and radicchio, turning the radicchio as necessary, until both are golden on both sides, about 10 minutes longer.

Arrange the polenta strips on a warmed platter, alternating them with the radicchio quarters. Season with pepper and serve very hot.

SERVES 6   *Photograph pages 32–33*

53

FRITTATA DI MACCHERONI
Maccheroni Frittata

Here is a good way to use leftover pasta that has been dressed with any kind of sauce except a seafood one. The frittata is so delicious in itself that Neapolitans often prepare pasta, usually dressed simply with tomato sauce, just to have some to make the frittata. It should be crunchy on the outside and soft on the inside.

about 2½ cups (12 oz/360 g) leftover cooked and dressed
    pasta (see note)
2 eggs, lightly beaten
½ cup (2 oz/60 g) grated Parmesan cheese
salt and freshly ground pepper
2 tablespoons extra-virgin olive oil
5 oz (150 g) mozzarella cheese, diced
5 oz (150 g) smoked provola cheese, diced

In a bowl, combine the pasta, eggs and Parmesan cheese. Mix well and season to taste with salt and pepper.

In a deep nonstick frying pan over high heat, warm 1 tablespoon of the oil. When it begins to bubble, reduce the heat to medium and pour in half of the pasta mixture, spread-

Clockwise from top: Maccheroni Frittata; Cold Cream of Cucumber Soup; Grilled Bread with Shredded Red Cabbage

Toscana

CROSTONI DI CAVOLO CAPPUCCIO

Grilled Bread with Shredded Red Cabbage

More and more frequently, Tuscans are serving thick slices of grilled bread with a variety of toppings as a first course in place of pasta, risotto or gnocchi. This recipe is a winter specialty of the restaurant at Badia a Coltibuono. The preparation is extremely simple. The decisive factor is the quality of the olive oil.

6 slices coarse country bread, each about ½ in (1 cm) thick
½ cup (4 fl oz/120 ml) extra-virgin olive oil
6 cloves garlic, chopped
10 oz (300 g) red cabbage, finely shredded
2 tablespoons red wine vinegar
salt and freshly ground pepper

🦎 Preheat a broiler (griller). Place the bread slices on a broiler pan (tray) and broil (grill), turning once, until lightly golden on both sides, just a few minutes. Remove from the broiler and brush lightly with olive oil on one side. Transfer to 6 individual plates, oiled side up.

🦎 In a large frying pan over high heat, warm the remaining oil with the garlic. When the garlic becomes translucent, after a couple of minutes, add the cabbage and mix well. Pour in the vinegar and season to taste with salt and pepper. Immediately remove from the heat. The cabbage should be barely warm and slightly wilted.

🦎 Place an equal portion of the cabbage on top of each crostoni. Serve immediately.

SERVES 6

CREMA FREDDA AL CETRIOLO

Cold Cream of Cucumber Soup

On hot summer days, this soup is wonderfully cooling. You can add 1 tablespoon plain yogurt to the top of each serving. Vegetable stock can be used in place of the chicken stock for a vegetarian first course; to prepare it, follow the directions included in the light chicken stock recipe.

2 tablespoons unsalted butter
1 small yellow onion, sliced
1¼ lb (600 g) cucumbers, peeled and sliced
2 cups (16 fl oz/480 ml) light chicken stock, plus additional stock as needed (recipe on page 40)
pinch of salt
¼ cup (2 fl oz/60 ml) heavy (double) cream or milk
handful of small fresh mint leaves

🦎 In a deep saucepan over medium heat, melt the butter. Add the onion and cook, stirring, until translucent, about 3 minutes. Add the cucumbers, mix well and pour in 2 cups (16 fl oz/480 ml) stock. Reduce the heat to low and cook, uncovered, until the cucumbers are tender, about 20 minutes.

🦎 Remove from the heat and let cool slightly. Working in batches, purée the cucumber mixture in a blender, adding a little stock to thin, if necessary. Pour into a bowl, cover and refrigerate for at least 3 hours to chill thoroughly.

🦎 Just before serving, add the salt and the cream or milk, mixing well. Ladle into chilled bowls, sprinkle with the mint and serve immediately.

SERVES 6

ing it to form an even surface and borders. Scatter the mozzarella and smoked provola cheeses evenly over the surface and cook for about 4 minutes. Pour in the remaining pasta mixture, reduce the heat to low, cover and cook, shaking the pan occasionally to prevent the frittata from sticking, until the bottom is nicely browned, about 4 minutes.

🦎 Invert the frittata browned side up onto the pan lid or a flat plate. Add the remaining 1 tablespoon oil to the pan and, when hot, slide in the frittata browned side up. Cook, uncovered, over low heat until the second side is golden but the center is still moist, about 5 minutes longer. Slide the frittata onto a warmed round platter or serve from the pan.

SERVES 6

GNOCCHI ALLE BIETOLE

Swiss Chard Gnocchi

You can also make these gnocchi with beet (beetroot) greens as shown or with spinach. They can be prepared up to one day in advance and kept in the refrigerator in an oven dish; when ready to serve, heat in a 350°F (180°C) oven. Tomato sauce (recipe on page 94) can be used in place of the butter.

2 lb (1 kg) Swiss chard (silverbeet), stalks removed
1¼ cups (10 oz/300 g) ricotta cheese

1 cup (4 oz/120 g) all-purpose (plain) flour
1 teaspoon freshly grated nutmeg
1 cup (4 oz/120 g) grated Parmesan cheese
3 egg yolks
salt and freshly ground pepper
6 tablespoons (3 oz/90 g) unsalted butter

☙ In a saucepan, combine the Swiss chard and a little salted water and bring to a boil. Cook until the Swiss chard is wilted and tender, about 3 minutes. Drain well and squeeze dry. Chop finely and place in a bowl.

☙ Add the ricotta, the flour, the nutmeg, half of the Parmesan cheese and the egg yolks. Season to taste with salt and pepper.

56

Clockwise from top: Spaghetti with Bread Crumbs and Garlic; Polenta with Fontina Sauce; Swiss Chard Gnocchi

With well-floured hands, shape the mixture into little ovals each about 2 in (5 cm) in length. As the gnocchi are formed, arrange in a single layer on a floured surface.

✺ Bring a large pot of salted water to a boil. Working in batches, add the gnocchi and boil until they float. Using a slotted spoon, lift out the gnocchi, allowing them to drain over the pot. Place on a warmed platter and keep warm. Repeat with the remaining gnocchi.

✺ Melt the butter in a small saucepan. Sprinkle the gnocchi with the remaining cheese, then pour the melted butter over the top. Serve immediately.

SERVES 6

Puglia

SPAGHETTI CON LA MOLLICA E AGLIO

Spaghetti with Bread Crumbs and Garlic

In the south, a topping of fried bread and garlic is often used instead of Parmesan. Here, a little of both makes for a simple but unforgettable pasta sauce.

1¼ lb (600 g) spaghetti
⅓ cup (2½ fl oz/80 ml) extra-virgin olive oil
1⅔ cups (6½ oz/200 g) fine dried bread crumbs
3 cloves garlic, chopped
¼ cup (2 oz/60 g) unsalted butter, melted and kept warm
6 tablespoons (1½ oz/45 g) grated Parmesan cheese
salt and freshly ground pepper

✺ Bring a large pot filled with salted water to a boil. Add the pasta, stir well and cook until al dente.

✺ Meanwhile, in a saucepan over medium heat, warm the oil. Add the bread crumbs and garlic and fry, stirring, until golden, about 3 minutes.

✺ Drain the pasta and transfer to a warmed bowl. Add the butter, Parmesan cheese and bread crumbs and season to taste with salt and pepper. Toss well and serve immediately.

SERVES 6

Piemonte

POLENTA ALLA CREMA DI FORMAGGIO

Polenta with Fontina Sauce

This ancient Piedmontese recipe is traditionally prepared with fonduta, a sauce made from only eggs and cheese. Today, the polenta is often dressed more simply with a light béchamel sauce enriched by egg yolks and Fontina cheese. When white truffles are in season, shave them over the top.

6 cups (48 fl oz/1.5 l) water
salt
2 cups (10 oz/300 g) polenta (coarse-grained cornmeal)
2 tablespoons unsalted butter
¼ cup (1 oz/30 g) all-purpose (plain) flour
2 cups (16 fl oz/480 ml) milk
freshly ground pepper
1 cup (4 oz/120 g) shredded Fontina cheese
2 egg yolks, lightly beaten

✺ In a deep saucepan, bring the water to a boil and add salt to taste. Then add the polenta in a slow, steady stream, whisking constantly to prevent lumps from forming. Reduce the heat to low, cover and cook, stirring occasionally with a wooden spoon, until the polenta thickens and pulls away from the side of the pan, about 30 minutes.

✺ Meanwhile, in a saucepan over medium heat, melt the butter. Stir in the flour and cook and stir for 1–2 minutes; do not allow to brown. Add the milk, a little at a time, stirring constantly. Continue to stir until a light béchamel sauce forms, just a few minutes. Season to taste with salt and pepper and stir in the cheese until melted. Remove from the heat.

✺ Transfer the polenta to a bowl moistened with cold water. Press down well and immediately invert onto a platter.

✺ Whisk the egg yolks into the sauce, mixing well, and pour the hot sauce over the polenta. Serve at once.

SERVES 6

CREMA DI ZUCCA E MELE
Cream of Pumpkin and Apple Soup

This soup makes a light and elegant start to an evening meal. It can also be garnished with croutons and grated Parmesan cheese, served separately, or sprinkled with crumbled amaretti *(almond cookies) just before serving. If a small pumpkin is unavailable, use a piece cut from a larger pumpkin. To make a vegetarian version, use vegetable stock (see directions included with light meat stock recipe).*

1 small pumpkin, 2 lb (1 kg)
¼ cup (2 oz/60 g) unsalted butter
2 yellow onions, sliced
6 cups (48 fl oz/1.5 l) light meat stock (recipe on page 40)
2 Golden Delicious or other sweet golden apples, peeled, cored and sliced
salt and freshly ground pepper
pinch of freshly grated nutmeg

☞ Using a sharp knife, cut the pumpkin through the stem end into thick slices. Scoop out and discard the seeds and fibers and peel off the skin. Cut the flesh into small pieces.
☞ In a soup pot over medium heat, melt the butter. Add the onions and cook, stirring, until translucent, about 3 minutes. Add the stock, pumpkin and apples and bring to a boil. Reduce the heat to low and cook, uncovered, until the pumpkin and apples are very soft, about 1½ hours.
☞ Remove from the heat and pour the soup through a food mill placed over a clean saucepan. Or purée in batches in a food processor fitted with the metal blade; return to the saucepan.
☞ Season to taste with salt and pepper and bring back to a boil. Add the nutmeg and pour into a warmed tureen. Serve immediately.

SERVES 6

FARFALLINE IN BRODO
Farfalline in Stock

The stock for this soup is made with good-quality meat. You can use the leftover meat for making croquettes by grinding (mincing) it finely and then mixing it with puréed potatoes and sautéing the croquettes in butter. Use only small pasta shapes.

1¼ lb (600 g) beef brisket
1¼ lb (600 g) beef shank
1 carrot, cut into pieces
1 celery stalk, cut into pieces
1 yellow onion, quartered
1 zucchini (courgette), cut into pieces
1 fennel bulb, quartered
1 bunch fresh flat-leaf (Italian) parsley
1 bunch fresh basil
2 fresh thyme sprigs
salt
2½ qt (2.5 l) water
1 egg white
3 tablespoons Vin Santo or any dessert wine
7 oz (210 g) farfalline or other small dried pasta shape
freshly ground pepper

☞ In a large pot, combine the beef brisket and beef shank with all the vegetables and herbs. Add salt to taste and the water and bring to a boil. Cover, reduce the heat to low and simmer, frequently skimming off any scum that rises to the surface, for about 2 hours.
☞ Strain the stock through a fine-mesh sieve into a bowl. (Reserve the meat for another use.) Refrigerate the stock until the fat rises to the surface, about 3 hours. Lift off the fat and discard.
☞ Pour the stock into a deep saucepan. Add the egg white, mix well and bring to a boil. Boil for 2 minutes to clarify the stock.
☞ Remove from the heat and strain through a fine-mesh sieve into a clean pan. Bring back to a boil. Add the Vin Santo or other dessert wine and the pasta and boil until the pasta is al dente. Season to taste with salt and pepper. Ladle into warmed bowls and serve immediately.

SERVES 6

Clockwise from top: Farfalline in Stock; Chick-pea Soup with Thyme; Cream of Pumpkin and Apple Soup

ZUPPA DI CECI E TIMO
Chick-pea Soup with Thyme

As in Tuscany, the Umbrians serve soup as a first course more often than pasta or rice. This soup is equally good the day after it is made. When some is left over, you can thin it with water or stock, add a little spaghetti broken into pieces or some form of short pasta, cook for about 8 minutes and let rest for another 5 minutes before serving.

2⅓ cups (1 lb/480 g) dried chick-peas (garbanzos), picked over and rinsed
8 cups (64 fl oz/2 l) water
⅓ cup (2½ fl oz/80 ml) extra-virgin olive oil
2 cloves garlic, chopped
pinch of red pepper flakes
1 bunch fresh flat-leaf (Italian) parsley, chopped
4 ripe plum (Roma) tomatoes, peeled and coarsely chopped, or canned tomatoes, coarsely chopped, with their juice
2 tablespoons fresh thyme leaves
salt

☞ Soak the chick-peas in cold water to cover for 24 hours. Remove and discard the ones that float to the top. Drain.
☞ In a soup pot over high heat, combine the chick-peas and water. Bring to a boil, reduce the heat to low, cover and simmer until tender, about 2 hours.
☞ Add the oil, garlic, pepper flakes, parsley, tomatoes and thyme and stir well. Season to taste with salt. Cover and continue to simmer over very low heat until the flavors are well blended, about 30 minutes longer. If the soup seems too thick, add hot water to thin to desired consistency.
☞ Ladle into warmed bowls and serve immediately.

SERVES 10

Penne ai Gamberetti e Fagiolini

Penne with Shrimp and
Green Beans

*This dish can also be served in a pastry shell: line a baking dish
with a thin sheet of pie pastry, and then bake the cooked and sauced
pasta in it. This way the two main elements of the dish can be
prepared well ahead of time and then combined and slipped into a
350°F (180°C) oven to bake for about 20 minutes (cover with
aluminum foil so that the pasta does not dry out) just before serving.*

1¼ lb (600 g) green beans
1¼ lb (600 g) penne or other dried pasta shape

warm the oil. Add the garlic and cook, stirring, until translucent, about 3 minutes.

🦎 Just before the pasta is ready, add the shrimp and green beans to the pan holding the garlic and cook over medium to high heat, stirring frequently, until the shrimp turn pink and curl, about 3 minutes.

🦎 Drain the pasta and transfer to a warmed bowl. Dress with the green beans and shrimp. Toss well and serve at once.

SERVES 6

Toscana

LASAGNE ALLE ZUCCHINE E DRAGONCELLO

Lasagna with Zucchini and Tarragon

This very contemporary dish features tarragon, a recent addition to the Tuscan table. If you like, prepare this lasagna several hours ahead of time and store in the refrigerator before baking. Peas, green beans, bell peppers (capsicums) or artichokes can be substituted for the zucchini, and basil or parsley can be used in place of the tarragon.

FOR THE DOUGH:

3 cups (12 oz/360 g) all-purpose (plain) flour
3 extra-large eggs

FOR THE FILLING:

1 tablespoon unsalted butter
½ cup (4 fl oz/120 ml) extra-virgin olive oil
6 zucchini (courgettes), finely chopped
handful of fresh tarragon leaves
salt and freshly ground pepper
2 cups (16 fl oz/480 ml) heavy (double) cream
1 cup (4 oz/120 g) grated Parmesan cheese

🦎 To make the dough, heap the flour in a mound on a work surface. Make a well in the center and break the eggs into it. Beat the eggs lightly with a fork, then gradually work the flour into the eggs until a loose ball of dough forms. Knead the dough on a lightly floured work surface until soft, smooth and elastic, about 5 minutes. Divide the dough into 6 equal portions. Using a pasta machine, roll out each portion into a very thin sheet. Allow to stand for a few minutes, then cut into long strips 4 in (10 cm) wide. Then cut the strips to form 4-in (10-cm) squares.

🦎 Bring a large pot of salted water to a boil. Add the pasta squares, a few at a time, and cook until al dente (they will float to the top). Using a slotted spoon, transfer the pasta squares to a bowl of cold water. Repeat with the remaining squares. When all are cooked and cooled, drain and spread out on a kitchen towel to dry.

🦎 Preheat an oven to 350°F (180°C). Grease a 12-by-16-in (30-by-40-cm) baking dish with the butter. To make the filling, in a frying pan over medium heat, warm the oil. Add the zucchini and sauté, stirring frequently, until tender, about 5 minutes. Add the tarragon and season to taste with salt and pepper. Remove from the heat.

🦎 In a bowl, stir together the cream and Parmesan cheese, then add the zucchini. Mix well until a creamy sauce forms.

🦎 Line the bottom of the prepared baking dish with a single layer of the pasta squares. Cover them evenly with one-third of the zucchini mixture. Repeat the layering twice, ending with a zucchini layer.

🦎 Bake until the sauce on the surface begins to bubble, about 20 minutes. Serve immediately.

SERVES 6

Left to right: Lasagna with Zucchini and Tarragon;
Penne with Shrimp and Green Beans

⅓ cup (2½ fl oz/80 ml) extra-virgin olive oil
1 clove garlic, sliced
24 shrimp (prawns), peeled and deveined

🦎 Bring a large pot filled with salted water to a boil. Add the green beans and boil for 1 minute. Using a slotted spoon, transfer the beans to a colander to drain. Keep the water boiling in the pot. Cut the beans into short lengths and set aside.

🦎 Add the pasta to the boiling water, stir well and cook until al dente. Meanwhile, in a deep saucepan over medium heat,

CANNELLONI FRITTI
Fried Cannelloni

These cannelloni are rich and very special. If you prefer not to fry them, they can be filled instead with the béchamel sauce, placed in a baking dish, dressed with a sauce of cream and Parmesan cheese and baked in a 350°F (180°C) oven for about 20 minutes. You can also serve them with tomato sauce (recipe on page 94).

¼ cup (2 oz/60 g) unsalted butter
½ cup (2 oz/60 g) all-purpose (plain) flour
1 cup (8 fl oz/240 ml) milk
salt and freshly ground pepper
5 oz (150 g) Fontina cheese, shredded
pinch of freshly grated nutmeg
12 lasagna squares made fresh according to recipe on
    page 61, or 6 dried lasagna noodles
2 eggs
2 cups (8 oz/240 g) fine dried bread crumbs
4 cups (32 fl oz/1 l) vegetable oil for deep-frying

In a saucepan over medium heat, melt the butter. Stir in the flour and cook and stir for 1–2 minutes; do not allow to brown. Add the milk, a little at a time, stirring constantly. Continue to stir until a thick béchamel sauce forms, about 10 minutes. Season to taste with salt and pepper. Remove from the heat and stir in the cheese and nutmeg until the cheese melts. Let cool, stirring occasionally.

Bring a large pot of salted water to a boil. Add the lasagna squares or noodles, a few at a time, and cook until al dente. Using a slotted spoon, transfer to a bowl of cold water. When all the pasta is cooked, drain well and spread out on a kitchen towel to dry. If using lasagna noodles, cut in half crosswise to make 12 squares.

Place an equal amount of the cooled sauce in the center of each lasagna square and roll it up to form a little tube, first folding in the ends slightly to hold in the sauce. Beat the eggs in a shallow bowl. Place the bread crumbs in a separate shallow bowl. Dip each pasta tube into the beaten eggs and then roll it in the bread crumbs.

In a deep frying pan, pour in the oil and heat to 340°F (170°C). Working in batches, slip the cannelloni into the hot oil, being careful not to crowd the pan. Fry, turning gently with a fork, until golden, about 5 minutes. Using tongs or a slotted spoon, transfer to paper towels to drain. Serve piping hot.

SERVES 6

CONCHIGLIE ALLA VODKA
Conchiglie with Vodka

All it takes to elevate a simple tomato sauce is a generous splash of vodka, thus refining the tone and taste of the finished plate of pasta.

3 tablespoons extra-virgin olive oil
6 ripe plum (Roma) tomatoes, peeled and chopped
1 small yellow onion, thinly sliced
1 clove garlic, thinly sliced
1 celery stalk, thinly sliced
1 carrot, thinly sliced
pinch of red pepper flakes
salt
½ cup (4 fl oz/120 ml) vodka
½ cup (4 fl oz/120 ml) heavy (double) cream
1¼ lb (600 g) conchiglie or other dried pasta shape
6 tablespoons (1½ oz/45 g) grated Parmesan cheese

In a large, deep saucepan over low heat, warm the oil. Add the tomatoes, onion, garlic, celery, carrot and pepper flakes and cook, stirring frequently, until the liquid has evaporated, about 30 minutes. Season to taste with salt. Add the vodka and cream and cook, stirring, until slightly thickened, about 5 minutes.

Meanwhile, bring a large pot filled with salted water to a boil. Add the pasta, stir well and cook until al dente.

Drain the pasta and pour it into the saucepan holding the sauce. Toss well, transfer to a warmed bowl, sprinkle with the Parmesan and serve.

SERVES 6

L o m b a r d i a

RISOTTO AGLI SPINACI
Risotto with Spinach

You can prepare this risotto with carrots, broccoli rabe, radicchio (red chicory) and other greens or vegetables in place of the spinach, and you can also use vegetable stock, if you prefer. The risotto should have a porridgelike consistency.

1¼ lb (600 g) spinach
½ cup (4 fl oz/120 ml) milk
8 cups (64 fl oz/2 l) light meat stock or vegetable stock
    (recipe on page 40)
6 tablespoons (3 oz/90 g) unsalted butter
1 yellow onion, finely sliced
3⅓ cups (1¼ lb/600 g) Arborio rice
6 tablespoons (1½ oz/45 g) grated Emmentaler cheese
salt and freshly ground pepper

In a saucepan, combine the spinach and a little salted water and bring to a boil. Cook until the spinach is wilted and tender, about 3 minutes. Drain well and squeeze dry. Place in a blender and add the milk. Blend until smooth and set aside.

Pour the stock into a saucepan, bring to a boil and adjust the heat to maintain a low boil. In a deep saucepan over medium heat, melt half of the butter. Add the onion and cook, stirring frequently, until translucent, about 3 minutes. Add the rice and cook, stirring frequently, until the rice is warm and coated with the butter, about 3 minutes. Add 1 or 2 ladlefuls of the stock, enough just to cover the rice, and cook, stirring frequently but not constantly. As the liquid is absorbed, add a little more simmering stock, again stirring frequently.

Continue to add the stock in this manner, making sure the rice is always covered with a veil of liquid. The risotto is done when the rice is tender but firm and the risotto flows but is not runny. This should take about 15 minutes in all from the moment the stock is added.

Add the puréed spinach, mix well and cook for another 2 minutes. Remove from the heat and stir in the Emmentaler cheese and the remaining butter. Season to taste with salt and pepper. Serve immediately.

SERVES 6   *Photograph pages 32–33*

Top to bottom: Fried Cannelloni; Conchiglie with Vodka

SFORMATO DI MELANZANE
Eggplant Mold

The idea for this recipe, which can be served as an appetizer or a first course, comes from all the different ways I have eaten eggplant in Greek homes. I sometimes serve it accompanied with a freshly made tomato sauce (see page 94 for recipe).

1¼ lb (600 g) eggplants (aubergines)
3 tablespoons extra-virgin olive oil
4 cloves garlic, chopped
1 tablespoon dried oregano
salt and freshly ground pepper
2 whole eggs plus 2 egg yolks
¾ cup (6 fl oz/180 ml) heavy (double) cream
1 tablespoon unsalted butter

☞ Preheat an oven to 350°F (180°C).
☞ Wrap each eggplant individually in aluminum foil and place in the oven. Bake for about 30 minutes. Remove from the oven, unwrap and set aside until cool enough to handle. Peel off the skins and place the pulp in a bowl. Using a fork, mash the pulp. Leave the oven set at 350°F (180°C).
☞ In a saucepan over low heat, warm the oil. Add the garlic and cook, stirring, until translucent, about 3 minutes. Add the mashed eggplant and the oregano, and season to taste with salt and pepper. Cook, stirring frequently, until the eggplant is creamy, about 10 minutes. Taste and adjust the seasonings; set aside to cool.
☞ In a mixing bowl, whisk together the whole eggs and egg yolks with a fork until blended. Add the cream and the eggplant, mixing well. Grease a 4-cup (32–fl oz/1-l) mold with the butter and pour in the eggplant mixture. Place the mold in a baking dish and pour hot water into the baking dish to a depth of 1 in (2.5 cm). Bake until set, about 1 hour.
☞ Run a thin, sharp knife blade around the edges of the mold and invert onto a serving platter. Serve in wedges.

SERVES 6

Piemonte

AGNOLOTTI AI FUNGHI
Agnolotti Stuffed with Mushrooms

Traditionally, a vegetable stuffing for pasta includes an equal portion of ricotta cheese to give it more body. Today, the trend is toward using just the cooked vegetable or, at the most, to mix it with a little potato that first has been sliced, sautéed in olive oil and then finely chopped.

FOR THE DOUGH:

2 cups (8 oz/240 g) all-purpose (plain) flour
2 extra-large eggs

FOR THE FILLING AND SAUCE:

½ cup (4 fl oz/120 ml) extra-virgin olive oil
2 cloves garlic
10 oz (300 g) fresh porcini mushrooms or button mushrooms, stemmed and sliced
salt and freshly ground pepper
1 tablespoon fresh marjoram or thyme leaves
3 tablespoons grated Parmesan cheese
1 egg yolk

Top to bottom: Tagliatelle with Sage and Chicken; Eggplant Mold; Agnolotti Stuffed with Mushrooms

☞ To prepare the dough, heap the flour in a mound on a work surface. Make a well in the center and break the eggs into it. Beat the eggs lightly with a fork, then gradually work the flour into the eggs until a loose ball of dough forms. Knead the dough on a lightly floured work surface until soft, smooth and elastic, about 5 minutes. Cut the dough into 4 equal portions. Using a pasta machine, roll out each portion into a very thin sheet. Allow to stand for a few minutes, then cut into long strips 4 in (10 cm) wide.
☞ To make the filling, in a frying pan over medium heat, warm half of the oil. Add the garlic and cook, stirring, until translucent, about 5 minutes. Discard the garlic. Add the mushrooms and cook, stirring frequently, until tender, about 5 minutes. Season to taste with salt and pepper and add the marjoram or thyme. Remove from the heat and let cool a little, then stir in the Parmesan cheese and egg yolk, mixing well.
☞ Place small mounds of the filling at regularly spaced intervals down one-half of each strip of pasta. The mounds should be about 2 in (5 cm) apart. Brush the edges of the dough with a little water, then fold over the strip to cover the filling. Press the edges together to seal. Using a fluted pastry cutter, cut between the mounds to form squares.
☞ Bring a large pot filled with salted water to a boil. Add the agnolotti, stir gently and cook until al dente (they will float to the top). Drain carefully and transfer to a warmed bowl. Dress with the remaining oil and serve.

SERVES 6

Toscana

TAGLIATELLE ALLA SALVIA E STRACCETTI DI POLLO
Tagliatelle with Sage and Chicken

For best results, slice the chicken into very thin strips so that it will cook quickly over high heat. That way the meat will stay tender and juicy, thus enhancing the full, rich flavor of this dish. Freshly made pasta is the best choice for this dish; fettuccine can be substituted for tagliatelle.

½ cup (4 fl oz/120 ml) extra-virgin olive oil
3 cloves garlic, finely chopped
6 tablespoons (1½ oz/45 g) fine dried bread crumbs
20 fresh sage leaves, shredded
10 oz (300 g) boneless, skinless chicken breast halves, cut into very thin strips
juice of 1 lemon
1¼ lb (600 g) fresh tagliatelle (see fresh pasta, page 246)
salt and freshly ground pepper

☞ In a small frying pan over medium heat, warm half of the oil. Add the garlic, bread crumbs and sage and cook, stirring constantly, until golden, about 5 minutes. Remove from the heat and set aside.
☞ In a large frying pan over high heat, warm the remaining oil. Add the chicken and cook, stirring frequently, until tender, about 2 minutes. Sprinkle with the lemon juice.
☞ Meanwhile, bring a large pot filled with salted water to a boil. Add the pasta, stir well and cook until al dente. Drain the pasta and pour it into the pan holding the chicken.
☞ Warm over medium heat, mixing gently, for a couple of minutes. Season to taste with salt and pepper.
☞ Transfer to a warmed bowl, sprinkle the garlic-bread mixture over the top and serve at once.

SERVES 6

RISO E FAGIOLI AL BASILICO
Rice and Beans with Basil

A dish of rice, beans and tomatoes is typical fare in the countryside of the Veneto. This version is updated with the addition of garlic and basil. It can be made strictly vegetarian by using vegetable stock; see directions included with the meat stock recipe.

4 lb (2 kg) fresh cranberry (borlotti) beans, shelled
6 tablespoons (3 fl oz/90 ml) extra-virgin olive oil
3 cloves garlic
2 lb (1 kg) small, ripe tomatoes, peeled and quartered
2½ qt (2.5 l) light meat stock (recipe on page 40)
1¼ cups (7 oz/210 g) Arborio rice
pinch of red pepper flakes
2 tablespoons chopped fresh basil
salt

☞ Bring a saucepan filled with water to a boil. Add the beans, reduce the heat to low and cook, uncovered, until tender, about 1 hour. Drain the beans. Place half of them in a food processor fitted with the metal blade or in a blender and purée until smooth. Set the puréed beans and the whole beans aside.

☞ In a deep saucepan over low heat, warm half of the oil. Add the garlic and cook, stirring occasionally, until golden, about 3 minutes. Discard the garlic. Add the tomatoes, raise the heat to medium and cook, stirring frequently, for about 10 minutes.

☞ Add the whole and the puréed beans and the stock. Reduce the heat to low, cover and cook for 30 minutes to blend the flavors. Add the rice and the pepper flakes and cook until the rice is tender yet firm to the bite, about 15 minutes longer.

☞ Remove from the heat and stir in the basil and the remaining oil. Season to taste with salt. Transfer to a warmed bowl and serve.

SERVES 6 *Photograph pages 32–33*

2 tablespoons finely chopped fresh chives
freshly ground pepper

Bring a large pot filled with salted water to a boil. Add the pasta, stir well and cook until al dente.

While the pasta is cooking, in a bowl, stir together the cheese and oil until combined, then mix in the chives. Add ¼ cup (2 fl oz/60 ml) of the hot pasta water and stir until smooth. Season generously with pepper.

Drain the pasta and place in a warmed bowl. Add the goat cheese mixture, toss well and serve immediately.

SERVES 6

Emilia-Romagna

RAVIOLI AI FIORI DI ZUCCA

Ravioli Stuffed with Zucchini Flowers

Zucchini flowers are available for only a very brief period right before the plant begins to produce the squashes, usually from July through September. The blossoms should be very fresh and tightly closed.

FOR THE DOUGH:

3 cups (12 oz/360 g) all-purpose (plain) flour
3 extra-large eggs

FOR THE FILLING AND SAUCE:

10 oz (300 g) zucchini (courgette) flowers
6 tablespoons (3 oz/90 g) unsalted butter
salt and freshly ground pepper
5 oz (150 g) coarse country bread, soaked in milk to cover
    and squeezed dry
1 extra-large egg
3 tablespoons grated Parmesan cheese
pinch of freshly grated nutmeg

To make the dough, heap the flour in a mound on a work surface. Make a well in the center and break the eggs into it. Beat the eggs lightly with a fork, then gradually work the flour into the eggs until a loose ball of dough forms. Knead the dough on a lightly floured work surface until soft, smooth and elastic, about 5 minutes. Divide the dough into 6 equal portions. Using a pasta machine, roll out each portion into a very thin sheet. Cut into long strips about 2 in (5 cm) wide.

To make the filling, remove and discard the pistil from inside each flower and chop the flowers into pieces. In a frying pan over medium heat, melt 1 tablespoon of the butter. Add the flowers and sauté until tender, about 3 minutes. Season to taste with salt and pepper and set aside to cool.

In a bowl, mix together the bread, egg, zucchini flowers and Parmesan cheese. Scoop out small spoonfuls of the filling and arrange them at 2-in (5-cm) intervals down the pasta strips. Brush the edges of the strips and between the mounds with a little water, then cover with the remaining strips. Press the edges together to seal. Cut around the mounds of filling with a fluted pastry cutter to form round ravioli.

Bring a large pot of salted water to a boil. Add the ravioli and cook until al dente (they will float to the top). Drain the ravioli carefully and transfer to a warmed bowl.

Melt the remaining butter in a small saucepan and pour it evenly over the top of the ravioli. Sprinkle with the nutmeg and serve immediately.

SERVES 6

Left to right: Ravioli Stuffed with Zucchini Flowers; Pennette with Goat Cheese

PENNETTE ALLA CREMA DI CAPRINO

Pennette with Goat Cheese

Today, Italian food producers are more curious about different foods than they were in the past, and that includes not only ingredients from other Italian regions but from neighboring countries as well. Italians now turn out delicious goat's milk cheeses that rival even the fine French products. For this recipe I use a goat cheese coated with ash, but a plain one will do as long as it is fresh and soft.

1¼ lb (600 g) dried pennette or other dried pasta shape
4 oz (120 g) fresh goat cheese
6 tablespoons (3 fl oz/90 ml) extra-virgin olive oil

Abruzzo

TORTINO DI SPAGHETTINI CON OLIVE NERE E ZAFFERANO

Saffron Spaghetti Pie with Black Olives

The saffron of Abruzzo is among the best in the world, but unfortunately the production is very limited. Spanish saffron can be substituted. Eat this dish either hot or at room temperature for a buffet or brunch.

1 teaspoon powdered saffron
1 tablespoon water
1¼ lb (600 g) spaghettini
1⅓ cups (6½ oz/200 g) Gaeta or other Mediterranean-style small black olives, pitted and halved
7 tablespoons (3½ fl oz/100 ml) extra-virgin olive oil
salt

☞ In a small cup, dissolve the saffron in the water. Set aside.
☞ Bring a large pot filled with salted water to a boil. Add the pasta, stir well and cook until al dente. Drain and transfer to a bowl. Add the olives, 1 tablespoon of the oil, salt to taste and the saffron and toss thoroughly.
☞ In a 12-in (30-cm) nonstick frying pan over medium heat, warm half of the remaining oil. Add the pasta mixture and cook, shaking the mixture occasionally, until a golden crust forms on the bottom, about 5 minutes. Carefully invert the pie onto a flat plate, browned side up. Add the remaining oil to the pan and, when hot, slide in the pie browned side up. Cook until a crust forms on the second side, about 5 minutes longer.
☞ Transfer the pie to a platter and cut into wedges to serve.

SERVES 6

FARFALLINE ALLE VERDURE

Farfalline with Vegetable Sauce

Today, vegetable sauces for dressing pasta are enjoying great popularity. Some of these sauces, like this one, are cooked, while others can be made from raw vegetables, such as finely cut tiny zucchini (courgettes), puréed with a little olive oil.

½ cup (4 fl oz/120 ml) extra-virgin olive oil
6 carrots, diced
1 yellow onion, diced
3 celery stalks, diced
1 clove garlic, chopped
pinch of red pepper flakes
½ cup (4 fl oz/120 ml) water
salt
handful of fresh flat-leaf (Italian) parsley leaves
handful of fresh basil leaves
6 tablespoons (1½ oz/45 g) grated Parmesan cheese
1¼ lb (600 g) farfalline or other small dried pasta shape

☞ In a saucepan over medium heat, warm the oil. Add the carrots, onion, celery, garlic and pepper flakes and sauté, stirring frequently, until the vegetables begin to soften, about 5 minutes. Add the water and salt to taste, reduce the heat to low and continue cooking, stirring occasionally, until tender, about 10 minutes.
☞ Remove from the heat and place in a food processor fitted with the metal blade. Add the parsley, basil and Parmesan cheese and process until creamy.

☞ Meanwhile, bring a large pot filled with salted water to a boil. Add the pasta, stir well and cook until al dente. Meanwhile, reheat the sauce in a clean pan. If it is too thick, dilute with a little of the pasta water.
☞ Drain the pasta and transfer to a warmed bowl. Pour the sauce on top, toss well and serve.

SERVES 6

Toscana

TAGLIOLINI AI CARCIOFI

Tagliolini with Artichokes

The heat from the pasta will "cook" the eggs. The pasta must be tossed well so that the strands are thoroughly coated with the sauce.

juice of 1 lemon
6 artichokes
¼ cup (2 oz/60 g) unsalted butter
¼ cup (2 fl oz/60 ml) extra-virgin olive oil
salt and freshly ground pepper
1¼ lb (600 g) fresh tagliolini (see fresh pasta, page 246)
3 eggs
⅔ cup (2½ oz/80 g) grated Parmesan cheese

☞ Fill a bowl with cold water and add the lemon juice. Cut off the top one-third of each artichoke, then cut or snap off the tough outer leaves. Cut each artichoke in half lengthwise. Using a sharp spoon, dig out the chokes and discard. As each artichoke is trimmed, place it in the lemon water to prevent discoloring. When they have all been trimmed, drain and dry.
☞ In a deep saucepan over low heat, melt the butter with the oil. Add the artichokes, cover and cook until tender, about 10 minutes, adding water to moisten from time to time. Season to taste with salt and pepper.
☞ Bring a large pot of salted water to a boil. Add the pasta, stir well and cook until al dente. While the pasta is cooking, lightly beat together the eggs with half of the Parmesan cheese. When the pasta is ready, drain and transfer to a warmed bowl. Add the beaten eggs and the artichokes. Toss immediately, sprinkle with the remaining Parmesan cheese and serve at once.

SERVES 6

Below, top to bottom: Tagliatelle with Mussels and Broccoli (recipe page 71); Farfalline with Vegetable Sauce

At right, left to right: Saffron Spaghetti Pie with Black Olives; Tagliolini with Artichokes

Clockwise from top: Cream of Bean and Spelt Soup; Rice with Savoy Cabbage and Sausage; Meat Sauce with Celery

Lombardia

RISO CON VERZE E SALSICCE

Rice with Savoy Cabbage and Sausage

A riso dish differs from a risotto in that the broth is added all at once rather than a little at a time. To serve this as a main course, surround the rice with a few more cooked sausages. Crinkly-leaved Savoy cabbage has a stronger flavor than regular green cabbage.

¼ cup (2 fl oz/60 ml) extra-virgin olive oil
1 head Savoy cabbage, about 2 lb (1 kg), finely chopped
1 yellow onion, chopped
10 oz (300 g) fresh sweet pork sausages, casings removed
  and meat crumbled
6 ripe plum (Roma) tomatoes, peeled and chopped, or
  canned tomatoes, chopped, with their juice
salt and freshly ground pepper
3⅓ cups (1¼ lb/600 g) Arborio rice

70

In a saucepan over low heat, warm the oil. Add the cabbage and onion and stir to coat. Cook over low heat for about 10 minutes. Add the crumbled sausage, mix well and allow it to absorb the flavors for about 3 minutes, stirring occasionally. Add the tomatoes, cover and continue to cook over low heat for about 30 minutes. If necessary, add a little water during cooking to keep the mixture moist and to prevent sticking. Season to taste with salt and pepper.

When the cabbage mixture is about half done, bring a saucepan filled with salted water to a boil. Add the rice and cook until tender yet firm to the bite, about 14 minutes.

Drain the rice and add to the cabbage mixture. Cook for another couple of minutes to blend the flavors, then pour onto a warmed platter and serve.

SERVES 6

Sardegna

RAGÙ DI CARNE AL SEDANO
Meat Sauce with Celery

A simple dish for a family meal, this hearty sauce can be served at room temperature on top of thick pieces of grilled bread, or it can be tossed with cooked and drained pasta. It also makes a delicious stuffing for cabbage rolls.

⅓ cup (2½ fl oz/80 ml) extra-virgin olive oil
1 small yellow onion, chopped
3 celery stalks, chopped
3 carrots, chopped
1⅓ lb (700 g) lean ground (minced) beef
2 cups (16 fl oz/480 ml) light meat stock (recipe on page 40)
salt
1 tablespoon chopped fresh flat-leaf (Italian) parsley

In a saucepan over low heat, warm the oil. Add the onion, celery and carrots and cook, stirring occasionally, until softened, about 10 minutes. Add the beef and continue to cook, stirring occasionally, until the meat is browned, another 10 minutes. Add the stock, bring to a boil, reduce the heat to low, cover and cook until the liquid has evaporated and the flavors are blended, about 1 hour. Season to taste with salt.

Remove from the heat and add the parsley. Mix well and serve hot or at room temperature.

SERVES 6

CREMA DI FAGIOLI E FARRO
Cream of Bean and Spelt Soup

In the past, spelt, an ancient variety of reddish wheat called farro *in Italian, was mostly used in the kitchens of Umbria and the Lucchesia area of Tuscany. Now it has become popular all over Italy, especially as an ingredient in soups. When I serve this creamy soup to guests, I often briefly sauté shrimp (prawns) in a little oil and add a few of them to each bowl at the last minute.*

1½ cups (10 oz/300 g) dried cranberry (borlotti) beans
½ cup (3 oz/90 g) spelt (emmer)
1 carrot, roughly chopped
1 yellow onion, roughly chopped
1 celery stalk, roughly chopped
½ fennel bulb, roughly chopped
7 fresh rosemary sprigs
1 bunch fresh sage
1 fresh thyme sprig
1 clove garlic
8 cups (64 fl oz/2 l) water
salt and freshly ground pepper
6 tablespoons (3 fl oz/90 ml) extra-virgin olive oil

Rinse the beans and spelt separately and place in separate bowls. Add water to cover each generously. Let stand for about 12 hours.

Drain the beans. In a deep saucepan, combine the beans, carrot, onion, celery and fennel. Using kitchen string, tie together 1 sprig of rosemary, the sage and the thyme. Add to the beans along with the garlic and water. Bring to a boil. Cover, reduce the heat to low and cook until the beans are tender, about 1½ hours.

Remove from the heat and discard the herb bundle. Pass the beans and vegetables through a food mill into a clean saucepan. Drain the spelt, add to the saucepan and place over low heat. Cook, stirring occasionally, until the spelt is tender, about 20 minutes. Season to taste with salt and pepper.

Ladle into warmed bowls and place 1 rosemary sprig atop each bowl. Drizzle the oil evenly over the bowls and serve immediately.

SERVES 6

TAGLIATELLE ALLE COZZE E BROCCOLI
Tagliatelle with Mussels and Broccoli

When I do not feel like making fresh pasta at home, I buy factory-produced dried tagliatelle, which are generally superior to the fresh pasta you find in shops. Be sure, however, that you buy a reputable Italian brand, such as De Cecco or Barilla.

4 lb (2 kg) mussels, scrubbed and debearded
2 lb (1 kg) broccoli
1¼ lb (600 g) fresh tagliatelle (see fresh pasta, page 246)
large pinch of saffron threads
6 tablespoons (3 fl oz/90 ml) extra-virgin olive oil

Place the mussels in a large pot with the water clinging to them, cover and place over high heat. As the pot begins to heat, briskly move it back and forth over the burner several times. The mussels will open after a few minutes. Using a slotted spoon, remove the shellfish from the pot, then extract the mussels from the shells, discarding any that did not open. Discard the shells and set aside the mussels, covering them to keep them warm. Pour the liquid remaining in the pot through a fine-mesh sieve lined with cheesecloth (muslin) into a small saucepan. Place the pan over low heat until the liquid is reduced to about ½ cup (4 fl oz/120 ml). Set aside.

Trim the stems from the broccoli and reserve for another use. Cut the tops into small florets.

Bring a large pot filled with salted water to a boil. Add the broccoli. As soon as the water returns to the boil, add the pasta, stir well and cook until al dente.

Meanwhile, place the saffron threads in the hot reduced mussel liquid to soften, then transfer to a blender and add the oil. Process until fully blended.

Drain the pasta and broccoli and place in a warmed bowl. Add the mussels and oil sauce. Toss well and serve.

SERVES 6   *Photograph page 68*

6 cups (48 fl oz/1.5 l) water
1 tablespoon curry powder
salt
6 tablespoons (3 oz/90 g) sour cream or plain yogurt

🐇 First, clean the squid: Pull the tentacles from each body. Discard the entrails, ink sac and cartilage from the body. Cut the tentacles off at the point just above the eyes and discard the head. Rinse the body and tentacles under cold running water. When all of the squid are cleaned, cut the bodies crosswise into rings and chop the tentacles. Set aside.

🐇 In a saucepan over low heat, warm the oil. Add the onion and carrot and cook, stirring occasionally, until the vegetables begin to soften, about 10 minutes. Do not allow the onion to take on color. Raise the heat, add the squid and cook for just a few minutes. Add the cabbage, tomato purée, water and curry powder and stir well. Season to taste with salt. Reduce the heat to low, cover and cook until the cabbage is very soft, about 1 hour.

🐇 Ladle into warmed bowls and top each serving with 1 tablespoon sour cream or yogurt. Serve immediately.

SERVES 6

Squid and Savoy Cabbage Soup

MINESTRA DI CALAMARETTI E VERZA

Squid and Savoy Cabbage Soup

I acquired a taste for curry powder when I visited India and have found that it goes well with many Italian dishes. For this soup I use moscardini, *the tiny, almost minuscule octopus available in Italy. Small squid, cut into pieces, are a good substitute, however. You can use canned tomato purée or peeled fresh tomatoes put through a food mill.*

1¼ lb (600 g) small squid
3 tablespoons extra-virgin olive oil
1 yellow onion, chopped
1 carrot, chopped
1 head Savoy cabbage, 1¼ lb (600 g), cored and finely chopped
1 cup (8 fl oz/240 ml) tomato purée

Liguria

INSALATA DI RISO AL PESTO

Rice Salad with Pesto

Here is a summer dish that uses pesto—the traditional sauce of Liguria—in an untraditional way. To use the pesto on pasta, cook 1¼ pounds (600 g) linguine and toss the sauce with the noodles (thin with reserved pasta water, if necessary). The salad can be prepared several hours beforehand and kept in the refrigerator, but should be brought to room temperature before serving. If the cherry tomatoes are large, cut them in half.

FOR THE SALAD:

2 cups (12 oz/360 g) Arborio or long-grain white rice
12 cherry tomatoes, stemmed (see note)
12 Gaeta or other Mediterranean-style small black olives, pitted and halved
½ lb (240 g) mozzarella cheese, diced

FOR THE PESTO:

1 cup (1 oz/30 g) lightly packed fresh basil leaves
¼ cup (1 oz/30 g) pine nuts
¼ cup (1 oz/30 g) grated pecorino cheese
¼ cup (1 oz/30 g) grated Parmesan cheese
4 cloves garlic, chopped
½ cup (4 fl oz/120 ml) extra-virgin olive oil
salt and freshly ground pepper

🐇 To make the salad, bring a saucepan filled with lightly salted water to a boil and add the rice. Cook until tender yet firm to the bite, about 15 minutes. Drain, reserving ½ cup (4 fl oz/120 ml) of the water, and spread the rice on a kitchen towel to dry and cool.

🐇 Transfer the rice to a salad bowl and add the tomatoes, olives and mozzarella.

🐇 To make the pesto, in a blender, combine the basil, pine nuts, pecorino and Parmesan cheeses, garlic, oil and a little salt and pepper. Blend to form a dense cream. Thin with the reserved rice water.

🐇 Pour the pesto dressing over the rice, mix well and let stand for at least 30 minutes before serving to allow the flavors to blend.

SERVES 6

Rice Salad with Pesto

Il Nord-Est

VENETO, TRENTINO–ALTO ADIGE, FRIULI–VENEZIA GIULIA

The northeastern corner of Italy may be the country's most diverse area. The Veneto, the northeast's dominant region, itself is a collection of singular cities—Venice, Verona, Padua, Vicenza, Treviso, Bassano—surrounded by fertile farmland flooded with numerous rivers that flow into the Adriatic Sea. The cities of the Veneto were often historic rivals, although most at some point or other were under the sway of Venice. Yet the varieties of food, wine, people, lifestyles and traditions of the region are more numerous than in many nations.

Bordering on the Veneto are two more regions: Friuli–Venezia Giulia and Trentino–Alto Adige. The hyphenations indicate that these regions also are amalgamations of smaller entities. Friuli–Venezia Giulia borders on Austria, Slovenia and Croatia. The western part of the region, including the handsome city of Udine, is Venetian in architecture, language and culinary tradition. The eastern part, with the port city of Trieste as its focus, is more Slavic than Italian. In Trieste, long an international city, one encounters people whose first language is Serbo-Croatian, Hungarian, German or perhaps even Italian. Most of Friuli–Venezia Giulia became part of Italy following World War I, and the boundaries were redrawn in 1954, at which point Trieste became part of

Previous pages: The quiet soul of Venice is reflected in one of the 400 bridges than span its 150 canals. At left: Keeping up on local news is as widely practiced in a caffe as drinking or socializing.

Italy and large portions of the surrounding area were given to the nation then called Yugoslavia.

Trentino–Alto Adige joins the southerly province of the city of Trento (fully within Italian territory) with the Teutonic province that Italians call Alto Adige (the high reaches of the Adige River), but which Germans and Austrians refer to as Südtirol. To northern Europeans, this region may technically be within Italian borders, but it is an unwilling captive yearning to break free and return to the Germanic fold. In the Alto Adige no one will speak Italian to you unless that is the language in which you address them. Even at that point, they may be unable to respond. Although the province is officially bilingual, Italian is seldom heard outside of the capital city of Bolzano. The Trentino can best be described as Italian Alpine, drawing traditions from the Veneto as well as Lombardy and Alto Adige. The two provinces were combined for administrative purposes in 1948, when they became part of Italy.

What then unifies all of these diverse cities and lands in Italy's northeast? This is the area of Italy that has, for most of its history, been under the influence of empire, and with that comes a loyalty to one larger political entity, one way of thinking and one form of economics. In ancient times, the Romans constructed the formidable cities of Verona (where they created the largest arena outside of the Coliseum in Rome) and Padua. As they did everywhere, the Romans built roads and established trade routes. One route headed straight north through the Alps, hugging the banks of the Adige River for much of the way. The road traversed what is now called the Brenner Pass and dropped into territories that centuries later would be called Austria and Germany. Pilgrims and merchants traveled it to Rome in ancient times, in the Middle Ages and the Renaissance, and their modern counterparts still use it today. The creation of this access enabled German peoples to travel south during the centuries, sometimes with peaceful intentions, but at many other times with the purpose of occupation. The traditional foods of this area were and are *canederli* (bread dumplings), *speck* (smoked cured bacon), game, mountain herbs and berries and excellent wines.

The road passing through Padua went east and somewhat north and brought the Romans to a land they called Forum Julii (the name later evolved to Friuli), where they established the city of Aquileia. The area became one of the high points of Roman civilization, filled with scholars, farmers and wine makers who produced a drink much favored in Rome. Friulians never lost their knack for wine making, and today their vintages stand alongside those of Piedmont and Tuscany as Italy's best.

When, in the fifth century, Aquileia was sacked by invaders from the north, its citizens fled to a group of undeveloped islands in a lagoon on the Adriatic Sea. Here, long after the fall of the Roman Empire, these survivors built a glorious city that rose like Venus from the sea: Venezia (Venice).

In time, Venice grew to become the greatest commercial republic of the late Middle Ages and the Renaissance, surpassing even Genoa during this time. Its ships sailed the Mediterranean and beyond, bringing back exotic foods such as rice from Asia. The Venetians also became

An unassuming sign leads visitors to the eighteenth-century Villa Widmann-Foscari-Rezzonico along the Brenta Canal in the Veneto.

Right: Remarkable costumes appear annually in St. Mark's Square in Venice as revelers celebrate carnevale, *the pre-Lenten festival.*

Iron, lead, glass, stone and brick find harmony in a house front in Venice.

the world's leading spice traders, so that black pepper, cinnamon, cloves and other flavors (including chocolate and coffee) quickly entered the Venetian kitchen. From 1420 to 1797, Venice occupied almost all of the mainland territory that surrounded it, spreading the foods it imported and drawing the products of the fertile soil.

The Veneto was, and is, one of the most agriculturally productive regions in Italy. Rice became a staple first course of the area, and cornmeal, in the form of polenta, was always a *primo* and now is also a side dish. Both

ingredients were used to make breads and pastries. Radicchio (red chicory) came from Treviso, asparagus from Bassano, cherries from Marostica, apples from Verona and Trento, wild mushrooms from Trentino, and olives and their oil, grapes, raisins and wine from Lake Garda. Cheeses arrived from Alpine valleys, and fish and seafood sprang from lakes, rivers and the sea. All of this food made its way to Venice, where local chefs combined it with spices and flavorings, creating a style of cooking that remains distinct throughout Italy.

The Venetian Empire collapsed in 1797, and Napoléon and the French took control until 1815. They were followed by the Austrians, then at the zenith of their empire, who occupied all of the northeast until the 1860s, gradually relinquishing pieces when Italy was unified. But all of the pieces of the Italian "occupation" of this territory would not be in place until 1954. In the meantime, Austrian cookery and commerce dominated, and Trieste became the principal port of the Austro-Hungarian Empire. During this period, the new spice route flowed from Trieste through Udine to Vienna and Budapest. Cinnamon, nutmeg, poppy seeds, cacao and coffee all passed along this road, and the flavors became central to Friulian cuisine.

Cinnamon is an interesting example of how a simple spice has been widely adopted throughout northeastern Italy. *Baccalà mantecato* is salt cod blended with cinnamon and anchovies. A popular Venetian pasta sauce combines cinnamon and fresh ricotta cheese. In the Veneto countryside, one can find mutton spiced with cinnamon, while in Friuli there is *toc de purcit,* pork stewed with white wine, cinnamon and cloves. The spice is invariably paired with apples in this area (this seems to be the earliest example of this flavor match), and is a common protagonist in local breads and pastries. Such heavy use of exotic spicing is virtually unknown in the rest of Italy.

What is equally interesting is how impervious the northeast has been to what is traditionally thought of as Italian food. The tomato has never made great inroads there, and pasta is a third-class citizen, except when long strands are occasionally combined with seafood in Venice. Exquisite olive oil is produced around Lake Garda, but it does not have great impact on the foods of the region. The breads reflect the hearty flavors of Central Europe more than those of Italy.

What must be understood, then, is that although the food of the northeast is not like that of the rest of the peninsula, it is Italian food as much as that of Tuscany, Campania or Sicily. And the cuisine of the region fits in well with the model of how Italians eat now: Venetians have always enjoyed small portions of tasty food washed down by a glass of friendly wine. Food for them becomes an occasion to gather for quick, though meaningful, social interaction. The food of Friuli and Trentino–Alto Adige, with its slow-cooked soups and stews accompanied by unusually spiced delicate foods such as cinnamon and fruit gnocchi, or savory crisps made with mountain cheeses, makes for tasty complete meals that can be prepared in advance and served when needed.

This expediency of food preparation is essential in northeastern Italy today. Especially in the economically vibrant Veneto, industrialists and craftsmen no longer wish to tarry at the table if there is money to be made.

Shoppers converge on Padua's central market for the finest seasonal produce.

Le Verdure

All summer long, Italian cooks celebrate the versatility of fiori di zucca—*zucchini flowers—by filling them, stuffing them into pastas and eating them as a side dish.*

Le Verdure

VEGETABLES

For centuries Italy has been known as the garden of Europe. Italians, more than most people, have an innate knowledge of the properties of vegetables, whether it is how they taste raw and cooked or how they pair with other foods and flavorings. One of the reasons that Italians know vegetables so well is because they usually live close to where they are grown.

With the exception of Milan and, to a lesser extent, Turin, Italian cities have productive gardens within a short distance of the city walls. Some, such as Genoa, even have vegetable and herb plots within city limits. So

Meaty caps and bulbous stems form the distinctive profiles of Boletus eduli *or* porcini mushrooms.

Italians not only have contact with the cultivation process, but also can often select vegetables that have been newly picked, when all of their flavor properties are at their peak.

Similarly, most Italians, despite increasingly busy lives, purchase vegetables the day they plan to eat them. They know that the freshness of the produce invariably makes the difference between an average meal and a great one. Vegetables acquired for consumption three days hence are muted by the time they are eaten and, for most Italians, that simply will not do.

In their pursuit of excellence in vegetables (and fruits), Italians are culinary geographers and timekeepers. They know through experience that particular places produce better-quality produce, owing to reasons of soil and climate. The basil from Liguria tastes better because the strong sun and the sea air combine in a way that could not happen in landlocked regions such as Lombardy or Umbria. The volcanic soil near Naples imparts a flavor to tomatoes that no other place can rival. These tomatoes, known as San Marzano, are prized throughout the country, and Italians will pay more to have them carefully shipped as quickly as possible.

Another famous example is radicchio. To foreigners, this invariably is a tight ball of red-and-white leaves. In fact, radicchio in Liguria and Friuli is a pleasant green-leaved vegetable, while in Treviso (in the Veneto) it is

Previous pages: Left to right: Eggplant with Herbs (recipe page 94); Fennel with Olive Oil and Parsley (recipe page 93); Zucchini Marinated in Olive Oil and Wine Vinegar (recipe page 106)

In Bologna, a produce vendor takes pride in his wares, carefully selecting the best specimens for his customers.

the traditional red and white but is shaped more like romaine (cos) lettuce. In other places it looks like a flowering head of lettuce, and in still others, such as Chioggia (in the Veneto), it is a little solid sphere.

Italians also know when to purchase vegetables. Unlike people in other nations who often show little regard for what naturally appears each season, Italians look forward to the annual return of foods with eager anticipation. Late winter brings artichokes in Albenga (Liguria) and exquisite potatoes from Avezzano (Abruzzo). Asparagus (especially from the Veneto) is a harbinger of spring, and new peas (from Lazio) speak of summer. Later in the summer there are purple onions from Tropea (Calabria), followed by the year's finest tomatoes. Autumn is the best time for wild mushrooms throughout the country and truffles in Piedmont and Umbria. Late autumn brings the olive harvest. Most will be used for oil and others will be preserved in brine or salt. But in some regions (including Tuscany), a part of the olive harvest is cooked or baked in breads for immediate consumption.

Many Italians even distinguish between the early and later appearances of a particular vegetable each year. The first arrivals are called *primizie,* and they are cooked with utmost care, usually just blanched or gently sautéed, so that their delicate flavors can shine through. Baby eggplants (aubergines) from Calabria and baby zucchini (courgettes) from Sicily are among the most popular *primizie.* In much of Italy, people customarily make a wish when eating a vegetable for the first time each year, a gesture that serves as a moment of thanks and recognition of nature's generosity.

When choosing which vegetable dishes to prepare, try to think with the seasons as the Italians do—that will lead you to the best results. To serve *verdure,* be bold about where they fit into the meal. Some of these dishes can be interchanged from antipasto to plated first course to side dish—even to a light main course.

Ultimately, the joy of eating an Italian vegetable is hard to pinpoint: is it in the selection, in the anticipation of tasting it, in the cooking, in the eating or in the happy reflection? It is a bit of all of these.

INSALATA DI ZUCCHINE E PARMIGIANO

Zucchini and Parmesan Cheese Salad

It is essential that the zucchini you use for this recipe be small, young and very fresh. In the winter months, finely cut fresh artichoke hearts can be used in place of the zucchini. This salad can also be served as an antipasto.

10 small zucchini (courgettes), cut into thin rounds
3 tablespoons extra-virgin olive oil
juice of 2 lemons
salt and freshly ground pepper
3 oz (90 g) Parmesan cheese, cut into fine shavings with a
    vegetable peeler or sharp knife

🖝 In a bowl, combine the zucchini, oil, lemon juice and salt and pepper to taste. Toss to coat the zucchini rounds evenly. Let stand at room temperature for 1 hour.

🖝 Drain the zucchini. In a salad bowl, arrange a layer of zucchini rounds. Top with a layer of Parmesan cheese. Repeat the layers until all the ingredients have been used, ending with the cheese. Serve at once.

SERVES 6

PEPERONI AI CAPPERI E ACCIUGHE

Peppers Stuffed with Rice, Capers and Anchovies

In summer, I serve these stuffed peppers on their own as a first course. They are also excellent picnic fare. Select peppers that are not too large and have solid "walls" for holding the stuffing.

6 large red or yellow bell peppers (capsicums) or other
    sweet peppers
2 cups (12 oz/360 g) Arborio or long-grain white rice
2 tablespoons chopped fresh flat-leaf (Italian) parsley
1 tablespoon chopped fresh basil
2 cloves garlic, chopped
2 tablespoons drained brine-cured capers, chopped
6 olive oil–packed anchovy fillets, drained and chopped
½ cup (4 fl oz/120 ml) extra-virgin olive oil
1 ripe tomato, peeled and diced
salt and freshly ground pepper

🖝 Preheat an oven to 350°F (180°C).

🖝 Place the sweet peppers in a baking dish. Bake until tender when pierced with the tip of a knife, about 40 minutes. Remove from the oven and, when cool enough to handle, cut off the tops and reserve. Carefully scrape out the seeds and ribs without tearing the peppers, then set aside.

🖝 Meanwhile, bring a saucepan filled with salted water to a boil. Add the rice and boil until tender, about 18 minutes. Drain well and rinse under cold water to cool. Transfer to a bowl. Add the parsley, basil, garlic, capers and anchovies and mix gently. Drizzle on the oil and stir to coat all the ingredients evenly. Add the tomato, mix once again and season to taste with salt and pepper.

🖝 Fill the peppers with the rice mixture and replace their tops. Arrange on a platter and serve.

SERVES 6

FRITTATA DI POMODORI

Tomato Frittata

A frittata should never be put into an oven to cook, as it will dry out. Although this version is best made with cherry tomatoes—the smallest ones you can find—sliced plum (Roma) tomatoes can be substituted. I often serve this frittata as a first course or as an appetizer, at room temperature and cut into small wedges.

Clockwise from top: Tomato Frittata; Zucchini and Parmesan Cheese Salad; Peppers Stuffed with Rice, Capers and Anchovies

6 eggs
1 tablespoon chopped fresh basil
salt and freshly ground pepper
10 oz (300 g) ripe cherry tomatoes (about 1½ cups, stemmed; see note)
2 tablespoons extra-virgin olive oil

❧ In a bowl, lightly whisk the eggs with the basil. Season to taste with salt and pepper. Gently stir in the tomatoes.
❧ In a deep nonstick frying pan over medium heat, warm 1 tablespoon of the oil. When it begins to bubble, pour in the egg mixture and cook for about 2 minutes. Then reduce the heat to low, cover and cook until the eggs are almost set, about 5 minutes. Invert the frittata browned side up onto the pan lid or a flat plate. Add the remaining oil to the pan and, when hot, slide in the frittata browned side up. Cook, uncovered, over low heat until the second side is golden but the center is still moist, no more than about 2 minutes longer. Slide the frittata onto a platter and serve hot, warm or at room temperature.

SERVES 6

Left to right: Asparagus with White Wine Sauce;
Grilled Radicchio with Pancetta

Piemonte

ASPARAGI CON SALSA AL VINO BIANCO
Asparagus with White Wine Sauce

Until 1861, Piedmont was part of the Savoy lands that extended into France. Many of the dishes typical of the area—including this one—are a testament to the elegant cuisine of that era. It can be made more substantial with the addition of fried eggs, arranging them on top of the asparagus spears. Green or white asparagus can be used.

4 lb (2 kg) asparagus spears
6 egg yolks
1½ cups (12 fl oz/360 ml) dry white wine
salt
2 tablespoons unsalted butter

☙ Snap or cut off the tough ends of the asparagus. Select a tall, narrow saucepan that will accommodate the asparagus standing with the tips facing upward and that can be tightly covered. Fill the pan half full with salted water and bring to a boil. Stand the asparagus in the pan, cover tightly and cook until tender when pierced with a knife, 7–10 minutes. Drain and keep warm.

☙ In the top pan of a double boiler, whisk together the egg yolks and wine and season to taste with salt. Place over boiling water in the bottom pan and cook, beating constantly, until the mixture coats a spoon, about 5 minutes. Whisk in the butter, mixing well.

☙ Arrange the asparagus on a platter with their tips toward the center. Transfer the sauce to a warmed bowl and offer alongside or spoon over the asparagus.

SERVES 6

Toscana

FUNGHI PORCINI ALL'ALLORO
Porcini Mushrooms with Bay Leaves

Funghi porcini, meaty wild mushrooms, grow abundantly in the fall in Italy and occasionally pop up during warm, humid spells in late spring. Like all mushrooms, they must be carefully brushed clean. If they are rinsed in water, they absorb the liquid and their distinctive flavor is destroyed. Fresh shiitake or button mushrooms can be used in place of the porcini.

1¼ lb (600 g) fresh porcini mushrooms
6 tablespoons (3 fl oz/90 ml) extra-virgin olive oil
salt and freshly ground pepper
2 bay leaves
juice of 1 lemon
2 tablespoons chopped fresh flat-leaf (Italian) parsley

☙ Preheat a broiler (griller).
☙ Cut off the stems of the porcini and save them for another use. Gently brush away any dirt from the porcini caps. Select a flameproof baking dish large enough to accommodate the mushrooms in a single layer and lightly brush it with a little of the oil. Arrange the mushroom caps in the prepared dish, rounded side up, and brush with some of the

oil. Season to taste with salt and pepper, and tuck the bay leaves around the mushrooms. Slip under the broiler about 4 in (10 cm) from the heat and broil (grill) until tender and slightly golden, about 10 minutes.

☙ In a small bowl, stir together the remaining oil, the lemon juice and the parsley. Season the dressing to taste with salt and pepper.

☙ Transfer the mushrooms to a warmed platter, discarding the bay leaves. Pass the dressing in a bowl.

SERVES 6   *Photograph page 186*

Veneto

RADICCHIO ALLA PANCETTA
Grilled Radicchio with Pancetta

If possible, use the long, red-leaved Treviso variety of radicchio. Belgian endive (chicory/witloof) can be substituted. If you cannot find pancetta, bacon will give the dish a pleasingly smoky flavor.

6 heads radicchio (red chicory), ¼ lb (120 g) each (see note)
1 tablespoon extra-virgin olive oil
6 slices pancetta

☙ Preheat a broiler (griller).
☙ Place the radicchio on a broiler pan (tray) and place under the broiler about 4 in (10 cm) from the heat. Broil (grill), turning once, for about 2 minutes on each side. Alternatively, grill on a preheated gas grill.
☙ Preheat an oven to 400°F (200°C). Oil a baking pan with the olive oil. Unfurl the pancetta slices and roll each radicchio head in a strip of the pancetta. Place them side by side in the prepared baking pan.
☙ Bake until the pancetta begins to turn golden, about 10 minutes. Transfer to a platter and serve.

SERVES 6

Toscana

POMODORI ALLE ERBE
Baked Tomatoes with Herbs

For the herbal mix, use oregano, mint, basil, parsley, tarragon and thyme in any combination. This recipe can be prepared with grated Parmesan cheese in place of the bread crumbs, in which case you should use only one herb in the filling.

6 large, ripe tomatoes
6 tablespoons (½ oz/15 g) chopped mixed fresh herbs (see note)
6 tablespoons (1½ oz/45 g) fine dried bread crumbs
6 tablespoons (3 fl oz/90 ml) extra-virgin olive oil
salt and freshly ground pepper

☙ Preheat an oven to 350°F (180°C).
☙ Halve the tomatoes crosswise and squeeze gently to eliminate some of the juice and the seed sacs.
☙ In a small bowl, stir together the herbs, bread crumbs and oil and season to taste with salt and pepper. Spoon the mixture into the tomato halves, dividing it evenly, and arrange the halves in a baking dish.
☙ Bake until tender, about 30 minutes. Serve hot, warm or at room temperature.

SERVES 6   *Photograph pages 90–91*

Campania

PEPERONCINI AL FILETTO
Green Peppers in Tomato Sauce

These little green peppers have a bittersweet taste all their own. In Naples, where the locals are particularly fond of them, they are called "the peasants' chocolate." It may be difficult to find the identical pepper outside of Italy; in some areas, a small, sweet "Italian frying pepper" is available. The closest substitute would be the mild Anaheim chili pepper, which is much larger and should be cut into chunks. Strips of green bell pepper (capsicum) can be prepared in the same way, but the taste is quite different. Serve warm or at room temperature.

2 lb (1 kg) mild green peppers (see note)
2 cloves garlic, chopped
6 tablespoons (3 fl oz/90 ml) extra-virgin olive oil
6 small, ripe tomatoes, peeled and chopped, or 1 cup (6 oz/ 180 g) chopped canned tomatoes
salt and freshly ground pepper
small handful of fresh basil leaves, torn into pieces

Cut off the stem from each pepper and pry out the seeds with the tip of a small, sharp knife; set the peppers aside. In a deep saucepan over medium heat, warm the garlic in the oil until it begins to take on color, about 5 minutes. Add the peppers, cover and cook, stirring occasionally, until the peppers begin to soften, about 10 minutes.

Add the tomatoes, season to taste with salt and pepper and mix well. Cover, reduce the heat to low and cook until the peppers are tender and the sauce has thickened slightly, another 10 minutes.

Remove from the heat, stir in the basil and transfer to a serving dish.

SERVES 6

Campania

MELANZANE A "FUNGETIELLO"
Sautéed Eggplant

The name of this dish, a quick and delectable Neapolitan classic, derives from the word fungo, *or "mushroom," because eggplant prepared in this way recalls the earthy character of mushrooms.*

⅓ cup (2½ fl oz/80 ml) extra-virgin olive oil
2 cloves garlic, finely chopped
pinch of red pepper flakes
2 lb (1 kg) eggplants (aubergines), diced
5 ripe plum (Roma) tomatoes, peeled and finely chopped, or canned tomatoes, finely chopped
salt
about 24 small fresh basil leaves

In a saucepan over medium heat, warm the oil. Add the garlic and pepper flakes and cook, stirring, until the garlic begins to take on color, about 3 minutes. Add the eggplants and cook, stirring occasionally, until they begin to soften, about 10 minutes.

Add the tomatoes, season to taste with salt and mix well. Continue to cook over medium heat for another 5 minutes. Reduce the heat to low, cover and simmer until the eggplants are tender and the liquid evaporates, about 10 minutes longer.

Remove from the heat and stir in the basil leaves. Transfer to a warmed dish and serve.

SERVES 6

Clockwise from left: Baked Tomatoes with Herbs (recipe page 89); Sautéed Eggplant; Green Peppers in Tomato Sauce

MIGLIO AL POMODORO

Millet with Tomatoes

Here is a good example of an old recipe rediscovered for today's kitchen. Millet, a tiny yellow seed with a pleasant crunch, has resurfaced because it is so nutritious; originally it was favored because it was plentiful and filling. It is easily found in any health-food store. You can also transform this

recipe into a soup by adding some light chicken or vegetable stock (recipe on page 40).

generous 2 cups (13 oz/400 g) millet
4 cups (32 fl oz/1 l) water
1 lb (480 g) plum (Roma) tomatoes, peeled and chopped
1 yellow onion, chopped
salt and freshly ground pepper
2 tablespoons unsalted butter
handful of fresh basil leaves

Left to right: Sweet-and-Sour Cabbage; Millet with Tomatoes

🐇 In a saucepan, combine the millet and water and bring to a boil. Reduce the heat to low, cover and cook until tender, about 40 minutes.

🐇 Add the tomatoes and onion, season to taste with salt and pepper and continue to cook, covered, until all the liquid is absorbed and the millet has the consistency of risotto, about 20 minutes longer.

🐇 Add the butter, sprinkle with the basil and mix well. Transfer to a warmed dish and serve very hot.

SERVES 6

Friuli

CAVOLO IN AGRODOLCE
Sweet-and-Sour Cabbage

Cabbage has a slightly Nordic flavor that goes well with pork. It has long been popular in Fruili, a legacy from the days when the area was under Austro-Hungarian dominion. I also like to serve this dish with roast veal. The sour taste of the vinegar makes it a good partner to fish as well.

1 tablespoon unsalted butter
1 tablespoon extra-virgin olive oil
1 head green or red cabbage, about 2 lb (1 kg), cored and shredded
¼ cup (2 fl oz/60 ml) white wine vinegar
½ cup (4 fl oz/120 ml) water, plus more if needed
2 Golden Delicious or similar sweet, juicy apples, peeled, halved, cored and sliced
salt
2 tablespoons red currant jelly (optional)

🐇 In a deep saucepan over medium heat, melt the butter with the oil. Add the cabbage, cover and cook, stirring occasionally, until wilted, about 10 minutes. Uncover, add the vinegar and cook until evaporated, just a few minutes.

🐇 Add the water, reduce the heat to low, cover and cook until the cabbage is very tender, about 1 hour. If necessary, add more water during cooking to keep the mixture moist.

🐇 Add the apples and cook until just tender, about 5 minutes longer. Season to taste with salt and stir in the jelly (if using), mixing well.

🐇 Transfer to a warmed dish and serve immediately.

SERVES 6

Lombardia

FINOCCHI ALL'OLIO E PREZZEMOLO
Fennel with Olive Oil and Parsley

Italian cooks identify fennel by gender. The elongated bulbs are female and are stronger in flavor than the rounder, more tender male bulbs. The latter are preferred for dishes calling for raw fennel and for such uncomplicated recipes as this one. This dish can be eaten hot, at room temperature or cold and would be a good addition to an antipasto selection.

6 fennel bulbs (see note)
1 tablespoon fresh lemon juice
6 tablespoons (3 fl oz/90 ml) extra-virgin olive oil
1 tablespoon chopped fresh flat-leaf (Italian) parsley
salt and freshly ground pepper

🐇 Cut off the fennel tops and discard or reserve for another use. Cut each bulb lengthwise into quarters. Bring a saucepan filled with salted water to a boil. Add the fennel, reduce the heat to medium, cover and cook until tender, about 10 minutes.

🐇 Drain the fennel and arrange on an oval serving platter. Drizzle with the lemon juice and the oil, sprinkle with the parsley and season to taste with salt and pepper. Serve.

SERVES 6   *Photograph pages 82–83*

POLPETTE DI SPINACI
Spinach Balls

These are delicious on a platter surrounding a meat dish. You can also serve them as a first course dressed with tomato sauce (see recipe below). When you clean the spinach, it is not necessary to eliminate the stems unless they are very tough.

2 lb (1 kg) spinach
4 tablespoons (2 oz/60 g) unsalted butter
¾ cup (3 oz/90 g) finely shredded Fontina cheese
2 eggs
pinch of freshly grated nutmeg
1 cup (4 oz/120 g) all-purpose (plain) flour
salt and freshly ground pepper
¼ cup (2 fl oz/60 ml) extra-virgin olive oil

✆ In a large saucepan, cook the spinach in a little boiling salted water until wilted, about 5 minutes. Drain and squeeze dry.

✆ In a saucepan over medium heat, melt 2 tablespoons of the butter. Add the spinach and cook, stirring frequently, until any liquid it gives off evaporates, about 10 minutes. Transfer the spinach to a cutting board and chop very finely. Place in a bowl and add the cheese, eggs, nutmeg and half of the flour. Season to taste with salt and pepper and mix well. The mixture should be quite dry.

✆ Flour your hands and form the spinach mixture into ovals about 2 in (5 cm) long. As they are formed, roll them in the remaining flour and set aside on a tray.

✆ In a nonstick frying pan over medium heat, melt the remaining 2 tablespoons butter with the oil. Add the spinach balls and cook, turning frequently, until golden on all sides, about 10 minutes. Transfer to a warmed dish and serve hot.

SERVES 6

SALSA DI POMODORO
Tomato Sauce

In summertime when tomatoes are ripe and full of flavor, Italian cooks use them for making this sauce. During the rest of the year, canned tomatoes are used because they are tastier than the fresh cool-weather tomatoes in the market. Be sure to buy good-quality canned Italian tomatoes; lesser brands lack the desirable deep red color and generally contain too much juice.

4 tablespoons (2 fl oz/60 ml) extra-virgin olive oil
2 cloves garlic, chopped
2 lb (1 kg) ripe plum (Roma) tomatoes, peeled and roughly chopped, or canned tomatoes, with their juice
salt
handful of fresh basil leaves or 1 tablespoon dried oregano

✆ In a saucepan over low heat, warm 3 tablespoons of the oil. Add the garlic and sauté until translucent, about 3 minutes. Add the tomatoes and cover with the lid ajar so the steam can escape. Cook, stirring occasionally, until all the excess liquid has evaporated and a thick sauce has formed, about 50 minutes.

✆ Season to taste with salt and stir in the remaining 1 tablespoon oil and the basil or oregano. Use as directed in individual recipes.

MAKES ABOUT 2 CUPS (16 FL OZ/480 ML)

MELANZANE ALLA SARDA
Eggplant with Herbs

While there are many styles of pecorino cheese made in Italy, the one from Sardinia is particularly tasty and salty. It gives this dish the distinction of being called alla sarda. Offer this as an accompaniment to fish, or serve as an antipasto.

4 ripe tomatoes, peeled and chopped
6 fresh sage leaves, chopped
1 yellow onion, chopped
1 tablespoon dried oregano
3 tablespoons grated aged pecorino cheese
3 tablespoons extra-virgin olive oil
2 cloves garlic, chopped
salt and freshly ground pepper
6 small globe eggplants (aubergines), about 6 oz (180 g) each
2 tablespoons water

✆ Preheat an oven to 350°F (180°C).

✆ In a bowl, stir together the tomatoes, sage, onion, oregano, pecorino cheese, oil and garlic. Season to taste with salt and pepper.

✆ Cut the eggplants in half lengthwise and make several deep incisions in the pulp of each half. Fill the slits with the tomato mixture and place the eggplants in a baking dish. Add the water to the dish.

✆ Bake until tender when pierced with a knife, about 40 minutes. Transfer to a warmed platter and serve.

SERVES 6   *Photograph pages 82–83*

CARDI ALLA CIPOLLA E POMODORO
Cardoon with Onion and Tomato

Cardoon, a pale green thistle that resembles a head of celery, is popular in central Italy, where it is commonly fried or sautéed. It is often served as an accompaniment to braised meats.

6 tablespoons (3 fl oz/90 ml) extra-virgin olive oil
2 yellow onions, finely chopped
12 plum (Roma) tomatoes, peeled and chopped
salt and freshly ground pepper
juice of 1 lemon
1 cardoon, about 2 lb (1 kg)

✆ In a saucepan over low heat, warm the oil. Add the onions and tomatoes, cover and cook, stirring occasionally, until the flavors are blended, about 10 minutes. Season to taste with salt and pepper.

✆ Meanwhile, fill a large bowl with water and add the lemon juice. Remove and discard the base from the cardoon and discard any tough outer stalks. Trim and discard the leaves and spurs from the tender stalks and then scrape stalks with a small knife to remove all strings and fibers. Cut into long, thin pieces. Place in the lemon water to prevent discoloring.

✆ When all the cardoon is cut, drain and add to the saucepan with the tomatoes. Cover and continue to cook over low heat until the cardoon is tender, about 30 minutes.

✆ Taste and adjust the seasoning, then transfer to a warmed dish to serve.

SERVES 6

Clockwise from top: Cardoon with Onion and Tomato; Tomato Sauce; Spinach Balls

Toscana

CARCIOFI RIPIENI DI RICOTTA

Artichokes Filled with Ricotta

Italian artichokes are small, so I usually plan on serving two per person. If you use large artichokes, one per person should be sufficient, but you will need to cook them longer.

juice of 1 lemon
12 artichokes
2 tablespoons extra-virgin olive oil
2 eggs, separated
¾ cup plus 2 tablespoons (7 oz/210 g) ricotta cheese
6 tablespoons (1½ oz/45 g) grated Parmesan cheese
salt and freshly ground pepper

❧ Fill a bowl with cold water and add the lemon juice. Trim off the top one-third of each artichoke, then cut off the tough outer leaves. Using a spoon, dig out the prickly choke from the center. Trim the stem even with the base. As each artichoke is trimmed, place it in the lemon water to prevent it from discoloring. Bring a saucepan filled with salted water to a boil. Drain the artichokes and add to the boiling water. Boil until tender when pierced with a fork, about 10 minutes. Drain, then invert the artichokes to drain thoroughly.

❧ Preheat an oven to 350°F (180°C). Select a baking dish large enough to accommodate the artichokes in a single layer and oil with the olive oil.

❧ In a bowl, using a fork, blend together the egg yolks and ricotta. Stir in the Parmesan cheese and season to taste with salt and pepper. In another bowl, beat the egg whites until firm peaks form. Fold them into the ricotta mixture, being careful not to overmix and deflate the mixture.

❧ Pat the artichokes dry and gently spread the leaves to form little cups. Spoon some of the ricotta mixture into the center of each artichoke, dividing it evenly. Stand the artichokes side by side in the prepared baking dish.

❧ Bake until the ricotta mixture swells and turns golden, about 20 minutes. Serve immediately.

SERVES 6

Venezia Giulia

PATATE ALLA S'CIAVA

Large Bacon-and-Potato Pancake

Here is a classic way potatoes are prepared in the area around Trieste where Austro-Hungarian influences are found in the local specialties. Traditionally, this dish is served as an accompaniment to pork, often along with sauerkraut. The latter is particularly popular in the surrounding region of Venezia Giulia.

2 lb (1 kg) baking potatoes, unpeeled
3 tablespoons extra-virgin olive oil
1 yellow onion, chopped
1 clove garlic, smashed
5 oz (150 g) bacon, diced
salt and freshly ground pepper

❧ Place the potatoes in a saucepan with salted water to cover generously. Bring to a boil and cook until tender when pierced with a fork, 20–30 minutes, depending upon size. Drain the potatoes and, when cool enough to handle, peel them and cut into thick pieces.

❧ Preheat an oven to 400°F (200°C).

❧ In a deep saucepan over medium heat, warm the oil. Add the onion, garlic and bacon and cook, stirring often, until the onion and garlic are translucent and the bacon is crisp, about 5 minutes.

❧ Reduce the heat to low. Add the potatoes, one piece at a time, mashing them with a fork and stirring well so they absorb the flavors. When a smooth mixture has formed, season to taste with salt and pepper and remove from the pan to a work surface. Shape the potato mixture into a large pancake about 12 in (30 cm) in diameter and place in a baking dish.

❧ Bake until a golden crust forms on the top, about 20 minutes. Invert the pancake onto a flat plate and return it to the baking dish, browned side up. Bake until a crust forms on the second side, about 10 minutes longer.

❧ Serve the pancake directly from the baking dish or turn out onto a platter. Serve immediately.

SERVES 6

Clockwise from top: Large Bacon-and-Potato Pancake; Artichokes Filled with Ricotta; Grilled Vegetables on Skewers (recipe page 111)

Left to right: Pecorino Cheese and Fava Bean Salad (recipe page 43); Tomato and Mozzarella Salad with Arugula (recipe page 99);
Yellow Peppers and Fennel with Cumin Seeds (recipe page 99)

Top to bottom: Baked Spinach Nests; Frittata of Sweet Onions

NIDI DI SPINACI
Baked Spinach Nests

These decorative nests complement chicken or rabbit dishes. If you like, spoon a little tomato sauce (recipe on page 94) over the top.

3 lb (1.5 kg) spinach
12 slices white bread
6 hard-cooked eggs
5 tablespoons (2½ oz/80 g) unsalted butter
1 tablespoon extra-virgin olive oil
salt and freshly ground pepper
2 tablespoons grated Parmesan cheese

❧ Remove the tough stems from the spinach. Place the leaves in a large pot with a little salted water and bring to a boil over medium heat. Cook, turning the leaves occasionally, until tender, about 5 minutes. Drain, squeeze dry thoroughly and chop. Set aside.

❧ Toast the bread slices until golden on both sides. Peel the hard-cooked eggs; discard the whites (or reserve for another use) and cut each yolk in half. Set the toasts and yolks aside.

❧ In a saucepan over medium heat, melt 2 tablespoons of the butter with the oil. Add the spinach and cook for several minutes, stirring often, while the spinach takes on flavor and the moisture evaporates. Remove from the heat, season to taste with salt and pepper and mix in the Parmesan cheese.

❧ Preheat an oven to 400°F (200°C). Grease a baking sheet (tray) with 1 tablespoon of the butter.

❧ Arrange a little nest of spinach on each toast and place half an egg yolk in the center of each nest. Place the nest-topped toasts on the prepared baking sheet.

❧ In a small saucepan over low heat, melt the remaining 2 tablespoons butter. Pour the butter evenly over the spinach nests. Cover with aluminum foil. Bake until heated through, about 10 minutes. Arrange on a warmed platter and serve at once.

SERVES 6

CAPRESE CON LA RUCOLA
Tomato and Mozzarella Salad with Arugula

Here is a variation on the celebrated caprese *salad, a summer specialty from the isle of Capri. In this version, arugula is used in place of the traditional basil, giving the salad a slightly nutty flavor. Top-quality mozzarella and flavorful ripe tomatoes are essential for the success of this simple recipe. Do not refrigerate before serving, or much of the flavor will be lost.*

1 lb (480 g) ripe tomatoes
1 lb (480 g) mozzarella cheese, preferably made from water buffalo's milk *(mozzarella di bufala)*
6 oz (180 g) arugula (rocket) leaves, stems discarded
salt and freshly ground pepper
¼ cup (2 fl oz/60 ml) extra-virgin olive oil

❧ Slice the tomatoes and mozzarella and arrange on a platter, alternating the slices with the arugula leaves. Alternatively, alternate only the tomatoes and cheese slices and cluster the arugula in the center of the platter. Season to taste with salt and pepper, drizzle with the oil and serve.

SERVES 6   *Photograph page 97*

PEPERONI GIALLI E FINOCCHI AL COMINO
Yellow Peppers and Fennel with Cumin Seeds

These same seasonings complement finely sliced leeks and onions. The quantity of cumin and fennel can be varied to taste. Cumin, a spice originally adopted from the Middle East, used to be found only occasionally in Italian cooking. It is now becoming more common in newer dishes such as this one.

4 yellow bell peppers (capsicums), seeded and cut into pieces
4 fennel bulbs, sliced lengthwise
1 tablespoon cumin seeds
1 tablespoon fennel seeds
3 tablespoons extra-virgin olive oil
pinch of salt, or as needed
¼ cup (2 fl oz/60 ml) water
freshly ground pepper

❧ In a deep saucepan, combine the bell peppers, sliced fennel, cumin and fennel seeds, oil and salt. Stir well, pour in the water and place over medium heat. Cover and cook until the vegetables are very tender, about 20 minutes.

❧ Uncover, stir well and raise the heat to evaporate the excess liquid. Some cooking juices should remain. Adjust the salt and season to taste with pepper. Transfer to a warmed platter and serve.

SERVES 6   *Photograph page 97*

FRITTATA DI CIPOLLE
Frittata of Sweet Onions

If the onions are allowed to cook slowly for a long time, they render this Italian omelet not only very tasty, but also very light. The frittata should be about 1½ inches (4 cm) thick, and firm on the outside yet moist on the inside. Serve as an antipasto, a light lunch or a brunch dish.

4 tablespoons (2 fl oz/60 ml) extra-virgin olive oil
4 lb (2 kg) red (Spanish) onions, finely chopped
½ cup (4 fl oz/120 ml) dry white wine
4 eggs, lightly beaten
salt and freshly ground pepper

❧ In a saucepan over very low heat, warm 2 tablespoons of the oil. Add the onions, stir to coat with the oil, cover and cook for at least 1 hour. Stir occasionally with a wooden spoon and add a little white wine every 20 minutes or so to keep them moist. When the onions are very soft, transfer them to a bowl and let cool. Mix in the eggs and season to taste with salt and pepper.

❧ In a deep nonstick frying pan over medium heat, warm 1 tablespoon of the remaining oil. When it begins to bubble, pour in the egg mixture and cook for about 2 minutes. Then reduce the heat to low, cover and cook until the eggs are almost set, about 5 minutes. Invert the frittata browned side up onto the pan lid or a flat plate. Add the remaining 1 tablespoon oil to the pan and, when hot, slide in the frittata browned side up. Cook, uncovered, over low heat until the second side is golden but the center is still moist, no more than 2 minutes longer.

❧ Slide the frittata onto a platter and serve hot, warm or at room temperature.

SERVES 6

ZUCCHINE ALLA MENTA E FORMAGGIO

Zucchini with Mint and Cheese

Select small zucchini, as their flavor is superior to that of larger ones. This dish is especially suitable for a summer luncheon.

2 lb (1 kg) small zucchini (courgettes)
1 tablespoon unsalted butter
3 tablespoons extra-virgin olive oil

1 cup (4 oz/120 g) grated Parmesan cheese
2 tablespoons chopped fresh mint
1 egg
salt and freshly ground pepper

☙ Bring a saucepan filled with salted water to a boil. Add the zucchini and parboil for about 3 minutes. Using a slotted spoon, lift out the zucchini and set aside to cool.

☙ Preheat an oven to 350°F (180°C). Using the butter, grease a baking dish large enough to accommodate the zucchini in a single layer and then drizzle with the oil.

☙ Cut the cooled zucchini in half lengthwise and carefully scrape out the pulp into a bowl, forming shells with sturdy

100

Lombardia

CAVOLFIORE CON CAPPERI ED UOVO SODO

Cauliflower with Hard-Cooked Egg and Caper Sauce

In this recipe, small heads of cauliflower are presented with a pungent topping. If you like, substitute a sauce made from melted butter, grated Parmesan cheese and dried bread crumbs for the one given here.

2 small cauliflowers, about 1 lb (480 g) total weight
¼ cup (2 fl oz/60 ml) extra-virgin olive oil
3 tablespoons salt-cured capers, rinsed and drained
pinch of salt
2 hard-cooked egg yolks, crumbled

Trim away the leaves and the tough stem ends of the cauliflowers; break heads into large pieces.
Bring a pot filled with salted water to a boil. Add the cauliflowers, cover and cook until tender but firm, about 10 minutes.
Drain well and place on a serving platter. Drizzle immediately with the oil and sprinkle with the capers, salt and egg yolks. Serve immediately.

SERVES 6

CETRIOLI RIPIENI

Baked Cucumbers with Goat Cheese Stuffing

Select the cucumbers carefully. They should be ripe and not too watery. You can substitute Fontina cheese or grated Parmesan for the goat cheese, but you then must add a little butter to the stuffing to make it creamier. Chopped fresh flat-leaf (Italian) parsley can replace the chives.

4 tablespoons (2 fl oz/60 ml) extra-virgin olive oil
6 small cucumbers, each about 7 in (18 cm) long
½ lb (240 g) fresh goat cheese
2 tablespoons finely chopped fresh chives
salt and freshly ground pepper
2 egg whites

Preheat an oven to 350°F (180°C). Using 1 tablespoon of the oil, oil a baking dish large enough to hold the cucumbers in a single layer once they are cut in half.
Peel the cucumbers and cut in half lengthwise. Using a small spoon, scoop out and discard the seeds from each half. In a bowl, combine the goat cheese, chives, the remaining 3 tablespoons oil and salt and pepper to taste. Stir until smooth and well blended.
In a bowl, whip the egg whites to form stiff peaks. Fold the whites into the chive-cheese mixture until no white streaks remain; do not overmix.
Spoon the mixture onto the cucumber halves, dividing it evenly. Arrange the cucumber halves in the prepared baking dish. Bake until the stuffing has expanded and turned golden, about 40 minutes. Add a few tablespoons water to the baking dish if the cucumbers begin to stick during cooking.
Transfer the cucumbers to a warmed platter and serve immediately.

SERVES 6

Clockwise from left: Baked Cucumbers with Goat Cheese Stuffing; Cauliflower with Hard-Cooked Egg and Caper Sauce; Zucchini with Mint and Cheese

sides. Set aside the zucchini shells. Add the Parmesan cheese, mint and egg to the bowl and season to taste with salt and pepper. Mix well. Spoon the mixture into the zucchini shells, dividing it evenly.
Arrange the zucchini in a single layer in the prepared dish. Bake until the stuffing is golden and the zucchini are tender when pierced with a knife, about 30 minutes. Transfer to a warmed platter and serve hot or at room temperature.

SERVES 6

Rye Bread Salad with Balsamic Vinegar

Toscana

PANZANELLA AL PANE DI SEGALE E BALSAMICO
Rye Bread Salad with Balsamic Vinegar

In Italy, this salad is made with the coarse country bread that is a staple of the Italian table. It is difficult to find the same loaf outside the country, however. I have discovered that rye bread is a good substitute—you do not have to soak it in advance, which makes the dish even easier to prepare.

salt
2 tablespoons balsamic vinegar
freshly ground pepper
¼ cup (2 fl oz/60 ml) extra-virgin olive oil
3 ripe tomatoes, chopped
10 oz (300 g) rye bread, crusts removed and bread cut into
    ½-in (1-cm) cubes
1 large yellow onion, thinly sliced
handful of fresh basil leaves, torn into small pieces

✒ In a small bowl, dissolve salt to taste in the vinegar. Add pepper to taste and the oil and mix well.
✒ In a salad bowl, combine the tomatoes, bread, onion and basil. Drizzle with the vinegar mixture, toss well and serve.
SERVES 6

RAPANELLI, MELA E PROVOLONE IN INSALATA
Radish, Apple and Provolone Cheese Salad

This delicious, crunchy, healthful salad is a lovely first course or light main course in autumn, when the apples are at their best. Choose any flavorful apple variety in the market. To shave off calories, add a pinch of cumin seeds in place of the cheese. This can also be prepared with arugula (rocket) instead of the radishes, or even the slightly peppery radish greens themselves, as shown (be sure to choose young, tender radishes that have not been sprayed).

3 apples, peeled, cored and thinly sliced
7 oz (210 g) radishes, sliced or cut in half
7 oz (210 g) provolone cheese, cut into matchstick-sized pieces
juice of 1 lemon
salt and freshly ground pepper
¼ cup (2 fl oz/60 ml) extra-virgin olive oil

✒ Combine the apples, radishes and cheese on a large platter.
✒ In a small bowl, stir together the lemon juice and salt and pepper to taste, then stir in the oil, mixing thoroughly. Pour over the salad, toss well and serve.
SERVES 6

Radish, Apple and Provolone Cheese Salad

103

INSALATA DI SONGINO CON AVOCADO

Mâche Salad with Avocado

Avocados have become so popular in Italy that now you can even find them in market stalls. This salad can be served as a side dish with a meat course or as a first course. If mâche is unavailable, substitute cleaned, washed mixed field greens.

juice of 2 lemons
4 avocados, halved, pitted and peeled
½ lb (240 g) mâche (lamb's lettuce) or mixed field greens
1 teaspoon minced yellow onion
¼ cup (2 fl oz/60 ml) extra-virgin olive oil
salt and freshly ground pepper

Fill a bowl with water and add the lemon juice. Using a melon scoop, carve out small balls from the avocados, dropping them into the lemon water as they are formed to prevent discoloring. Alternatively, cut the avocados into chunks and drop into the water.

In a salad bowl, combine the mâche or field greens and onion. Using a slotted spoon, lift out the avocado balls or chunks and add to the bowl. Add the oil and season to taste with salt and pepper. Toss well and serve.

SERVES 6

INSALATA DI LATTUGA AL PROSCIUTTO

Prosciutto and Lettuce Salad with Honey Dressing

The addition of honey to this dressing is a contemporary innovation. The prosciutto should not overpower the taste of the lettuce, so select a mild product and do not add more than is indicated. Fontina cheese, which also goes well with honey, can be cut into matchstick-sized pieces and used in place of the prosciutto.

10 oz (300 g) lettuce such as romaine (cos) or other large-
   leaved variety, torn into bite-sized pieces
3 oz (90 g) prosciutto, cut into thin strips
1 teaspoon Dijon mustard
1 tablespoon red wine vinegar
1 tablespoon honey
salt and freshly ground pepper
¼ cup (2 fl oz/60 ml) extra-virgin olive oil
2 tablespoons chopped fresh chives

In a salad bowl, combine the lettuce and prosciutto. In a small bowl, stir together the mustard, vinegar and honey. Season to taste with salt and pepper.

Drizzle the mustard mixture over the lettuce and prosciutto and toss well. Add the oil and toss thoroughly again. Sprinkle with the chives and serve at once.

SERVES 6

Clockwise from left: Eggplant with Yogurt and Mint (recipe page 114); Prosciutto and Lettuce Salad with Honey Dressing; Mâche Salad with Avocado

CETRIOLI ALLA MENTA
Cucumbers with Mint

Ideally, cucumbers should be freshly picked and firm to the touch; otherwise, they have a bitter taste. For this recipe, I choose ones that are only about 6 inches (15 cm) long and thus do not have to discard their seeds.

6 cucumbers (see note)
1 tablespoon unsalted butter
2 tablespoons extra-virgin olive oil
2 cloves garlic, chopped
salt
handful of fresh mint leaves
1 teaspoon paprika

 Peel the cucumbers. Cut them lengthwise into quarters and then dice.

 In a saucepan over medium heat, melt the butter with the oil. Add the garlic and sauté until translucent, about 3 minutes. Do not allow it to take on color. Add the cucumbers and season to taste with salt. Cover and cook, stirring once gently, until the cucumbers are tender-crisp, about 5 minutes. Uncover and cook until all the liquid has evaporated.

 Sprinkle with the mint leaves and paprika, mix well and transfer to a warmed platter. Serve immediately.

SERVES 6

Lombardia

SOFFIATO DI CAROTE
Carrot Soufflé

French influences in the Lombardy region have led to a fondness for soufflés. This dish is an especially good accompaniment to red meat such as roast beef. It also makes an appealing first course. The pinch of nutmeg adds a subtle flavor.

1 lb (480 g) carrots, cut into large pieces
6 tablespoons (3 oz/90 g) unsalted butter
1 yellow onion, chopped
2 cups (16 fl oz/480 ml) milk
½ cup (2 oz/60 g) all-purpose (plain) flour
pinch of freshly grated nutmeg
1 teaspoon sugar
salt and freshly ground pepper
3 eggs, separated

 In a saucepan, combine the carrots with salted water to cover. Bring to a boil and cook until tender when pierced with a fork. The timing will depend upon the size of the carrots; check them occasionally for doneness after about 15 minutes of cooking. Drain well and pass through a food mill positioned over a bowl.

 Meanwhile, in a deep saucepan over medium heat, melt 2 tablespoons of the butter. Add the onion and sauté until translucent, about 3 minutes. Remove from the heat.

 Preheat an oven to 400°F (200°C). Grease a round baking dish 7 in (18 cm) in diameter and 3½ in (8.5 cm) deep with 1 tablespoon of the butter.

 Pour the milk into a saucepan and bring to just below a boil. In another saucepan over medium heat, melt the remaining 3 tablespoons butter. Add the flour and mix well with a wooden spoon. Add the hot milk a little at a time, stirring constantly. Cook, stirring, until smooth and thickened, 10–15 minutes. Add immediately to the carrots along with the onion, nutmeg, sugar and salt and pepper to taste.

 Add the egg yolks to the carrot mixture one at a time, stirring well after each addition until completely blended.

 In a bowl, beat the egg whites until stiff peaks form. Stir about one-fourth of the egg whites into the carrot mixture to lighten it. Then fold in the remaining whites just until no white streaks remain.

 Pour the carrot mixture into the prepared dish. Bake until the top has risen and is golden, about 30 minutes. Serve immediately.

SERVES 6

Campania

ZUCCHINE A "SCAPECE"
Zucchini Marinated in Olive Oil and Wine Vinegar

Like many traditional southern recipes, this dish takes a bit of time to prepare, but it can be kept in the refrigerator for up to three days before serving, during which time its flavors will intensify pleasantly. Serve it as part of an antipasto selection or as a side dish.

4 lb (2 kg) small zucchini (courgettes), cut into slices ¼ in (.5 cm) thick
salt
about 4 cups (32 fl oz/1 l) olive oil
2 handfuls of fresh mint leaves, about 1 cup (2 oz/60 g), loosely packed
red pepper flakes
½ cup (4 fl oz/120 ml) white wine vinegar
½ cup (4 fl oz/120 ml) water
2 cloves garlic, chopped

 Layer the zucchini slices in a colander, sprinkling each layer with salt. Set aside to drain for a couple of hours. Pat dry.

 Pour the oil into a large frying pan; the oil should be deep enough to immerse the zucchini slices completely. Heat to 340°F (170°C).

 When the oil is hot, add the zucchini slices a few at a time; do not crowd the pan. Fry until golden, 3–5 minutes. Using a slotted spoon, transfer to paper towels to drain. Repeat with the remaining zucchini slices.

 When all the slices are cooked, scoop out and reserve 2 tablespoons of the cooking oil; discard the remainder. Let the zucchini slices cool to room temperature.

 In a bowl, arrange the zucchini in layers, covering each with mint leaves, a pinch of pepper flakes and salt to taste.

 In a small pan, combine the vinegar and water and bring to a boil. Add the garlic, reduce the heat to medium and cook until the garlic softens and the flavors blend, about 10 minutes. Remove from the heat, add the 2 tablespoons reserved oil and immediately pour over the zucchini. Cover and refrigerate for at least 24 hours before serving, or for up to 3 days. Bring to room temperature before serving.

SERVES 10   *Photograph pages 82–83*

Top to bottom: Cucumbers with Mint; Carrot Soufflé

PATATE FRITTE
Deep-Fried Potatoes

Fried potatoes are a ubiquitous Italian contorno, *or accompaniment. This method for frying the potatoes has clear advantages: You don't have to interrupt your conversation at the dinner table to go and stand over the stove, as the potatoes fry without any attention. Less oil is used than for conventional deep-fried potatoes, and the potatoes come out particularly light and crispy on the outside and soft on the inside.*

2 lb (1 kg) boiling potatoes
about 4 cups (32 fl oz/1 l) olive oil for deep-frying
salt

Peel the potatoes and cut into long, uniform strips ½ in (1 cm) thick. Place the strips in a frying pan and pour in the oil to cover. Place over medium heat and, without ever stirring, fry uncovered until golden, about 30 minutes.

Using a slotted spoon, remove to paper towels to drain very briefly. Sprinkle with salt, transfer to a warmed platter and serve very hot.

SERVES 6

Campania

GATTO' DI PATATE
Gratin of Mashed Potato and Cheese

In the eighteenth century, when the Kingdom of Naples was ruled by the Bourbon monarchy, many French dishes were introduced to the area. In time, these dishes became thoroughly "Neapolitanized" and are now part of the local diet. This gratin, part of that French tradition, can be served as a first course or alongside a meat main course.

2 lb (1 kg) baking potatoes, unpeeled
4 tablespoons (2 oz/60 g) unsalted butter
3 tablespoons fine dried bread crumbs
⅓ cup (2½ fl oz/80 ml) milk
1 egg
½ cup (2 oz/60 g) grated Parmesan cheese
handful of chopped fresh flat-leaf (Italian) parsley
pinch of freshly grated nutmeg
salt and freshly ground pepper
3 oz (90 g) smoked provola cheese, sliced
3 oz (90 g) mozzarella cheese, sliced
3 oz (90 g) sliced prosciutto, cut into small pieces

Place the potatoes in a saucepan with salted water to cover generously. Bring to a boil and cook until tender when pierced, 20–30 minutes, depending upon size. Drain and, when cool enough to handle, remove the skins.

Preheat an oven to 350°F (180°C). Butter a 12-in (30-cm) round baking dish with 1 tablespoon of the butter. Coat with 2 tablespoons of the bread crumbs.

Cut up the potatoes and place in a large bowl. Add the milk, egg, half of the remaining butter, the Parmesan cheese, parsley, nutmeg and salt and pepper to taste. Using an electric mixer, beat until creamy. Pour half of the potato mixture into the prepared dish.

Top with the slices of provola and mozzarella cheeses and the prosciutto, covering evenly. Pour the remaining potato purée over the top and smooth the surface with a wooden spoon. Sprinkle evenly with the remaining 1 tablespoon bread crumbs. Cut the remaining 1½ tablespoons butter into small bits and dot the surface with the pieces.

Bake until golden, about 40 minutes. Serve hot, directly from the baking dish.

SERVES 6

Top to bottom: Deep-Fried Potatoes; Gratin of Mashed Potato and Cheese

PATATE RIPIENE DI GORGONZOLA

Baked Potatoes Stuffed with Gorgonzola

Stuffed potatoes in Italy are a contemporary adaptation of a dish popular in America. Use only good-quality, fresh Gorgonzola for this recipe. It should be very white and without any off odor. If you are unable to find satisfactory Gorgonzola, substitute grated Asiago or fresh goat's milk cheese.

6 large baking potatoes, about 7 oz (210 g) each
2 eggs
6 oz (180 g) Gorgonzola cheese
6 tablespoons (3 fl oz/90 ml) heavy (double) cream
salt and freshly ground pepper

❧ Preheat an oven to 350°F (180°C).

❧ Scrub each potato but do not peel. Wrap separately in pieces of aluminum foil. Place directly on an oven rack and bake until soft to the touch, about 1 hour.

❧ Remove from the oven . Leave the potatoes wrapped in foil and cut each one in half lengthwise. Scrape out some of the pulp from each half into a bowl, leaving shells about ½ in (1 cm) thick. Add the eggs, cheese and cream to the pulp and season to taste with salt and pepper. Mix well. Spoon the pulp back into the potato halves, dividing it evenly and mounding it slightly.

❧ Place in a baking pan and return to the oven. Bake until the surfaces begin to take on color, about 20 minutes. Remove from the oven, discard the aluminum foil and serve immediately.

SERVES 6

MELANZANE RIPIENE

Twice-Stuffed Eggplants

Hollowed eggplants hold a fluffy blend of the pulp mixed with besciamella (béchamel sauce); a boiled egg is cradled in the center of each, creating a double stuffing. This dish can be served with tomato sauce (recipe on page 94). It also makes a good main course for a vegetarian meal.

3 eggplants (aubergines), about 6 oz (180 g) each
4 cups (32 fl oz/1 l) olive oil
2 cups (16 fl oz/480 ml) milk
¼ cup (2 oz/60 g) unsalted butter
½ cup (2 oz/60 g) all-purpose (plain) flour
salt
2 tablespoons grated Parmesan cheese
1 teaspoon dried oregano
6 eggs

❧ Cut the eggplants in half lengthwise but do not peel. Pour the oil into a frying pan and heat to 340°F (170°C). When the oil is ready, place the eggplants in the pan cut sides down and fry for about 5 minutes, without stirring, until golden. Remove

Clockwise from top: Twice-Stuffed Eggplants; Tomato Sauce (recipe page 94); Baked Potatoes Stuffed with Gorgonzola

with tongs or a slotted spoon and drain on paper towels until cool. Using a spoon, scrape out the pulp into a bowl, taking care not to tear the skins. Reserve the skins.

❧ Transfer the pulp to a saucepan with 2 tablespoons of the frying oil and place over low heat. Warm the pulp, mashing it continuously with a fork, until smooth, about 10 minutes. Set aside to cool. Strain the remaining frying oil and save for another use.

❧ Prepare a béchamel sauce: Pour the milk into a saucepan and bring to just below a boil. In another saucepan over medium heat, melt the butter. Add the flour and stir until it is fully absorbed by the butter. Add the hot milk a little at a time, stirring constantly. Cook, stirring, until smooth and thickened, 10–15 minutes. Remove from the heat and let cool, stirring often to prevent a film from forming on the surface. Season to taste with salt.

❧ Preheat an oven to 400°F (200°C).

❧ Add 2 tablespoons of the cooled sauce to the mashed eggplant along with the Parmesan cheese and oregano. Taste and adjust with salt. Carefully spoon the eggplant mixture into the eggplant skins, dividing it equally and forming an indentation in the center.

❧ Bring a saucepan three-fourths full of water to a boil and carefully slip the eggs into the water. Boil for 5 minutes, then lift out the eggs with a slotted spoon and immerse in cold water until cool enough to handle. Carefully peel the eggs and place each egg in the center of a stuffed eggplant half.

❧ Transfer eggplant halves to a baking dish large enough to accommodate them in a single layer. Spoon the remaining sauce over the eggplant halves, dividing it evenly.

❧ Bake until the tops are golden, about 10 minutes. Arrange on a warmed platter and serve at once.

SERVES 6

SPIEDINI DI VERDURE ALLA GRIGLIA

Grilled Vegetables on Skewers

You can vary the look of this dish by alternating vegetables on skewers or grouping one or two kinds of vegetables on each skewer. Serve with grilled fish or grilled steak.

1 or 2 slender (Asian) eggplants (aubergines)
salt
12 small yellow or white onions, each about 1½ in (4 cm) in diameter
1 bell pepper (capsicum), seeded and cut into 1¼-in (3-cm) squares
12 cherry tomatoes
2 zucchini (courgettes), cut into slices ½ in (1 cm) thick
3 tablespoons extra-virgin olive oil
salt and freshly ground pepper

❧ Prepare a fire in a charcoal grill.

❧ Cut the eggplant crosswise into slices ½ in (1 cm) thick. Then cut the slices into 1¼-in (3-cm) pieces. Cut the onions into quarters.

❧ Using 6 skewers, thread on the vegetables—eggplants, onions, bell pepper, tomatoes, zucchini—alternating them. Brush with half of the oil and season to taste with salt and pepper. When the fire is ready, place the skewers on the grill rack. Grill, turning occasionally to ensure even cooking and brushing with remaining oil, until lightly golden on all sides, about 10 minutes. Transfer to a platter and serve.

SERVES 6 *Photograph page 96*

INSALATA DI SEDANO DI VERONA

Celeriac Salad

In Italy, celeriac is often called Verona celery because traditionally it was grown and consumed only in that Veneto city. It is also known as sedano rapa. *The easiest way to peel celeriac is to trim off the rough skin with a small, sharp knife.*

2 celeriacs (celery roots), about 1¼ lb (600 g) total weight
pinch of salt
1 tablespoon fresh lemon juice
¼ cup (2 fl oz/60 ml) extra-virgin olive oil
4 large lettuce leaves
freshly ground pepper
1 tablespoon cumin seeds

☙ Peel the celeriacs and cut them into matchstick-sized pieces. Place in a bowl. In a small bowl or cup, dissolve the salt in the lemon juice and pour over the celeriac. Toss to mix, add the oil and mix again.

☙ Line a salad bowl with the lettuce leaves and place the celeriac in the center. Sprinkle with pepper to taste and the cumin seeds and serve.

SERVES 6

Lombardia

INSALATA DI BARBABIETOLE E CIPOLLINE

Beet and Onion Salad

Throughout the northern regions of Italy, sturdy vegetables such as beets, potatoes and carrots are blended with mayonnaise and served as a salad or antipasto. You can also simplify the dish by tossing it with a dressing of extra-virgin olive oil and wine vinegar in place of the mayonnaise.

1 lb (480 g) beets (beetroots)
1 lb (480 g) boiling potatoes
1 whole egg, plus 1 egg yolk
pinch of salt
1 tablespoon white wine vinegar
¾ cup (6 fl oz/180 ml) extra-virgin olive oil
½ cup (4 fl oz/120 ml) milk
7 oz (210 g) drained small white onions pickled in vinegar

☙ Trim off each beet stem about ½ in (1 cm) from the crown but do not peel. Place in a saucepan with water to cover, bring to a boil and boil until tender, 20–30 minutes. Drain and, when cool enough to handle, peel and dice.

☙ Meanwhile, place the unpeeled potatoes in a saucepan with water to cover, bring to a boil and boil until tender, 30–40 minutes. Drain and, when cool enough to handle, peel and dice.

☙ In a blender or food processor fitted with the metal blade, combine the whole egg and egg yolk, salt and vinegar. Process briefly to mix. With the motor running, add the oil in a slow, steady stream, continuing to blend until a mayonnaise forms. (Alternatively, make the mayonnaise with an electric mixer or by hand with a whisk.) Stir in the milk.

☙ In a bowl, mix together the beets, potatoes, onions and mayonnaise. Transfer to a serving dish and serve at room temperature.

SERVES 6

Left to right: Beet and Onion Salad; Celeriac Salad

113

Piemonte

CESTINI DI PATATE E PISELLI
Potato Baskets with Peas

These decorative baskets are easy to make and can be formed a few hours ahead of baking. It is important that all the moisture has evaporated from the potatoes before you form them into baskets.

1⅔ lb (800 g) baking potatoes, unpeeled
4 tablespoons (2 oz/60 g) unsalted butter
2 eggs
pinch of freshly grated nutmeg
½ cup (2 oz/60 g) grated Parmesan cheese
2 lb (1 kg) peas, shelled (2 cups/10 oz/300 g shelled)
¼ cup (2 fl oz/60 ml) water
2 tablespoons extra-virgin olive oil
salt

☞ Place the potatoes in a saucepan with water to cover generously. Bring to a boil and boil until tender when pierced with a fork, 20–30 minutes, depending upon size. Drain the potatoes and, when cool enough to handle, peel them. Pass the warm potatoes through a ricer into a clean saucepan.
☞ Place over low heat and warm the mashed potatoes, stirring constantly, until dry, about 10 minutes. Stir 2 tablespoons of the butter into the potatoes and remove from the heat. Let cool a little. Add the eggs, nutmeg and Parmesan cheese to the potatoes and stir to mix well.
☞ Preheat an oven to 350°F (180°C). Using the remaining 2 tablespoons butter, grease a standard baking sheet (tray).
☞ Spoon the potato mixture into a pastry (piping) bag fitted with a star tip. Pipe out 6 disks 2 in (5 cm) in diameter onto the prepared baking sheet, spacing them a little bit apart. Pipe a border onto the edge of each disk to make a basket shape. Bake until just golden, about 20 minutes.
☞ Meanwhile, in a saucepan, combine the peas and water. Place over low heat and bring to a boil. Cover and cook until tender, about 5 minutes. Drain and place in a bowl. Add the oil and season to taste with salt.
☞ Remove the potato baskets from the oven and divide the peas evenly among them. Return to the oven until warm, another 5 minutes. Arrange the potato baskets on a warmed platter and serve at once.

SERVES 6

Venezia Giulia

CIPOLLE AL CHIODO DI GAROFANO
Baked Onions with Cloves

The practice of studding onions with cloves comes from an old Venezia Giulia recipe. The sharp flavor of the spice is softened by the sweetness of the onions. This dish goes well with any number of main courses such as pork roast with peaches (recipe on page 188) or nearly any meat stew.

6 medium to large yellow onions
18 whole cloves
3 tablespoons balsamic vinegar
3 tablespoons extra-virgin olive oil
salt and freshly ground pepper

☞ Preheat an oven to 350°F (180°C).
☞ Leave the onion skins intact. Using a sharp knife, make 3 incisions, each ½ in (1 cm) deep, around the stem end of each onion. Insert 1 clove into each incision. Wrap each onion in a

piece of aluminum foil and secure the foil tightly closed. Bake until tender to the touch, about 40 minutes.
☞ Remove from the oven and discard the foil wrappers. Peel the onions and arrange them on a warmed platter; keep warm.
☞ In a saucepan, warm the vinegar for a minute or two. Add the oil, season to taste with salt and pepper and mix well. Pour over the onions and serve at once.

SERVES 6

Campania

FRIARIELLI "STRASCINATI"
Broccoli Rabe and Garlic Sauté

Friarielli are a particularly small and tender variety of broccoli found only in the fields of Campania. Broccoli rabe makes a good substitute.

2 lb (1 kg) broccoli rabe
6 tablespoons (3 fl oz/90 ml) extra-virgin olive oil
2 cloves garlic, chopped
pinch of red pepper flakes
salt

☞ Trim off and discard the tough stems from the broccoli rabe. Bring a large pot of salted water to a boil. Add the broccoli rabe and cook for 1 minute. Drain immediately and pat dry with paper towels.
☞ In a large frying pan over medium heat, warm the oil. Add the garlic and pepper flakes and cook, stirring occasionally, until the garlic begins to take on color, about 3 minutes. Add the broccoli rabe and continue to cook over medium heat, stirring frequently, until the greens are tender, about 5 minutes longer.
☞ Season to taste with salt and serve immediately.

SERVES 6

MELANZANE ALLO YOGURT
Eggplant with Yogurt and Mint

This contemporary vegetable dish makes a refreshing salad for summer. The eggplant can instead be grilled over a charcoal fire; dried oregano or fresh basil, chives or parsley can replace the mint.

3 eggplants (aubergines), about 1¼ lb (600 g) total weight
½ cup (4 oz/120 g) plain yogurt
3 tablespoons extra-virgin olive oil
1 teaspoon paprika
salt and freshly ground pepper
2 tablespoons chopped fresh mint

☞ Preheat a broiler (griller).
☞ Cut the unpeeled eggplants into slices about ¼ in (.5 cm) thick. Place on a broiler pan (tray) and broil (grill), turning once, until tender when pierced with a knife, about 3 minutes on each side. Transfer to a serving dish and let cool to room temperature.
☞ In a bowl, stir together the yogurt, oil and paprika. Season to taste with salt and pepper. Pour the yogurt mixture over the eggplant slices. Sprinkle with the mint.
☞ Let the eggplant stand for about 30 minutes to absorb the flavors, then serve.

SERVES 6   *Photograph pages 104–105*

Clockwise from top left: Baked Onions with Cloves; Broccoli Rabe and Garlic Sauté; Potato Baskets with Peas

Fried Potatoes and Sage

Toscana

FRITTURA DI PATATE E SALVIA

Fried Potatoes and Sage

This is a delicious and aromatic combination. The same batter can be used to fry other vegetables such as zucchini (courgettes), carrots, artichokes or fennel. The secret of a good batter is to achieve a consistency that is thick enough to coat the vegetables.

1¼ lb (600 g) baking potatoes
½ cup plus 2 tablespoons (2½ oz/80 g) all-purpose
   (plain) flour
1 egg
½ cup (4 fl oz/120 ml) water
salt
4 cups (32 fl oz/1 l) olive oil for deep-frying
30 large fresh sage leaves, carefully rinsed and well dried

Peel the potatoes and cut into long strips ½ in (1 cm) thick. Place in a bowl with cold water to cover and let stand for about 2 hours. (The soaking removes starch from the potatoes, making them crispier when fried.)

In a food processor fitted with the metal blade, combine the flour, egg, water and a pinch of salt. Process to form a creamy consistency. Pour into a bowl.

Drain the potatoes and dry thoroughly.

Pour the oil into a large, deep frying pan and heat to 340°F (170°C). When the oil is ready, add the potatoes and fry, carefully turning from time to time, until they begin to turn golden, about 20 minutes. Then dip the sage leaves into the batter and drop them into the oil. Continue to fry until the potatoes and sage turn a deep gold, about 5 minutes longer. Using a slotted spoon, transfer the potatoes and sage to paper towels to drain briefly.

Place on a platter, adjust with salt and serve piping hot.

SERVES 6

Campania

TORTA DI SCAROLA E OLIVE

Escarole and Olive Pie

This classic Neapolitan vegetable pie can be served as a first course, light main course or as an accompaniment. It is also good cold. The filling of escarole seasoned with garlic, olives and capers makes a perfect pizza topping.

FOR THE PASTRY:

3 cups (12 oz/360 g) all-purpose (plain) flour
¾ cup (6 oz/180 g) unsalted butter, chilled, cut into pieces
3 tablespoons water

FOR THE FILLING:

2 heads escarole (Batavian endive), about 1¼ lb (600 g) total
   weight, coarsely sliced
¼ cup (2 fl oz/60 ml) extra-virgin olive oil
⅓ cup (2 oz/60 g) Gaeta or other Mediterranean-style small
   black olives, pitted and chopped
¼ cup (2 oz/60 g) drained brine-cured capers
1 clove garlic, chopped

To make the pastry, heap the flour onto a work surface. Place the butter in the center and, using your fingertips, work the ingredients together until the mixture resembles cornmeal. Add the water and work it in with your hands until the mixture comes together to form a rough mass. Gather the dough into a ball, wrap securely in plastic wrap and refrigerate for 1 hour.

To make the filling, bring a large pot of salted water to a boil. Add the escarole and boil for 1 minute. Drain and squeeze dry; set aside to cool.

Preheat an oven to 350°F (180°C).

Divide the dough into 2 portions, one twice as large as the other. Rewrap the smaller portion and return it to the refrigerator. On a lightly floured board, roll out the larger dough portion into a round about 14 in (35 cm) in diameter. Carefully transfer the dough round to a 12-in (30-cm) tart pan with a removable bottom. Set aside.

In a frying pan over medium heat, warm the olive oil. Add the olives, capers and garlic and cook, stirring, until the garlic begins to take on color, about 3 minutes. Add the escarole and continue to cook over medium heat, tossing to coat with the oil, until tender, about 3 minutes. Spread the escarole over the bottom of the tart pan.

Roll out the remaining portion of dough and carefully transfer it to the tart pan, positioning it over the filling. Trim the pastry overhang as needed and press the edges of the top and bottom crusts together attractively to seal.

Bake until lightly golden, about 40 minutes. Set aside to cool slightly, then remove the pan sides. Slide the tart off the base onto a platter and serve hot or at room temperature.

SERVES 6

Escarole and Olive Pie

*Top to bottom: Celeriac with Balsamic
Vinegar; Ricotta Pie with Chives*

Lombardia

SEDANO RAPA AL BALSAMICO

Celeriac with Balsamic Vinegar

The use of balsamic vinegar transforms the classic Lombardian summertime dish of celeriac salad into a contemporary Italian accompaniment to fish or cold meat. It can also be set out as part of a selection of antipasti.

juice of 2 lemons
2 lb (1 kg) celeriacs (celery roots)
salt
¼ cup (2 fl oz/60 ml) extra-virgin olive oil
2 tablespoons balsamic vinegar

↪ Fill a bowl with water and add the lemon juice. Using a sharp knife, peel the celeriacs and cut into matchstick-sized pieces. Place them in the lemon water to prevent discoloring.
↪ In a small bowl, stir together salt to taste, the oil and vinegar. Drain the celeriac and pat dry. Place in a serving dish and drizzle with the oil mixture. Toss and serve.

SERVES 6

Toscana

TORTINO DI RICOTTA ED ERBA CIPOLLINA

Ricotta Pie with Chives

There are many ways to vary this pie. I sometimes add a little puréed spinach, artichokes or Swiss chard (silverbeet); some blanched peas; or diced ham and cheese. Serve the pie hot; it is also good warm or even cold, but not refrigerated. If you do not have a food mill, whirl the ricotta in a food processor to make it smooth.

1 tablespoon unsalted butter
1 cup (4 oz/120 g) grated Parmesan cheese
1 lb (480 g) ricotta cheese, passed through a food mill
3 eggs, separated
3 tablespoons chopped fresh chives

pinch of freshly grated nutmeg
salt and freshly ground pepper

↪ Preheat an oven to 350°F (180°C). Grease a 9-in or 21-cm springform pan with the butter and coat the bottom and sides with ¼ cup (1 oz/30 g) of the Parmesan cheese.
↪ In a bowl, combine the ricotta cheese, egg yolks, chives, nutmeg and the remaining Parmesan cheese. Mix well. In another bowl, beat the egg whites until they are soft and foamy, then carefully blend them into the ricotta mixture. Do not overmix. Season to taste with salt and pepper.
↪ Pour the ricotta mixture into the prepared pan and smooth the surface. Bake until golden, about 50 minutes. Remove from the oven and let cool for a few minutes. Run the tip of a knife around the edges of the pan, then release the sides. Slide the pie off the base onto a platter and serve.

SERVES 6

RUCOLA IN INSALATA CON LE PERE

Arugula and Pear Salad

To transform this salad into an inviting antipasto, add a little finely sliced Parmesan cheese and a few chopped nuts. The blend of good olive oil and fresh lemon juice is a classic Italian dressing.

7 oz (210 g) arugula (rocket)
3 firm Bosc pears
¼ cup (2 fl oz/60 ml) extra-virgin olive oil
juice of ½ lemon
salt

↪ Remove the tough stems from the arugula and arrange the leaves in a bed in a shallow salad bowl. Peel the pears, then halve, core and slice lengthwise. Arrange the pear slices on top of the arugula.
↪ In a small bowl, stir together the oil, lemon juice and salt to taste. Drizzle over the pears and arugula, toss and serve immediately.

SERVES 6

CARCIOFI ALLA MAIONESE
Artichokes with Mayonnaise

Homemade mayonnaise is a light, delicious accompaniment to many Italian dishes. It is popular on vegetables and is also used as the basis for the classic Piedmontese sauce for vitello tonnato, *cold veal with tuna mayonnaise.*

juice of ½ lemon
12 small- to medium-sized artichokes

FOR THE MAYONNAISE:

1 whole egg, plus 1 egg yolk
salt
juice of ½ lemon
¾ cup (6 fl oz/180 ml) extra-virgin olive oil
1 teaspoon grated orange zest
freshly ground pepper

Fill a bowl with cold water and the lemon juice. Trim off the top one-third of each artichoke, then cut or pull off the tough outer leaves. Using a spoon, dig out the prickly choke from the center. Trim the stem even with the base. As each artichoke is trimmed, place it in the lemon water to prevent it from discoloring.

Bring a saucepan filled with salted water to a boil. Drain the artichokes and add to the boiling water. Boil until tender when pierced with a fork, about 10 minutes. Drain and pass under cold running water to halt the cooking. Invert to drain well.

To make the mayonnaise, in a blender or a food processor fitted with the metal blade, combine the whole egg and egg yolk. Season with salt and add the lemon juice. Process briefly to blend. With the motor running, add the olive oil in a very slow, steady stream, continuing to process until a mayonnaise forms. Mix in the orange zest and season to taste with pepper.

Pat the artichokes dry and gently spread the leaves to form little cups. Spoon some of the mayonnaise into the center of each artichoke, dividing it evenly. Serve at once.

SERVES 6

ASPARAGI ALLA POLPA DI GRANCHIO
Asparagus with Crabmeat

Shrimp (prawn) or lobster meat can be used instead of crabmeat for this recipe. Indeed, this recipe is a good way to use any leftover cooked shellfish you may have on hand.

4 lb (2 kg) asparagus
6 oz (180 g) fresh-cooked crabmeat, finely chopped
6 tablespoons (3 fl oz/90 ml) extra-virgin olive oil
juice of 1 lemon
1 tablespoon unsalted butter, melted and cooled slightly
salt and freshly ground pepper
1 tablespoon fennel seeds

Snap or cut off the tough ends of the asparagus. Select a tall, narrow saucepan that will accommodate the asparagus standing with the tips facing upward and that can be tightly covered. Fill the pan half full with salted water and bring to a boil. Stand the asparagus in the pan, cover tightly and cook until tender when pierced with a knife, 7–10 minutes. Drain, transfer to a serving platter and let cool to room temperature.

Place the crabmeat in a bowl. Add the oil, lemon juice and butter and stir to mix well. Season to taste with salt and pepper.

Spoon the crab sauce over the asparagus, sprinkle with the fennel seeds and serve.

SERVES 6

Left to right: Asparagus with Crabmeat; Artichokes with Mayonnaise

Clockwise from top: Onions Stuffed with Fontina Cheese; Potato and Pumpkin Purée; Fennel with Tomato and Raisins

FINOCCHI AL POMODORO E UVETTA

Fennel with Tomato and Raisins

The combination of tomatoes and raisins is a hallmark of Sicilian cooking. For cooked fennel dishes such as this, you can use either the round "male" bulb or the more elongated "female" bulb.

6 fennel bulbs
2 tablespoons extra-virgin olive oil
1 small yellow onion, chopped
6 ripe plum (Roma) tomatoes, peeled and chopped
scant ¼ cup (1 oz/30 g) raisins
1 teaspoon cumin seeds
salt

🦐 Cut off the fennel tops and discard or reserve for another use. Cut each bulb lengthwise into quarters. Set aside.
🦐 In a deep saucepan over medium heat, warm the oil. Add the onion and sauté until translucent, about 3 minutes. Add the fennel, tomatoes, raisins and cumin seeds and season to taste with salt. Cover and cook over low heat until the fennel is tender, about 20 minutes.
🦐 Uncover and allow the excess cooking liquid to evaporate. Transfer to a warmed platter and serve immediately.

SERVES 6

PASSATO DI PATATE E ZUCCA

Potato and Pumpkin Purée

It is a good idea to keep a pumpkin or two in the house. Like onions and apples, they stay fresh for many days and can be used in a variety of ways: in soups, as an accompaniment to meat dishes, as a stuffing for pasta or to make a pie.

2 lb (1 kg) pumpkin or other hard-shelled squash such as acorn or butternut
1¼ lb (600 g) baking potatoes
2 tablespoons unsalted butter
½ cup (4 fl oz/120 ml) milk
pinch of freshly grated nutmeg
1 tablespoon crumbled amaretti (see glossary)
salt and freshly ground pepper

🦐 Preheat an oven to 350°F (180°C).
🦐 Using a sharp knife, cut the pumpkin or other squash into large pieces. Scoop out the seeds and fibers, then peel the pieces. Place in a baking dish and bake until tender when pierced with a knife, about 30 minutes. Remove from the oven and pass the pieces through a food mill or a ricer into a deep saucepan.
🦐 Meanwhile, place the potatoes in a saucepan with water to cover generously. Bring to a boil and boil until tender when pierced with a fork, 20–30 minutes, depending upon size. Drain the potatoes and, when cool enough to handle, peel them. Pass them through the food mill or ricer into the pan holding the pumpkin.
🦐 Add the butter, milk, nutmeg and amaretti crumbs to the purée, mix well and season to taste with salt and pepper. Place over medium heat and cook, stirring frequently, until thickened and warmed through, about 5 minutes.
🦐 Transfer to a warmed dish and serve immediately.

SERVES 6

CIPOLLE ALLA FONTINA

Onions Stuffed with Fontina Cheese

Asiago and Parmesan cheese are both satisfactory substitutes for Fontina in this recipe, which is a traditional preparation of Italy's northwest region.

1 tablespoon extra-virgin olive oil
8 large yellow onions, peeled but left whole
1 cup (2 oz/60 g) bread crumbs, soaked in milk to cover and squeezed dry
¾ cup (3 oz/90 g) shredded Fontina cheese
2 eggs
salt and freshly ground pepper
2 tablespoons toasted and chopped almonds

🦐 Preheat an oven to 350°F (180°C). Oil a baking pan with the oil.
🦐 Bring a large saucepan filled with salted water to a boil. Add the onions and parboil for about 10 minutes. Drain, pat dry and, when cool enough to handle, cut off the tops. Using a teaspoon, scrape about 1 tablespoon pulp out of each onion. In a bowl, combine the bread crumbs, Fontina cheese and eggs. Season to taste with a little salt and pepper and mix well.
🦐 Spoon the bread crumb mixture into the hollow of each onion, dividing it evenly and mounding it over the top. Place the onions side by side in the prepared pan and sprinkle the tops with the almonds. Bake until the onions are soft when pierced, about 30 minutes, adding a little water to the pan as needed to keep the onions moist. Transfer to a platter and serve hot.

SERVES 4

CAVOLFIORE AL PROSCIUTTO E OLIVE

Cauliflower with Prosciutto and Olives

Cauliflower is popular everywhere in Italy. The variations come in the sauces; it is dressed differently from region to region. This version goes well with pork. Broccoli can be substituted for the cauliflower.

2 large cauliflowers, about 2 lb (1 kg) total weight
¼ cup (2 fl oz/60 ml) extra-virgin olive oil
3 tablespoons water, plus more as needed
18 Gaeta or other Mediterranean-style small black olives, pitted and halved
3 oz (90 g) prosciutto, cut into small pieces
salt and freshly ground pepper

🦐 Cut off the leaves and divide the cauliflowers into florets. Place the florets in a deep saucepan large enough to hold them in a single layer. Add the oil and 3 tablespoons water and sprinkle with the olives and prosciutto. Season to taste with salt and pepper.
🦐 Cover and cook over low heat for about 10 minutes, adding water as needed to moisten and shaking the pan every few minutes to prevent the florets from sticking. Do not stir.
🦐 Carefully transfer the florets and seasonings to a warmed platter. Serve at once.

SERVES 6　　　　　*Photograph pages 126–127*

TORTINO DI CARCIOFI AL FORNO

Artichoke Pie

For a brunch or a buffet, serve this pie together with the zucchini mold (recipe below) and the escarole and olive pie (recipe on page 116), and follow them with a light dessert. You can make this a meatless menu by leaving the beef out of the mold. This tortino also makes a tasty antipasto or first course and can be served at room temperature as well.

juice of 1 lemon
8 artichokes
½ cup (4 fl oz/120 ml) extra-virgin olive oil
1 cup (4 oz/120 g) all-purpose (plain) flour
salt and freshly ground pepper
6 eggs
1 tablespoon chopped fresh mint leaves

Fill a bowl with cold water and add the lemon juice. Trim off the top one-third of each artichoke, then cut or pull off the tough outer leaves. Cut in half lengthwise and, using a spoon, dig out the prickly chokes. Trim the stem even with the base. As each artichoke is trimmed, immediately drop it into the lemon water to prevent it from discoloring. Drain well, pat dry and cut lengthwise into slices ¼ in (.5 cm) thick.

Preheat an oven to 400°F (200°C). Using a little of the oil, oil a 9-in (23-cm) baking dish.

Dust the artichoke slices with the flour, coating evenly and tapping off any excess. In a frying pan over medium heat, warm the remaining oil. Add the artichoke slices and cook, turning once, until golden on both sides, about 10 minutes total. Using a slotted spoon, transfer to paper towels to drain. Season to taste with salt and pepper.

In a bowl, beat the eggs until blended. Add the artichokes and mint and mix well. Pour the mixture into the prepared baking dish.

Bake until soft inside and lightly golden on the outside, about 15 minutes. Remove from the oven and serve immediately from the baking dish.

SERVES 6

SFORMATO DI ZUCCHINE

Zucchini Mold

The ground beef in this recipe gives the mold substance and, of course, a heartier flavor, but the dish is equally good prepared without the meat. Traditionally, a mold such as this one is served as a middle course for a formal dinner. If you want to offer it as an accompaniment to a main course of fish or meat, form it in individual molds and reduce the baking time to 20 minutes.

¼ cup (2 fl oz/60 ml) extra-virgin olive oil
2 lb (1 kg) zucchini (courgettes), finely diced
1 yellow onion, chopped
2 cloves garlic, chopped
1 tablespoon unsalted butter
¼ cup (1 oz/30 g) fine dried bread crumbs
¼ lb (120 g) ground (minced) beef
4 eggs
1 cup (4 oz/120 g) grated Parmesan cheese
1 tablespoon chopped fresh flat-leaf (Italian) parsley
salt and freshly ground pepper

In a saucepan over medium heat, warm the oil. Add the zucchini, onion and garlic and cook, stirring frequently, until tender, 10 minutes. Add a little water, if needed, to keep the mixture moist. Remove from the heat and let cool.

Preheat an oven to 350°F (180°C). Grease a 9-in (23-cm) ring mold with the butter and coat the bottom and sides with the bread crumbs.

Transfer the zucchini mixture to a bowl and add the beef, eggs, cheese and parsley. Season to taste with salt and pepper and mix well. Spoon into the prepared mold.

Bake until firm, about 50 minutes. Remove from the oven and invert the mold onto a platter. Serve immediately.

SERVES 6

INDIVIA DEL BELGIO CON OLIVE VERDI

Belgian Endive with Green Olives

Serve this dish as a first course or as an accompaniment to the main course. Black olives can be substituted for the green. I have used Belgian endive here, as it has a much longer season than its cousin, the highly seasonal radicchio (red chicory) from Treviso.

6 heads Belgian endive (chicory/witloof), halved lengthwise
3 cups (13 oz/400 g) green olives, pitted and cut into pieces
⅓ cup (2½ fl oz/80 ml) extra-virgin olive oil
½ cup (4 fl oz/120 ml) light chicken stock (recipe on page 40)
salt and freshly ground pepper

Preheat an oven to 350°F (180°C).

In an oven dish, place the endive halves side by side. Sprinkle the olives evenly over the endives, then pour in the oil and stock. Season to taste with salt and pepper. Bake until the endives are tender, about 20 minutes.

Remove any excess cooking liquid from the baking dish with a spoon and serve directly from the dish.

SERVES 6

Clockwise from top: Belgian Endive with Green Olives; Artichoke Pie; Zucchini Mold

TORTA DI BIETOLE

Swiss Chard Pie

Although I often serve this lovely savory pie as a first course for a luncheon, it is also the perfect main dish for a brunch or a light supper. Spinach, asparagus, artichokes, fennel or broccoli can be used in place of the Swiss chard. Any leftover pie is delicious eaten cold the next day.

FOR THE PASTRY:

2 cups (8 oz/240 g) all-purpose (plain) flour
½ cup (4 oz/120 g) unsalted butter at room temperature, cut into pieces
2 tablespoons water

FOR THE FILLING:

1¼ lb (600 g) Swiss chard (silverbeet), tough stems removed
3 tablespoons unsalted butter
¼ lb (120 g) Emmentaler cheese, cut into matchstick-sized pieces

Meanwhile, to make the filling, bring a large pot with a little salted water to a boil. Add the Swiss chard and boil until wilted, about 3 minutes. Drain well and, when cool enough to handle, squeeze thoroughly dry. Chop roughly. In a saucepan over medium heat, melt 2 tablespoons of the butter. Add the Swiss chard and sauté until it softens and takes on some flavor, about 3 minutes. Remove from the heat and stir in the cheese, ham, eggs and nutmeg. Season to taste with salt and pepper and mix well.

Preheat an oven to 350°F (180°C). Use the remaining 1 tablespoon butter to grease a 10-in (25-cm) tart pan with a removable bottom.

On a lightly floured work surface, roll out the dough into a round large enough to fit the pan. Carefully transfer it to the pan and press it gently into the bottom and sides. Trim the edges even with the rim. Spread the Swiss chard mixture in the tart shell.

Bake until the crust is lightly golden, about 40 minutes. Transfer to a rack to cool slightly, then free the pie from the pan sides and slide it off the base onto a serving plate. Serve warm or cold.

SERVES 6

Umbria

PASSATO DI FAVE CON I CARDI

Fava Bean Purée with Cardoon

This recipe combines two distinctly Italian vegetables that are particularly popular in il centro—*the center. Cardoon discolors very quickly. To prevent it from browning, promptly add the trimmed pieces to the lemon water.*

juice of 2 lemons
2 lb (1 kg) cardoon
4 cups (1¼ lb/600 g) shelled fava (broad) beans (4 lb/2 kg unshelled)
6 tablespoons (3 fl oz/90 ml) extra-virgin olive oil
1 yellow onion, chopped
salt and freshly ground pepper

Fill a large bowl with water and add the juice of 1 lemon. Remove and discard the base from the cardoon and discard any tough outer stalks. Trim and discard the leaves and spurs from the tender stalks and then scrape the stalks with a small knife to remove all strings and fibers. Thinly slice the stalks and place in the lemon water until needed. Bring a saucepan filled with salted water to a boil. Drain the cardoon and add to the pan with the remaining lemon juice. Cook until tender, about 10 minutes. Drain and keep warm.

Meanwhile, bring another saucepan filled with salted water to a boil. Add the fava beans and cook until tender, about 10 minutes. Drain and pass through a food mill positioned over a bowl.

Preheat an oven to 350°F (180°C). Lightly grease a 2-qt (2-l) baking dish with 1 tablespoon of the oil.

In a saucepan over low heat, warm the remaining oil. Add the onion and sauté until translucent, about 5 minutes. Add the puréed favas and salt and pepper to taste and continue to cook over low heat for about 10 minutes, adding a little water if needed to keep the mixture moist. Remove from the heat.

Arrange the cardoon in the prepared baking dish. Pour the bean purée evenly over the top. Bake until heated through, about 20 minutes. Serve immediately.

SERVES 6

Clockwise from left: Swiss Chard Pie; Cauliflower with Prosciutto and Olives (recipe page 123); Fava Bean Purée with Cardoon

¼ lb (120 g) ham, cut into matchstick-sized pieces
2 eggs
pinch of freshly grated nutmeg
salt and freshly ground pepper

To make the pastry, on a work surface, mound the flour and add the ½ cup (4 oz/120 g) butter. Using your fingertips, work the ingredients together until the mixture has the consistency of fine crumbs. Drizzle on the water and knead quickly until well blended. Shape the dough into a ball and cover with plastic wrap. Refrigerate for about 1 hour.

Emilia-Romagna

FINOCCHI GRATINATI

Fennel Stuffed with Smoked Provola and Parmesan

Since this dish is quite substantial, it is suitable either as an accompaniment to a meat dish or as a main course for supper. Use the larger, rounder fennel bulbs, which are more tender than the slender ones. Provola is a smaller version of provolone cheese made from cow's milk.

5 fennel bulbs
5 oz (150 g) smoked provola cheese, thinly sliced
1 cup (4 oz/120 g) grated Parmesan cheese
1 egg
1 cup (4 oz/120 g) fine dried bread crumbs
2 tablespoons extra-virgin olive oil
2 tablespoons unsalted butter
salt and freshly ground pepper

☛ Trim off the stalks from the fennel bulbs and cut the bulbs in half lengthwise. Bring a saucepan filled with salted water to a boil, add the fennel bulbs, cover and cook for 10 minutes. Drain and pat dry. Cut each fennel half in half again, so that each bulb is quartered. Slip a slice of provola cheese and some

*Clockwise from left: Fennel Stuffed with Smoked Provola and Parmesan;
Pearl Onions in Sweet-and-Sour Tomato Sauce;
Layered Potato and Cheese Casserole*

Campania

CIPOLLINE IN AGRODOLCE AL POMODORO

Pearl Onions in Sweet-and-Sour Tomato Sauce

Those who like piquant dishes will appreciate this recipe. It goes especially well with braised meat dishes. Sweet-and-sour sauces are enjoyed particularly in the deep south and in the north.

2 lb (1 kg) pearl onions
¼ cup (2 fl oz/60 ml) extra-virgin olive oil
¼ cup (2 fl oz/60 ml) dry white wine
1 tablespoon sugar
2 tablespoons tomato sauce (homemade, recipe on page 94, or store-bought)
salt
3 tablespoons red wine vinegar

❧ Bring a saucepan filled with water to a boil. Add the pearl onions and boil for 2–3 minutes. Drain and, when cool enough to handle, trim off the root ends and stem ends. Slip off the skins.

❧ In the same saucepan over medium heat, warm the oil. Add the onions and cook, stirring frequently, for about 10 minutes.

❧ Add the wine, sugar and tomato sauce and season to taste with salt. Reduce the heat to low, cover and continue to cook until the onions are tender, about 20 minutes.

❧ Add the vinegar, mix well and cook for 3 minutes longer to blend the flavors. Transfer to a warmed bowl and serve.

SERVES 6

Piemonte

TEGLIA DI PATATE AL FORMAGGIO

Layered Potato and Cheese Casserole

Seek out authentic Italian Fontina, the semisoft mild cheese from the Valle d'Aosta. Offer this classic baked dish as a substantial first course or as a simple main course at lunch, perhaps accompanied by a green salad.

2 lb (1 kg) baking potatoes, of uniform size
1 tablespoon unsalted butter
salt
1 cup (4 oz/120 g) shredded Fontina cheese
⅔ cup (2½ oz/80 g) grated Parmesan cheese
1 cup (8 fl oz/240 ml) light meat stock (recipe on page 40)

❧ Have ready a large bowl of water. Peel the potatoes and slice them into thin rounds. As soon as they are sliced, place them in the water. When they have all been sliced, drain well and lay out on a kitchen towel to dry.

❧ Preheat an oven to 300°F (150°C). Grease a baking dish about 9½ in (24 cm) in diameter with the butter. In the prepared dish, layer some of the potato slices in a circle, with the slices slightly overlapping, to form a flower. Sprinkle with a pinch of salt and a small handful of each of the cheeses. Repeat the layering until you have used up all the potatoes, finishing with the cheeses. Pour the meat stock over the surface.

❧ Bake until potatoes are tender when pierced with a toothpick and the top is slightly golden, about 1½ hours. Be careful that they do not become too brown on top, covering the dish with aluminum foil if necessary. Serve hot directly from the dish.

SERVES 6

grated Parmesan cheese between each rib of fennel. In a shallow bowl, beat the egg. Place the bread crumbs in a separate shallow bowl. Dip each fennel quarter first in the beaten egg and then in the bread crumbs, coating completely.

❧ In a large nonstick frying pan, heat the oil and butter together over medium heat. Add half the fennel, cover and cook, turning occasionally to brown on all sides, until the fennel is golden, about 5 minutes. Transfer the fennel to a warmed platter; keep warm. Continue with remaining fennel.

❧ Season to taste with salt and pepper. Serve hot.

SERVES 6

Il Centro

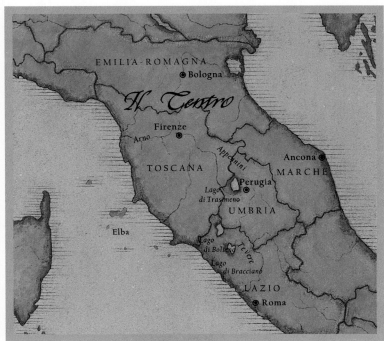

Il Centro

EMILIA-ROMAGNA, TOSCANA,
MARCHE, UMBRIA, LAZIO

For most travelers to Italy, the first visit to the country includes portions of central Italy, plus a visit to Venice in the northeast. As such, the center captures a large part of the foreign imagination about what Italy might be, and later forms the most enduring memory of what Italy is.

The regions of central Italy, moving from north to south, are Emilia-Romagna, Tuscany, the Marches, Umbria and Lazio. These were the lands of the original Etruscan towns, long before there was a Rome. The Etruscans cultivated the ancient Mediterranean trilogy of wheat, grape and olive, so that bread, rudimentary pasta, wine and oil were foundations of the ancient diet.

Later, with the advent of the Roman Empire, these lands took on a new aspect. The Romans, who built their capital in Lazio in 753 B.C., were master engineers who revolutionized civic and agricultural design. Towns were laid out with central squares that could be points of commerce and social interchange, a function they still serve today. Aqueducts were constructed to carry water to cities and to farms. Roads were built that led to Rome from all points in the Empire, so that merchandise could easily be transported. Every food product to be found anywhere in the Empire made its way to Rome, and the city became the cradle of gastronomic experimentation and excess.

Previous pages: The Piazza del Campo in Siena is one of Italy's most-loved squares. At left: In the Vatican Museums, the Scala di Bramante, one of the greatest architectural treasures of Rome, gracefully climbs five tiers in a gentle spiral to an arched loggia at its top.

133

In Chianti, the viticultural heart of Tuscany, a lacework of vineyards and olive groves drapes the hills as far as the eye can see.

The Romans had a tradition of feasting that would often last for days, in which long sessions of eating and drinking would be broken up by interludes of sex and other recreations. Long before the Seven Deadly Sins were codified, the Romans managed to partake fully of them and probably several others that did not make the final list. In their search for new things to eat, the chefs of Rome were adventurous in combining sweet, sour, spicy and sharp flavors. Honey and fruit were paired with meat and cheese, and sourness might be tried with green vegetables. Some of these dishes have come down to us because of Marcus Gavius Apicius, a first-century gourmet who squandered his fortune on epic feasts. His recipe collection is usually considered the first cookbook ever created.

The legacy of this tradition, and what is important to those of us who look at Italy today, is that it has always been customary to prize the highest-quality ingredients and to be very open to using them in innovative ways. Rome received foodstuffs from all over the Empire, but those closest at hand came from central and southern Italy.

Today, central Italy continues to be home to ingredients of extraordinary quality. This is noticeable in the markets of Bologna, Florence and Rome, in the shops of small towns in Umbria, at farm stands in Lazio and the Marches, and in restaurants throughout these regions. While more audacious cooking may be occurring in northern Italy, the place with the greatest potential for innovation is in the center, where the inherent skills of the cooks combine with outstanding materials.

This is not to say that there is a uniformity in the food of the center. In fact, one can journey only a short distance and find similar ingredients combined to create dishes that have little in common. Part of this is due to the fact that the area is largely mountainous, which results in natural and psychological boundaries between places. For example, Emilia-Romagna lies north and east of the Apennines and has an Adriatic coastline, while Tuscany is south and west with a long stretch of the Mediterranean. Lazio is largely west of the mountains and has a lengthy border on the Mediterranean, and the Marches is east of them and fronts the Adriatic. Umbria has one north-south system of mountains and another of hills, and is entirely landlocked.

With so many mountains, there are also river valleys and numerous exposures to the sun. Many towns sit atop or next to hills, each taking pride in local traditions as well as ancient fealties and hostilities. Umbria and the Marches maintained historic links to the Papacy and therefore have had a close relationship with Rome. Tuscany and Emilia-Romagna were composed of duchies and city-

Enduring since its inauguration in A.D. 80, the Coliseum has earned its reputation as the symbol of the Eternal City.

The mightiness of Renaissance Florence is still palpable today in the soaring tower of the Palazzo Vecchio.

A restaurateur near Modena works on his Trebbiano grapes for balsamic vinegar. The juice must be aged in casks of several different woods before earning the label of aceto balsamico tradizionale.

states that for much of their history warred with one another. The feelings of rivalry and disdain remain palpable to this day in such Tuscan cities as Florence, Siena, Pisa and Lucca. Certain places spent many years under foreign occupation, with the result that they acquired the tastes and customs of their occupiers. For example, Lucca and the Emilian cities of Parma and Piacenza show a strong preference for things French in food and taste in general. Parma and Piacenza are practically the only places in Italy where people bring butter to the dinner table to flavor not only bread, but also ham.

There is probably no region in Italy that offers the diversity and quality of ingredients to be found in Emilia-Romagna, nor the cooks skillful enough to use them. Its pork products are the best in the nation, starting with the delicate *culatello* and prosciutto hams of Parma and including an endless variety of salamis made in Felino and other towns, plus the mortadella of Bologna and the *zampone* (stuffed pig's trotter) of Modena. Parmigiano-Reggiano is indisputably the most exquisite cheese made in Italy, and it can be eaten on its own or as a flavoring with pasta or vegetables. This is also the region that produces balsamic vinegar, an elixir that glorifies the flavor of every food to which it is added.

The people of Emilia-Romagna are very exacting about the quality of the food they eat and do not abide imitations. Thus real Prosciutto di Parma is branded with that unmistakable designation. Similarly, Parmigiano-Reggiano that is not made under strict controls in the provinces of Parma, Reggio Emilia, Modena, Bologna or Mantua (in Lombardy) cannot bear the name of the cheese. Real balsamic vinegar, called *aceto balsamico tradizionale,* can come only from Modena or Reggio Emilia, and must be made from the juice of Trebbiano

A calming Umbrian view is contemplated in the late-afternoon light of Spoleto.

grapes and then aged in five different woods for at least twelve years. Most balsamic vinegar sold outside Emilia-Romagna does not meet these rigid standards.

Emilia-Romagna is also the homeland of fresh pasta: lasagne, tagliatelle, tortellini, cannelloni and filled pastas such as anolini and tortelli that might contain cheese, spinach, Swiss chard (silverbeet), fish, pumpkin, meat, poultry or fruit. The pasta is dressed with silken butter (the preferred fat of Emilia-Romagna); a rich sauce made of meat, cheese or vegetables; or perhaps with the porcini mushrooms that abound in the Apennines. While Emilia has herds of cattle and pens full of pigs, Romagna has some of the best apples, pears, cherries and other fruits and vegetables to be found in Europe. With its long coastline, Romagna also has excellent fish and seafood. All of these ingredients combine to create Italy's most sophisticated kitchen, one whose influence pervades the whole peninsula.

There is more gastronomic unity in the other regions of central Italy. Unlike in Emilia-Romagna, where extraordinary ingredients are used to make intricate preparations, cooks elsewhere tend to prepare foods more simply and in a way that reveals their natural states and flavors. In these areas, olive oil is the leading fat (the oils of Tuscany and Umbria, along with that of Liguria, are Italy's best). Pork is the leading meat, although it is more often roasted (as *porchetta*) or served in pieces than made into cold cuts. The pork butchers of Norcia in Umbria, however, are probably the finest in Italy outside of Emilia-Romagna, producing wonderful sausages and salamis. Prosciutto from the town of Carpegna in the Marches is exceeded only by those of Parma and San Daniele (in Friuli). Lamb is the second

most popular meat in central Italy, although the Tuscans enjoy excellent beef along with liver, poultry, small birds and game. People in Lazio are Italy's leading consumers of organ meats. All of this consumption of fatty proteins should give lie to the myth that Tuscans follow the moderate dictates of the so-called Mediterranean diet.

The coastlines are replete with good fish and seafood, especially in the Marches, which boasts 10 percent of the nation's catch. Traditional fish stews such as *brodetto* (the Marches) and *cacciucco* (Tuscany) offer respite from meat. There is a wide variety of unsurpassed vegetables and grains, including artichokes and peas in Lazio; lentils, chick-peas (garbanzos) and potatoes in Umbria and the Marches; and white beans, spinach and cabbage in Tuscany. *Farro* (called spelt or emmer in English) is a sturdy grain used since Etruscan times in Umbria and Tuscany. It has made an amazing comeback in recent years and is one of the stars of new Italian cooking. Hidden in the hills of Umbria is a huge cache of black and white truffles that lend perfume and irresistible flavor to pasta and other dishes, although they are hard to obtain outside of Italy.

The wines of central Italy rank among the country's best. Tuscan reds such as Chianti Classico, Brunello di Montalcino and Vino Nobile di Montepulciano deserve their world-class rankings. Whites such as Verdicchio (the Marches), Orvieto (Umbria), Vernaccia di San Gimignano (Tuscany) and some Frascati (Lazio) are eminently drinkable and pair well with local dishes.

Anyone interested in how Italians cook today must sample and understand the foods of central Italy. In other words, when near Rome, do as the Romans did.

I Pesci

A display of shimmering fish catches the shopper's eye in Milan. The art of presentation is nearly as important as quality in an Italian market.

I Pesci

SEAFOOD

The Italian peninsula extends into the Mediterranean like a gigantic pier from which fishing boats can depart to pursue the bounty of the sea. The shoreline is approximately 1,860 miles (3,000 km), and if one adds Sicily and Sardinia and numerous other coastal islands, the total rises to almost 3,000 miles (5,000 km). The country's major inland lakes (Maggiore, Como, Garda, Trasimeno, Bracciano) offer further possibilities, as do the Po and many of the rivers and streams in the Alps and the Apennines.

Since ancient times the peoples of the Italian peninsula have eaten the wealth of the waters with unmatched gusto. Seafood is seen in the mosaics of antiquity (such as those in Aquileia in Friuli) and of the early Christian Era (in Ravenna in Emilia-Romagna), in Venetian Renaissance paintings, and on plates and ceramics in Italy today. Italians eat a much wider range of products from the sea and rivers than most people, thanks to a combination of ingenuity and a lack of squeamishness. It is almost fair to say that if something swims near an Italian, it is a candidate to be eaten.

The royalty of the national seafood table are certainly the swordfish *(pesce spada)* and tuna *(tonno)* caught in the waters off Calabria and Sicily. These fish taste perfect

after a simple grilling, but they also marry well with many of the flavors of southern Italy: olives, almonds, capers, tomatoes, eggplants (aubergines) and so on. Other prized fish in Italy include gilt-head bream *(orata)*, monkfish *(pescatrice* or *rospo)*, Adriatic sole *(sogliola)* and sea bass *(branzino)*. All of these require little more

Freshness is paramount when it comes to seafood, and the steady turnover at the central market in Padua guarantees it.

Previous pages: Left to right: Mixed Grilled Fish (recipe page 158); Shellfish Stew with Garlic (recipe page 158)

A fishmonger advertises his historic calling in Camogli (Liguria).

than absolute freshness and an attentive eye while cooking. Some are even served raw today, as in the popular tuna carpaccio.

Lower down on the social scale but in no way less desirable is a category of fish called *pesce azzurro* (sky-blue fish). It includes fresh sardines and anchovies, which are very inexpensive and healthful and suffer an undeservedly bad reputation because of their salted, pickled and desiccated cousins. Fresh *pesce azzurro,* especially popular in Liguria and Sicily, is a delicious staple of the Italian diet that awaits full recognition abroad.

Italian fishermen also catch *paranza,* a generic term for the runts of the piscatorial litter, fish that are not pretty or easily served by themselves. But when they are fresh, properly cleaned, dipped in batter and fried in good olive oil, they can be as delicious as any other fish, and Italians eat quite a bit of them. *Paranza* and shellfish are often cooked together to make stews known as *zuppa di pesce, brodetto* (on the Adriatic) and *cacciucco* (in Tuscany). It is said that *cacciucco* must be made with five types of fish, one for each *c* in the name.

There is a comparable social register in the shellfish set. Lobster (*aragosta*) is not generally thought of as a native Italian food, but there are wonderful lobsters off the western coast of Sardinia that are boiled, chilled, cut into pieces in their shells and tossed with red (Spanish) onions, sliced oranges and olive oil, or, less classically, topped with a raw vegetable sauce. *Squisito!* Apulia has a generous supply of oysters that are eaten raw, baked or in pasta sauces. Venetians favor spider crabs (*granseole*), people in Trieste eat razor clams (*arselle*), Ligurians love mussels (*muscoli*) and Neapolitans enjoy littleneck clams (*vongole veraci*). Shrimp (prawns) come in all sizes and are

referred to variously as *gamberetti, gamberi* and *gamberoni* (small, medium and large). *Scampi* is the all-purpose term for crayfish and langoustines. Scallops (*capesante*) do not have widespread use, but are now gaining popularity.

Italians throughout the country enjoy baby octopus (*polpo*), either cooked with tomato and black pepper or boiled and served with potatoes. Squid becomes ever more popular. While people in other countries buy black pasta made with squid ink, Italians prefer a more intensely flavored dish of regular pasta dressed with a sauce of the ink.

Perhaps the most popular fish in Italy is not even Italian: cod. Since the Renaissance, Italian sailors have brought home dried cod (*stoccafisso*) and dried salt cod (*baccalà*) from northern Europe. After lengthy soaking, the fish is ready for cooking in numerous ways, such as in milk in Vicenza (the Veneto), with herbs and olives (Liguria) or in fritters all along the coasts. The other newly popular imported fish is salmon, to which Italians are now beginning to apply their own culinary magic.

From Italian rivers and lakes come trout, salmon trout (charmingly called *trota salmonata*) and perch. A prized fish in Emilia-Romagna is sturgeon from the Po. With that region's unmatched penchant for quality luxury ingredients, local cooks grill fresh sturgeon and dress it in olive oil, and remove eggs from the females for Italy's finest caviar. In ancient times, only Jews in Italy consumed caviar until others discovered how exquisite it is. Another delicacy that has gained favor in recent years is *bottarga,* the roe from red or gray mullet or tuna, found in western Sardinia. The roe is dried and then served with lemon as an antipasto. It is only a matter of time before Italians discover another fish (wolffish, mahi mahi, or char, for example) and, in their unmistakable fashion, make it their own.

At the port in Castelsardo, Sardinia, fishermen engage in a relatively new livelihood. Historically, Sardinian cooking was based on the sheep of the mountains and not the fish of the sea.

Liguria

ORATA AL VINO BIANCO

Gilt-head Bream Baked in White Wine

Present this fish on a serving platter decorated with Gaeta or other Mediterranean-style small black olives. A sea bass, salmon trout or similar whole fish can be substituted for the bream.

¼ cup (2 fl oz/60 ml) extra-virgin olive oil
3 cloves garlic, chopped
leaves from 2 fresh rosemary sprigs, chopped
salt and freshly ground pepper
1 whole gilt-head bream, about 5 lb (2.5 kg), cleaned
1 cup (8 fl oz/240 ml) dry white wine

Preheat an oven to 350°F (180°C). Using a little of the oil, oil a baking dish large enough to accommodate the fish.

In a small bowl, stir together the garlic and rosemary and season to taste with salt and pepper. Make a horizontal cut along the backbone of the fish and fill with some of the garlic and rosemary mixture. Stuff the remainder in the cavity of the fish. Place the fish in the prepared dish and pour the remaining oil over the top.

Place in the oven and bake until the oil begins to bubble, about 3 minutes. Add the wine and continue to bake, brushing the fish frequently with the cooking juices, until opaque when cut into at the thickest point, about 30 minutes in all.

Transfer the fish to a platter, pour the dish juices over the top and serve.

SERVES 6

FILETTI DI SOGLIOLA ALLE ZUCCHINE E MANDORLE

Fillets of Sole with Zucchini and Almonds

Sole, a fish popular throughout Italy, is topped with an updated sauce of zucchini, almonds and mint. The zucchini must be cooked very quickly over high heat so as not to release liquid.

2 lb (1 kg) sole fillets
1 cup (4 oz/120 g) all-purpose (plain) flour
6 tablespoons (3 oz/90 g) unsalted butter
salt and freshly ground pepper
1¼ lb (600 g) zucchini (courgettes), finely chopped
½ cup (2½ oz/80 g) almonds, very finely chopped
1 tablespoon chopped fresh mint

Dust the sole fillets with the flour, shaking off the excess.

In a frying pan over medium heat, melt 4 tablespoons (2 oz/60 g) of the butter. When it begins to brown, add the sole fillets and cook, carefully turning once, until golden on both sides and opaque in the center, about 3 minutes on each side. Season to taste with salt and pepper. Transfer to a warmed platter and keep warm.

Quickly wipe the frying pan with a paper towel. Place over high heat and add the remaining 2 tablespoons butter. When it begins to foam, add the zucchini and almonds. Cook, stirring frequently, until heated through, a couple of minutes. Season to taste with salt and pepper.

Spoon the zucchini and almonds over the sole fillets and sprinkle with the mint. Serve at once.

SERVES 6

142

Clockwise from left: Steamed Fish with Corn Salad (recipe page 148);
Fillets of Sole with Zucchini and Almonds; Gilt-head Bream
Baked in White Wine

Sardegna

ARAGOSTA IN CREMA DI VERDURE

Lobster with Vegetable Sauce

Lobster is a specialty of Sardinia's ancient port city of Alghero. The success of this vegetable sauce depends upon the tomatoes being firm but ripe.

1 green bell pepper (capsicum)
1 cucumber, peeled and cut into pieces
4 ripe tomatoes, peeled and cut into pieces
2 cloves garlic, chopped
salt and freshly ground pepper
¼ cup (2 fl oz/60 ml) extra-virgin olive oil
3 lobsters, about 1¼ lb (600 g) each

Preheat a broiler (griller). Cut the bell pepper in half lengthwise and discard the stem, seeds and ribs. Place cut side down on a broiler pan (tray) and broil (grill) until the skin is blistered and blackened. Remove from the broiler and place in a paper bag. Close tightly and let steam for about 10 minutes to loosen the skin. Using your fingers, peel off the skin and cut the pepper halves into pieces.

In a food processor fitted with the metal blade, combine the pepper pieces, cucumber, tomatoes and garlic. Season to taste with a pinch of salt and a generous pinch of pepper and add the oil. Purée until smooth and transfer to a bowl.

Bring a large pot of lightly salted water to a boil. Drop in the lobsters and cook until the shells turn red and the lobsters are done. Drain well and set aside to cool. Using a large, sharp knife, cut each lobster in half. Pull out the dark vein that runs the length of the body, as well as the sand sac near the lower part of the head. Arrange the lobster halves on a platter, meat side up. Dress with the vegetable sauce and serve.

SERVES 6

Marche

CAPESANTE CON PORRI E ZAFFERANO

Scallops with Saffron-Leek Sauce

While scallops are not common on the traditional Italian table, they are making appearances on today's menus, a testament to the enduring appeal for Italian cooks of all things from the sea. They are especially appreciated in the Marches region. Serve this saffron-scented dish with a green salad.

1 teaspoon powdered saffron
5 tablespoons (2½ fl oz/80 ml) water
3 leeks
2 tablespoons unsalted butter
¼ cup (2 fl oz/60 ml) dry white wine
½ cup (4 fl oz/120 ml) tomato sauce (recipe on page 94)
¾ cup (6 fl oz/180 ml) milk
12 sea scallops, cut in half horizontally
salt and freshly ground pepper

Preheat an oven to 350°F (180°C).

In a small bowl, dissolve the saffron in 1 tablespoon of the water. Discard the root ends, dark green tops and any tough outer leaves from the leeks. Slit along the shank and rinse well under running water, then slice crosswise.

In a saucepan over low heat, melt the butter. Add the leeks and the remaining 4 tablespoons (2 fl oz/60 ml) water and cook over low heat for about 10 minutes. Add the wine, raise the heat to medium and allow the liquid to evaporate for a few minutes. Add the tomato sauce, the saffron mixture and the milk, stir well, reduce the heat to low and cook until thickened, about 10 minutes. Pour into a baking dish large enough to hold the scallops in a single layer.

Season the scallops to taste with salt and pepper. Arrange them over the sauce. Bake until the scallops are opaque throughout, about 10 minutes. Serve very hot directly from the dish.

SERVES 6

Clockwise from left: Scallops with Saffron-Leek Sauce; Lobster with Vegetable Sauce; Grilled Swordfish with Herbs

Toscana

TAGLIATA DI SPADA ALLE ERBE

Grilled Swordfish with Herbs

While Tuscany is world famous for its inland towns such as Florence and Siena, it also has a beautiful coastline offering superb seafood. Briefly grilled with a blend of herbs, this aromatic dish makes a perfect main course for a light luncheon.

6 swordfish steaks, each about 6 oz (180 g)
1 teaspoon chopped fresh rosemary
1 teaspoon chopped fresh sage
1 teaspoon chopped fresh thyme
1 teaspoon dried oregano
2 cloves garlic, chopped
4 tablespoons (2 fl oz/60 ml) extra-virgin olive oil
2 tablespoons balsamic vinegar
1 teaspoon fresh lemon juice
salt and freshly ground pepper

☙ Arrange the fish on a deep platter. In a small bowl, stir together all the herbs, 3 tablespoons of the oil, the balsamic vinegar and the lemon juice. Season with salt and pepper. Pour the herbal mixture over the fish, cover and marinate in the refrigerator for about 3 hours, turning occasionally.

☙ Prepare a fire in a charcoal grill.

☙ Remove the fish steaks from the marinade; reserve the marinade. Brush a very hot grill rack with the remaining 1 tablespoon oil and place the fish on it. Grill, turning once, until golden brown on both sides and opaque in the center, 2–3 minutes on each side.

☙ Serve, drizzling with the reserved marinade, if desired.

SERVES 6

Filetti di Rombo con Pomodori e Cipolle

Turbot Fillets with Tomato and Onion Sauce

Serve this pleasantly rich dish with young, tender vegetables sautéed in butter. Sometimes the sauce of tomatoes and cream is called salsa rosa *because of its appealing pinkish color.*

¼ cup (2 oz/60 g) unsalted butter, cut into pieces
2 yellow onions, sliced

12 turbot fillets, about 3 oz (90 g) each
salt and freshly ground pepper
¼ cup (2 fl oz/60 ml) dry white wine
6 ripe plum (Roma) tomatoes, peeled and chopped
⅔ cup (5 fl oz/150 ml) heavy (double) cream

◦ Preheat an oven to 350°F (180°C).
◦ Select a baking dish large enough to hold the fillets in a single layer, slightly overlapping them, and scatter the butter pieces evenly over the bottom. Add the onions in an even layer. Bake, stirring once, until the onions are tender but not golden, about 10 minutes. Remove from the oven.
◦ Season the turbot fillets with salt and pepper to taste. Arrange the fillets over the onions and return to the oven for

146

another 10 minutes. Pour the wine into the dish and continue to cook for 3 minutes. The fillets should remain moist.

🍤 Remove the dish from the oven and remove the fillets from the dish. Set aside and keep warm. Using a slotted spoon, remove the onions from the sauce and discard. Pour the sauce through a fine-mesh sieve into a saucepan. Add the tomatoes and cream and cook over medium heat for about 3 minutes, stirring frequently. The sauce should be creamy, but the tomato pieces should remain intact.

🍤 Transfer the fillets to a warmed platter, spoon the sauce over them and serve.

SERVES 6

Sicilia

TONNO AL VINO ROSSO
Tuna in Red Wine

Two facts of Sicilian life unfold in this dish: tuna is considered one of the most prized catches there, and the island actually has more vineyards than any other region of Italy. Choose a good red wine that is fruity but not too heavy, such as the famed Sicilian Corvo.

6 tablespoons (3 fl oz/90 ml) extra-virgin olive oil
2 cloves garlic, chopped
1 small yellow onion, finely chopped
6 tuna steaks, about 6 oz (180 g) each and ½ in (1 cm) thick
salt and freshly ground pepper
2 tablespoons all-purpose (plain) flour
½ cup (4 fl oz/120 ml) dry red wine (see note)
2 tablespoons chopped fresh flat-leaf (Italian) parsley

🍤 In a frying pan large enough to hold the tuna in a single layer, warm the oil over medium heat. Add the garlic and onion and sauté until the garlic begins to take on color, about 3 minutes. Push the vegetables to the side of the pan, add the tuna and season to taste with salt and pepper. Cook, turning once, until browned on both sides and nearly opaque in the center, about 3 minutes on each side.

🍤 Meanwhile, in a small bowl, stir together the flour and wine. When the tuna is nicely browned, add the wine mixture and continue to cook until the wine has been absorbed, about 3 minutes. Sprinkle with the parsley. Transfer to a warmed platter and serve at once.

SERVES 6

Emilia-Romagna

TROTELLE AL BALSAMICO
Baked Trout with Balsamic Vinegar

Modena in Emilia-Romagna is the home of balsamic vinegar. Its complex, sweet flavors accent the delicate flesh of trout. Be careful not to overcook the fish. Their flesh should be opaque and moist.

4 tablespoons (2 oz/60 g) unsalted butter
6 whole trout, about ½ lb (240 g) each, cleaned
¼ cup (1 oz/30 g) all-purpose (plain) flour
salt and freshly ground pepper
2 tablespoons extra-virgin olive oil
3 tablespoons balsamic vinegar
leaves of 1 small bunch fresh flat-leaf (Italian) parsley, finely chopped

🍤 Preheat an oven to 400°F (200°C). Using 2 tablespoons of the butter, grease a baking dish large enough to hold the trout in a single layer.

🍤 Carefully remove the skin from each trout and then make 2 incisions, each 1 in (2.5 cm) long, along the backbone. Lightly dust the fish with the flour, shaking off the excess, and season to taste with salt and pepper.

🍤 In a frying pan over medium heat, warm the oil. Add the trout and cook, turning once, until golden on both sides, about 3 minutes on each side. Remove from the heat.

🍤 Transfer the fish to the prepared baking dish. Slip the remaining 2 tablespoons butter into the incisions in the trout, dividing it evenly. Bake, uncovered, until the trout are opaque at the center, about 10 minutes. A couple of minutes before the trout are ready, pour the vinegar over them and sprinkle with the parsley. Serve immediately.

SERVES 6

Campania

MUSSILLO IN UMIDO

Cod Stewed in Tomatoes

The term mussillo *refers to the best part of the cod—the fillet near the backbone. You can also use salt cod fillets for this recipe. If you do, however, you will need to soak the fish in several changes of cold water for 24 hours before using it. The length of soaking depends upon the thickness of the pieces and their saltiness.*

2½ lb (1.25 kg) cod fillets (see note) or other firm-fleshed
    white fish fillets
⅓ cup (2½ fl oz/80 ml) extra-virgin olive oil
2 cloves garlic
pinch of red pepper flakes
¼ cup (2 fl oz/60 ml) dry white wine
2 lb (1 kg) tomatoes, peeled and chopped
1 tablespoon chopped fresh flat-leaf (Italian) parsley

☞ Place the cod in a saucepan with water to cover generously. Bring to a boil and boil for 5 minutes. Using a slotted spoon, remove the fish from the water. When cool enough to handle, break them into small pieces, discarding any bones.
☞ In a deep saucepan over medium heat, warm the oil. Add the garlic and pepper flakes and cook, stirring, until the garlic begins to take on color, about 3 minutes. Add the cod pieces, reduce the heat to low and simmer, uncovered, for 5 minutes, stirring frequently with a wooden spoon and adding the wine a little at a time. Stir in the tomatoes and continue to cook until a thick, shiny sauce forms, about 20 minutes.
☞ About 5 minutes before the fish is ready, stir in the parsley. Transfer to a warmed bowl and serve.

SERVES 6

Toscana

INSALATA DI PESCE AL GRANTURCO

Steamed Fish with Corn Salad

Gilt-head bream has a delicate flavor that would be masked by a complicated preparation. Steaming, however, leaves all the subtle flavor of the fish beautifully intact. Sea bass, salmon or trout can be substituted for the bream. This recipe is a specialty of Da Antonio in Castelnuovo Berardenga in Chianti, one of the best fish restaurants I know.

2 ears of corn
1 large, ripe tomato, peeled, seeded and finely chopped
salt
6 tablespoons (3 fl oz/90 ml) extra-virgin olive oil
1 tablespoon chopped fresh chives
1 whole gilt-head bream, 2 lb (1 kg), cleaned, boned and
    thinly sliced

☞ Bring a saucepan filled with salted water to a boil. Add the ears of corn and boil until tender, 7–10 minutes. Drain, let cool and cut off the kernels from the cobs. Set aside. Meanwhile, place the tomato in a colander, sprinkle with salt and let drain for 30 minutes.
☞ In a small bowl, stir together the oil, chives and tomato. Taste and adjust the salt. Place the fish on a rack in a steamer above boiling water. Cover and steam for about 2 minutes.
☞ Arrange the fish on a warmed platter and sprinkle with the corn. Spoon the tomato mixture over the top and serve.

SERVES 6   *Photograph pages 142–143*

Cod Stewed in Tomatoes

Top to bottom: Stewed Squid with Potatoes and Parsley; Baked Hake with Artichokes

NASELLO AI CARCIOFI

Baked Hake with Artichokes

It is best to use six small hakes for this recipe, as they will deliver a more flavorful dish than a single large one. If you cannot find hake, use flaky, mild small whole fish such as perch, trout or whiting. Also use small, tender artichokes, as the larger ones tend to be too tough and dry for this recipe.

juice of 1 lemon
6 small, tender artichokes
3 tablespoons extra-virgin olive oil

6 whole hakes, about ½ lb (240 g) each, cleaned
salt and freshly ground pepper
¼ cup (2 fl oz/60 ml) dry white wine

Fill a bowl with cold water and add the lemon juice. Trim off the top one-third of each artichoke, then cut or pull off the tough outer leaves. Using a spoon, dig out the prickly choke from the center. Trim the stem even with the base. As each artichoke is trimmed, place it in the lemon water to prevent it from discoloring.

Preheat an oven to 400°F (200°C). Brush a baking dish large enough to accommodate the fish and artichokes with 1 tablespoon of the oil.

Arrange the fish in the prepared baking dish in a single layer. Drain the artichokes, cut each in half and then slice lengthwise. Arrange the slices around the fish. Season the fish and artichokes with salt and pepper to taste and pour the remaining 2 tablespoons oil and the white wine over all.

ᴄ⊀ Bake until the fish are opaque in the center and the artichokes are tender, about 15 minutes. Arrange the fish and artichokes on a warmed platter and serve immediately.

SERVES 6

Campania

CALAMARI ALLE PATATE E PREZZEMOLO

Stewed Squid with Potatoes and Parsley

If possible, use squid that weigh no more than about 3½ ounces (100 g) each. Tiny squid can actually be left whole, but are difficult to find in most areas. Serve this dish as a main course, or use it as a sauce for spaghetti or linguine.

3 lb (1.5 kg) squid (see note)
6 tablespoons (3 fl oz/90 ml) extra-virgin olive oil
3 cloves garlic
pinch of red pepper flakes
4 cups (1½ lb/750 g) canned tomatoes, roughly chopped, with their juice
3 large boiling potatoes, peeled and diced
salt
2 tablespoons chopped fresh flat-leaf (Italian) parsley

ᴄ⊀ To clean the squid, pull the tentacles from each body. Discard the entrails, ink sac and cartilage from the body. Cut the tentacles off at the point just above the eyes and discard the head. Rinse the body and tentacles under cold water.

ᴄ⊀ In a large saucepan over medium heat, warm the oil. Add the garlic and pepper flakes and cook, stirring, until the garlic begins to take on color, about 3 minutes. Add the squid. Cover the pan tightly, first with aluminum foil and then with a lid. Reduce the heat to low and simmer for 30 minutes.

ᴄ⊀ Add the tomatoes, potatoes and salt to taste and mix well. Re-cover and continue to simmer until the potatoes are tender and a thick, shiny sauce forms, about 40 minutes longer. Add the parsley and stir to mix, being careful not to break up the potatoes.

ᴄ⊀ Transfer to a warmed platter and serve.

SERVES 6

BRANZINO ALL'ARANCIA E PREZZEMOLO

Sea Bass in Orange and Parsley Sauce

Red snapper is a good substitute for the sea bass in this recipe. If you want to thin the sauce, purée it in a blender and strain it through a fine-mesh sieve before stirring in the orange zest.

zest of 1 orange, removed in large pieces
6 tablespoons (3 oz/90 g) unsalted butter
1 yellow onion, finely chopped
1 tablespoon all-purpose (plain) flour, plus ½ cup (2 oz/60 g) for dusting fish

½ cup (4 fl oz/120 ml) dry white wine
juice of 4 oranges
salt
6 sea bass fillets, about 5 oz (150 g) each
freshly ground pepper
3 tablespoons chopped fresh flat-leaf (Italian) parsley

ᴄ⊀ Bring a small pan of salted water to a boil, add the orange zest and boil for about 5 minutes. Drain, transfer to a bowl of cold water and let cool in the water for 5 minutes. Drain and cut into long, narrow strips. Set aside.

ᴄ⊀ In a frying pan over medium heat, melt 3 tablespoons of the butter. Add the onion and sauté until translucent, about 3 minutes. Add the 1 tablespoon flour, the wine and the orange juice. Season to taste with salt and allow to cook, stirring often, until thickened and creamy, about 10 minutes. Stir in the reserved orange zest strips.

ᴄ⊀ Meanwhile, using the ½ cup (2 oz/60 g) flour, dust the fish fillets with the flour, shaking off the excess. In a frying pan over medium heat, melt the remaining 3 tablespoons butter. When it begins to foam, add the fish fillets and cook, turning once, until golden brown on both sides and opaque in the center, about 3 minutes on each side. Season to taste with salt and pepper.

ᴄ⊀ Transfer to a warmed platter and spoon some of the orange sauce over the top. Sprinkle with the parsley and serve. Pass the remaining sauce in a bowl.

SERVES 6

Top to bottom: Trout Fillets with Almonds (recipe page 154); Sea Bass in Orange and Parsley Sauce

Sicilia

COSTOLETTE DI SPADA AL POMODORO CRUDO

Marinated Swordfish with Fresh Tomato Sauce

This especially light preparation from Sicily bears a certain resemblance to the seviche of Spain in that the fish is "cooked" in an acidic marinade. Use only the freshest fish and shellfish for this dish, purchased from a reputable fish shop with high turnover.

6 thin swordfish steaks, about 3 oz (90 g) each
10 oz (300 g) shrimp (prawns), peeled and deveined
juice of 10 lemons
3 ripe tomatoes, peeled, seeded and diced
salt
2 tablespoons extra-virgin olive oil
1 tablespoon chopped fresh flat-leaf (Italian) parsley
1 tablespoon chopped fresh basil
¼ teaspoon hot-pepper sauce such as Tabasco sauce

◆ Place the swordfish steaks on a deep glass or ceramic plate and the shrimp in a glass or ceramic bowl. Pour about half of the lemon juice over the swordfish and the remainder over the shrimp. Cover and marinate them both in the refrigerator for about 3 hours, carefully turning occasionally.
◆ Place the tomatoes in a colander, sprinkle with salt and let drain for 30 minutes. In a bowl, stir together the oil, parsley, basil, hot-pepper sauce and tomatoes.
◆ Drain the liquid from the swordfish steaks and arrange on a platter. Drain the shrimp and arrange them decoratively on the swordfish steaks. Spoon the tomato sauce over the fish and shrimp and serve.

SERVES 6

Sicilia

COSTOLETTE DI TONNO AL FINOCCHIO

Tuna Steaks with Sautéed Fennel

The fennel in this recipe sweetens the taste of the tuna, one of the prized catches of the Sicilian fisherman. Broccoli or artichokes, blanched and sautéed, would also be delicious with the fish.

6 tuna steaks, each about 6 oz (180 g) and ½ in (1 cm) thick
½ cup (2 oz/60 g) all-purpose (plain) flour
2 fennel bulbs, thinly sliced lengthwise
4 tablespoons (2 oz/60 g) unsalted butter
salt and freshly ground pepper

◆ Dust the tuna steaks with the flour, shaking off the excess.
◆ Bring a saucepan filled with salted water to a boil. Add the fennel and blanch for 30 seconds. Drain well and return to the saucepan. Add 1 tablespoon of the butter, cover and place over low heat. Cook until tender, about 5 minutes, adding a little water as needed to keep the fennel moist.
◆ Meanwhile, in a large frying pan over medium heat, melt the remaining 3 tablespoons butter. Add the tuna steaks and cook, turning once, until browned on both sides, about 3 minutes on each side. Drain off any fat from the pan and add the fennel. Season to taste with salt and pepper, cover, reduce the heat to low and cook for another 2 minutes or so to finish cooking the fish and to blend the flavors.
◆ Transfer to a warmed platter and serve.

SERVES 6

*Top to bottom: Marinated Swordfish with Fresh
Tomato Sauce; Tuna Steaks with Sautéed Fennel*

Tonno alla Melagrana
Tuna Steaks with Pomegranate Sauce

The slightly acidic taste of pomegranate seeds combines perfectly with the sweet flavor of tuna. For centuries, pomegranates have been popular in Middle Eastern dishes, and now are often used in Italian cooking as well, adding both flavor and color.

6 tuna steaks, about 6 oz (180 g) each and ½ in (1 cm) thick
½ cup (2 oz/60 g) all-purpose (plain) flour
¼ cup (2 oz/60 g) unsalted butter
2 tablespoons extra-virgin olive oil
¼ cup (2 fl oz/60 ml) dry white wine
seeds from 2 pomegranates
salt and freshly ground pepper

☞ Dust the tuna steaks with the flour, shaking off the excess. In a large frying pan over medium heat, melt the butter with the oil. When the butter foams, add the tuna steaks and cook, turning once, until golden on both sides, about 3 minutes on each side.

☞ Add the wine and pomegranate seeds and season to taste with salt and pepper. Cover, reduce the heat to low and allow the tuna to take on flavor for about 2 minutes, turning the steaks once at the halfway point.

☞ Arrange the tuna steaks on a warmed platter. Pour the pomegranate seeds and pan juices over the top and serve.

SERVES 6

Alto Adige

Filetti di Trota alle Mandorle
Trout Fillets with Almonds

Landlocked Alto Adige boasts wonderful trout from its pristine rivers. Sole or another delicately flavored fish of the sea can be substituted here, however. Hazelnuts (filberts), pine nuts or pistachios can be used in place of almonds.

12 trout fillets, about 3 oz (90 g) each
½ cup (2 oz/60 g) all-purpose (plain) flour
6 tablespoons (3 oz/90 g) unsalted butter
salt
6 tablespoons (2 oz/60 g) chopped almonds

☞ Dust the trout fillets with the flour, shaking off the excess. In a frying pan over medium heat, melt 3 tablespoons of the butter. When it begins to foam, add the trout fillets and cook, turning once, until golden on both sides, about 3 minutes on each side. Season with salt. Transfer to a warmed platter and keep warm.

☞ Quickly wipe the frying pan with a paper towel. Place over medium heat and add the remaining 3 tablespoons butter. When it foams, add the almonds and cook, stirring frequently, until they take on color, about 5 minutes; take care they do not burn. Remove from the heat.

☞ Drain off any cooking juices from the platter and neatly arrange the fillets on it. Pour the almonds and butter over the fillets and serve at once.

SERVES 6 *Photograph page 151*

Coda di Rospo con Salsa al Pernod e Dragoncello
Monkfish with Pernod and Tarragon Sauce

Monkfish is an unusual species: it has a large unsightly head that is always discarded, leaving the firm, sweet flesh of the tail (coda, in Italian) to be eaten. You can substitute another aniseed-flavored liqueur for the Pernod. Or you can leave out the liqueur and

Left to right: Tuna Steaks with Pomegranate Sauce;
Monkfish with Pernod and Tarragon Sauce

season the fish with a handful of finely chopped foliage clipped from a fennel bulb.

1 clove garlic, lightly smashed
½ cup (4 fl oz/120 ml) extra-virgin olive oil
1 monkfish, about 3 lb (1.5 kg)
2 lemons, thinly sliced
salt and freshly ground pepper
¼ cup (2 fl oz/60 ml) Pernod
2 tablespoons chopped fresh tarragon or 1 tablespoon dried tarragon

  In a small bowl, combine the garlic and oil and let stand for about 30 minutes to infuse the oil with the garlic flavor. Remove and discard the garlic.

  Preheat an oven to 400°F (200°C).

  Remove the skin from the monkfish and make 2 incisions, each 1 in (2.5 cm) long, along the backbone. Select an oven dish large enough to hold the monkfish and cover the bottom with the lemon slices. Place the monkfish on top of the lemons. Brush with half of the oil and season to taste with salt and pepper.

  Bake, uncovered, for 10 minutes. Remove from the oven and spoon out the excess cooking liquids from the dish. Pour in the remaining flavored oil and the Pernod and sprinkle with the tarragon.

  Return the monkfish to the oven and continue to bake until opaque at the center, about 10 minutes longer. Serve directly from the dish.

SERVES 6

SEPPIE AI PORRI

Sautéed Cuttlefish and Leeks

Cuttlefish are small mollusks with broad heads, suckered tentacles and ink sacs. They closely resemble squid, which may be used in their place in this recipe. Select the smallest cuttlefish or squid you can find, as they will be the most tender. If only large ones are available, use the body portion and save the rest for another use, or cut into tiny pieces before cooking.

1⅔ lb (800 g) cuttlefish, preferably small (see note)
2 lb (1 kg) leeks

¼ cup (2 fl oz/60 ml) extra-virgin olive oil
3 tablespoons all-purpose (plain) flour
salt and freshly ground pepper
½ cup (4 fl oz/120 ml) dry red wine
1 tablespoon chopped fresh flat-leaf (Italian) parsley

☙ Pull the tentacles from each cuttlefish body. Discard the entrails, ink sac and cartilage from the body. Cut off the tentacles at the point just above the eyes and discard each head. Rinse the bodies and tentacles under cold running water. Cut the bodies into long strips, and chop the tentacles, if desired.

GAMBERONI AL DRAGONCELLO E RICOTTA
Shrimp with Tarragon-Ricotta Stuffing

Here is a refreshing summer dish, as the shrimp are served cold. You can prepare a smaller quantity of the recipe and serve it as a first course on crostini, or "little toasts." While tarragon is not common throughout Italy, it is showing up in newer recipes such as this.

60 large shrimp (prawns) in the shell
rounded ¾ cup (6½ oz/200 g) ricotta cheese
3 tablespoons chopped fresh tarragon
1 tablespoon chopped fresh flat-leaf (Italian) parsley
pinch of salt
several lettuce leaves

❧ Bring a large saucepan of salted water to a boil. Add the shrimp and cook until they turn pink and curl slightly, about 5 minutes, or less if they are not large. Drain well and let cool, then peel. Using a sharp knife, make a deep incision lengthwise along the back of each shrimp. Set aside. In a bowl, stir together the ricotta, tarragon and parsley. Season with the salt. Pack the ricotta mixture into a pastry (piping) bag fitted with a star tip. Cover a platter with a bed of lettuce leaves.

❧ Open the incision in each shrimp and pipe a ribbon of the ricotta mixture into each opening. Arrange the shrimp on the lettuce-lined platter and serve.

SERVES 8–10

Sardegna

SARDE IN TORTIERA
Baked Sardines with Oregano

Although Sardinians traditionally have eaten more lamb than fish, sardines are abundant on the island. Fresh anchovies can be used in place of the sardines. They are smaller fish and have less fat.

¼ cup (2 fl oz/60 ml) extra-virgin olive oil
2 yellow onions, finely chopped
1 clove garlic, smashed
salt and freshly ground pepper
1 tablespoon chopped fresh oregano
3 tablespoons white wine vinegar
1½ lb (750 g) fresh sardines
juice of 1 lemon

❧ In a saucepan over medium heat, warm the oil. Add the onions and garlic and cook, stirring, until translucent, about 3 minutes. Season to taste with salt and pepper. Add the oregano and vinegar, reduce the heat, cover and simmer until the onions disintegrate, about 30 minutes, adding a little water for moisture, if necessary.

❧ Meanwhile, remove the heads from the sardines. Slit the bodies lengthwise along the belly and open them flat. Remove and discard the bones. Cover and refrigerate until needed.

❧ Preheat an oven to 400°F (200°C).

❧ Arrange the sardines in a baking dish in slightly overlapping layers, sprinkling each layer with lemon juice and some of the onions. Finish with a layer of onions.

❧ Bake, uncovered, until the fish are opaque at the center, about 10 minutes. Serve at once.

SERVES 6

Clockwise from left: Baked Sardines with Oregano; Sautéed Cuttlefish and Leeks; Shrimp with Tarragon-Ricotta Stuffing

❧ Discard the root ends, dark green tops and any tough outer leaves from the leeks. Slit along the shank and rinse well under running water, then thinly slice crosswise.

❧ In a saucepan over high heat, warm the oil. When hot, add the cuttlefish and leeks, sprinkle with the flour and sauté, stirring occasionally, for several minutes until the cuttlefish are opaque. Season to taste with salt and pepper, add the wine, cover, reduce the heat to low and cook until the flavors are blended, about 10 minutes longer.

❧ Uncover and let excess cooking liquid evaporate. Sprinkle with the parsley, transfer to a warmed platter and serve.

SERVES 6

Campania

PESCE ALLA GRIGLIA
Mixed Grilled Fish

In the summer, along the Amalfi coast, fish is cooked over outdoor grills. Small whole fish such as mullet, bream, sea bass and similar varieties from the nearby waters are presented in a mixed grill. Firm-fleshed fish fillets can be used in addition to the whole fish. The combination of vinegar and mint heightens the flavor of the catch.

4 lb (2 kg) assorted whole fish (see note), about 6 fish, each weighing about ¾ lb (360 g), cleaned but left whole
¼ cup (2 fl oz/60 ml) extra-virgin olive oil
¼ cup (2 fl oz/60 ml) white wine vinegar
2 tablespoons chopped fresh mint
salt and freshly ground pepper

🐟 Prepare a fire in a charcoal grill.
🐟 Place the whole fish on the grill rack over hot coals. Grill, turning once, until well browned on both sides but still soft in the center, about 10 minutes total. The timing will depend upon the size and type of fish.
🐟 Meanwhile, in a large, deep platter, stir together the oil, vinegar, mint, and salt and pepper to taste. As the fish are ready, carefully transfer them from the grill rack to the platter, immersing them in the sauce. Serve hot on the same platter.

SERVES 6   *Photograph pages 138–139*

ZUPPA DI MOLLUSCHI ALL'AGLIO
Shellfish Stew with Garlic

This is a surprisingly quick dish to prepare. It is important at the finish to reduce the cooking liquids very quickly so that the shellfish remain warm. While it is traditionally prepared just with mollusks, you could add crustaceans such as scampi or large shrimp, if desired.

2 lb (1 kg) assorted shellfish such as clams, mussels, scallops, shrimp (prawns) and scampi
6 slices coarse country bread, each about ½ in (1 cm) thick
6 cloves garlic
¼ cup (2 fl oz/60 ml) extra-virgin olive oil
pinch of red pepper flakes
1 cup (8 fl oz/240 ml) canned tomatoes passed through a food mill
2 tablespoons chopped flat-leaf (Italian) parsley

🐟 If using clams, soak in a large bowl of salted water for at least 2 hours to rid them of any sand. Rinse several times. If using mussels, scrub well and remove their beards. Rinse all other shellfish thoroughly.
🐟 Preheat a broiler (griller). Place the bread slices on a broiler pan (tray) and broil (grill) until golden on both sides. Remove from the broiler and rub the slices on one side with half of the garlic cloves; keep warm.
🐟 Chop the rest of the garlic and place in a deep pot with the olive oil and pepper flakes. Place over medium heat and sauté until the garlic begins to take on color, about 3 minutes. Add the tomatoes and continue to cook, stirring occasionally, until reduced and thickened, about 10 minutes. Add the shellfish, cover and cook until the shells of the mollusks open and all the other shellfish are cooked, about 3 minutes. Using

a slotted spoon, transfer the shellfish to a bowl and keep warm. Discard any mollusks that did not open. Raise the heat to reduce the cooking liquids quickly.
🐟 Place the grilled bread slices, garlic side up, in 6 shallow bowls and pour the tomato sauce over them. Top with the shellfish, sprinkle with the parsley and serve at once.

SERVES 6   *Photograph pages 138–139*

Veneto

SCAMPI ALLA GRIGLIA CON SALSA AL LIMONE
Broiled Shrimp with Lemon Sauce

You can make an extra batch of sauce and store it in the freezer for a quick meal. It is also excellent spooned over boiled rice. Scampi (also known as langoustines or Dublin Bay prawns) are hard to come by outside of Europe; large shrimp make a tasty substitute.

¼ cup (2 fl oz/60 ml) extra-virgin olive oil
juice of 2 lemons
salt and freshly ground pepper
36 scampi or large shrimp (prawns), peeled and deveined
2 tablespoons unsalted butter
2 tablespoons all-purpose (plain) flour
2 tablespoons dry white wine
1 tablespoon heavy (double) cream or milk, if needed

🐟 In a small bowl, stir together the oil, lemon juice, and salt and pepper to taste, mixing well. Arrange the scampi or shrimp on a deep platter and pour the oil mixture evenly over them. Marinate at room temperature for 1 hour, turning occasionally.
🐟 Preheat a broiler (griller).
🐟 To thread the scampi or shrimp onto 6 skewers, first remove from the marinade, reserving the marinade. Then bend each one almost in half and insert the skewer just above the tail so that it passes through the body twice. As the skewers are loaded, arrange them on a broiler pan (tray).
🐟 Place the scampi or shrimp under the broiler about 4 in (10 cm) from the heat and broil (grill), brushing occasionally with the marinade, until they turn pink, about 5 minutes. When the shellfish are cooked, dip them into the marinade and arrange on a serving platter; keep warm.
🐟 In a saucepan over medium heat, melt the butter and add the flour; blend well. Add the white wine and reserved marinade and whisk over medium heat for 5 minutes. If necessary, add the cream or milk to create a smoother sauce.
🐟 Transfer the sauce to a bowl and serve with the shellfish.

SERVES 6

Campania

SAUTÉ DI VONGOLE
Sautéed Clams with Garlic

The French word sauté *has been commonly used in Neapolitan recipes ever since Naples was ruled by the Bourbons. These clams can be served on their own or as a sauce for linguine.*

6 lb (3 kg) clams
6 tablespoons (3 fl oz/90 ml) extra-virgin olive oil
3 cloves garlic

Top to bottom: Sautéed Clams with Garlic;
Broiled Shrimp with Lemon Sauce

pinch of red pepper flakes
1 large bunch fresh flat-leaf (Italian) parsley, chopped

✍ Soak the clams in a large bowl of salted water for at least 2 hours to rid them of any sand. Rinse several times, then allow to dry.

✍ In a deep saucepan over medium heat, warm the oil. Add the garlic and pepper flakes and cook, stirring, until the garlic begins to take on color, about 3 minutes. Add the clams and sauté, stirring often, until the shells open, about 3 minutes. Add the parsley and mix well. Discard any clams that did not open.

✍ Transfer the clams with their liquid to a warmed bowl and serve.

SERVES 6

Salt Cod Cakes

Liguria

FOCACCINE DI BACCALÀ
Salt Cod Cakes

On Friday mornings in most regions of Italy, and especially in Liguria, you can still find shops that sell salt cod ready to cook. The shopkeepers have kept it under a steady stream of cold running water for 24 hours so that their customers will not have to rehydrate it at home. If you can't find salt cod, you can simmer the same amount of fresh cod with some aromatic herbs and mix it with the potatoes.

2½ lb (1.25 kg) salt cod
1 lb (480 g) boiling potatoes, unpeeled
1 tablespoon chopped fresh flat-leaf (Italian) parsley
2 egg whites
1 cup (4 oz/120 g) fine dried bread crumbs
4 cups (32 fl oz/1 l) vegetable oil for deep-frying

🐟 Soak the cod in water to cover in the refrigerator for 24 hours, changing the water 3 or 4 times. (Soaking time will depend upon the thickness of the pieces and their saltiness.)

🐟 Place the potatoes in a saucepan, add water to cover and bring to a boil. Boil until tender when pierced with a fork, 20–30 minutes. Drain and, when just cool enough to handle, peel them; keep warm.

🐟 Meanwhile, drain the salt cod. Place in a saucepan with water to cover and bring to a boil. Reduce the heat to medium-low and simmer until tender, about 15 minutes. Drain and, when cool enough to handle, remove the bones and skin.

🐟 Place the salt cod and potatoes in a bowl and mash with a fork until smooth. Add the parsley, mix well and form the mixture into cakes about 2 in (5 cm) in diameter and ½ in (1 cm) thick.

🐟 In a bowl, whisk the egg whites until frothy. Place the bread crumbs in another bowl. Dip the salt cod cakes first in the egg whites and then in the bread crumbs. Pour the oil into a deep frying pan and heat to 340°F (170°C). Working in batches, slip the salt cod cakes into the oil and fry, turning as needed, until well browned on all sides, about 5 minutes total. Using a slotted spoon, transfer to paper towels to drain briefly, then arrange on a warmed platter and serve at once.

SERVES 6

Veneto

TRANCE DI SALMONE AI PISELLI

Sautéed Salmon Steaks with Peas

Fresh peas—small, tender and barely cooked—are preferred for this dish. But on those occasions when they cannot be found, small frozen peas can be used instead. Place them under cold running water for a couple of minutes to thaw them.

2 lb (1 kg) peas, shelled (2 cups/10 oz/300 g shelled)
6 tablespoons (3 fl oz/90 ml) extra-virgin olive oil
salt
6 salmon steaks, about 6 oz (180 g) each

½ cup (2 oz/60 g) all-purpose (plain) flour
2 tablespoons unsalted butter
freshly ground pepper

❧ In a saucepan, combine the peas, 4 tablespoons (2 fl oz/ 60 ml) of the oil and a little salt. Place over low heat and cook until barely tender, about 5 minutes. Remove from the heat and keep warm. Dust the salmon steaks with the flour, shaking off the excess.

❧ In a frying pan over medium heat, warm the remaining 2 tablespoons oil with the butter. When hot, add the salmon and cook, turning once, until golden on both sides and barely opaque in the center, about 3 minutes on each side. Add the peas, season to taste with salt and pepper, reduce the heat to low, cover and cook for 2 minutes to blend the flavors.

❧ Transfer to a warmed platter and serve at once.

SERVES 6

Sautéed Salmon Steaks with Peas

Tuna Carpaccio with Capers

Campania

CARPACCIO DI TONNO AI CAPPERI

Tuna Carpaccio with Capers

Raw fish is becoming increasingly popular in Italy. Here, sword-fish can be substituted for the tuna. Whatever type you use, it must be of highest quality and unquestionable freshness.

2¼ lb (1.1 kg) tuna fillets
juice of 2 lemons
2 tablespoons drained and chopped brine-cured capers

2 tablespoons chopped fresh basil
1 tablespoon chopped fresh flat-leaf (Italian) parsley
6 tablespoons (3 fl oz/90 ml) extra-virgin olive oil
salt and freshly ground pepper

Very finely chop the tuna fillets. In a bowl, stir together the lemon juice, capers, basil, parsley and 3 tablespoons of the oil. Season to taste with salt and pepper. Add the fish and mix very well, taking care not to mash the fish.

Divide the tuna mixture into 6 equal portions and, using your hands, shape each portion into a round "steak." Arrange the steaks on a platter and drizzle the remaining olive oil over the top. Serve at once.

SERVES 6

Marche

TROTA SALMONATA ALLE OLIVE

Baked Salmon Trout with Olives

This very tasty way to prepare fish can be adapted to salmon, bream or red mullet. Adjust the cooking time depending upon the size of the fish. This trout is excellent accompanied with sautéed broccoli rabe (recipe on page 114).

1 whole salmon trout, about 5 lb (2.5 kg), cleaned
¼ cup (2 fl oz/60 ml) extra-virgin olive oil
juice of 4 lemons
4 cloves garlic, lightly smashed
½ cup (4 fl oz/120 ml) dry white wine
1 tablespoon finely chopped fresh flat-leaf (Italian) parsley
salt and freshly ground pepper

12 Gaeta or other Mediterranean-style small black olives, pitted and halved
2 bay leaves

🐟 Using a sharp knife, slice along the backbone of the salmon trout, cutting from the point of the dorsal fin to the tail. Then cut across the tail and back along the opposite side from the tail to the point at which the head is attached. Slip the knife under the backbone and free the top fillet from the bone, then free the bottom fillet. Rinse and pat dry.

🐟 Preheat an oven to 350°F (180°C).

🐟 In a bowl, stir together the oil, lemon juice, garlic, wine, parsley and salt and pepper to taste. Spoon 2 tablespoons of the oil mixture into the bottom of a baking dish large enough to hold the fish fillets. Place the 2 fish fillets, cut sides up and side by side, in the dish. Cover with the olives and bay leaves and pour the remaining oil mixture over the top. Cover with aluminum foil and bake until the fish is opaque in the center, about 30 minutes.

🐟 Transfer to a platter and serve.

SERVES 6

Baked Salmon Trout with Olives

Il Sud

Il Sud

CAMPANIA, ABRUZZO, MOLISE, PUGLIA, BASILICATA, CALABRIA

Mamma, è pronta la cena (Mom, is dinner ready)?! This is arguably the most ubiquitous cry in the south of Italy, one that is indeed followed by a question mark and an exclamation point. While much of Italy today has moved to a more international way of eating, with smaller portions, faster consumption and less time spent sharing what used to be known as the pleasures of the table, in southern Italy the family meal is still greeted with eager anticipation.

Traditions are held dear in the south, not only because they are cherished, but also because they provide assurance in an uncertain world. Although the area is one of great beauty, especially on the long coastlines, the land has been difficult. Much of the area has been historically plagued with drought, unyielding soil, earthquake and, near Naples, eruptions from Mount Vesuvius, the only active volcano on continental Europe. All of this unpredictability, combined with centuries of foreign rule and grinding poverty, has made life difficult for the people of southern Italy.

In the late nineteenth century, just as Italy was being unified, many southerners felt the impulse to migrate in search of a better life. Men were often the laborers during the industrial buildup of northern Italy, of other European countries, and later of the United States, Canada, Argentina and Australia. Sometimes whole families moved abroad, but often only the men went, sending money to the women, children and elderly back

The contrasts of the south are evidenced in a serene view of Ravello along the Amalfi coast (previous pages) and in the colorful chaos of a florist's display in Naples (at left).

167

Vesuvius rises proudly above the Bay of Naples, a symbol of both the vigor and uncertainty of life beneath a volcano.

home. The women ran the families and, even in a traditional context, acquired more autonomy and self-determination than might be expected. It was *mamma* who worked, cleaned, raised and fed the children, and she received mythic status. Women also were protagonists in agriculture, and their links to the land and the kitchen helped them evolve what we now know as southern Italian food.

In the twentieth century, whole families often migrated, and the tradition of mother as social and economic engineer spread to other countries. For this reason, when people outside of Italy think of the archetypal Italian mother, it is the southern mother who comes to mind. And when foreigners think of Italian food, it is southern food that they think of—more specifically, the food of Naples.

Naples is the capital of Campania, the most densely populated region of Italy. It is the nation's third-largest city, after Rome and Milan, and has a culinary tradition that is second to none. Because Naples is right on the Mediterranean, it has always been favored with spectacular seafood. In addition, the volcanic eruptions of Vesuvius throughout the centuries have produced, just beyond the city limits, the most fertile soil in the south. The key to Campania's food is that everything consumed, whether from land or sea, is at the peak of freshness and flavor, so that very little complicated cooking is required. And unlike its imitations abroad, the food of Naples is light, healthful and fully digestible.

Although Neapolitans do eat meat dishes, they dote on pasta, fish, vegetables and fruit. If Campania made no other contribution to the world's food aside from spaghetti and macaroni, it would still be legendary. All of southern Italy prefers dried pasta to fresh. It can be stored until it is needed, and can be adapted to many sauces. The area also produces some of the world's best tomatoes, lemons and peaches, all of which are central to its cooking. The tomatoes are paired with pasta, are used in salads, give structure to sauces for meat and

fish and, most important, go atop pizza, yet another specialty of Campania.

The lemons of the Amalfi Coast are the size of small grapefruits and give off a bewitching fragrance. They are used for pasta sauces; to flavor meat, fish, fruit and vegetables; and are the backbone of limoncello, the most popular after-dinner drink in Italy today. But the Campanians probably love their peaches best of all. The area between Aversa and Giugliano produces a peach called the *percoca,* whose flavor and fragrance give new meaning to the word "arousal." Neapolitans use these peaches for nectar, jam, baking, sauces, to cut into wine and for plain eating. In Naples, Italy's most frenetic city, everything comes to a halt when it is time to eat a peach.

Campania is also the home of the water buffalo. In the marshes near the Volturno River in the southern part of the region, white buffalo travel in herds. A herder calls each buffalo one by one to be milked and, after a mother lets her calf suckle to its heart's delight, the remaining milk is drawn for making mozzarella di bufala, a slightly sour and exquisite cheese that bears little resemblance to its pallid cow's milk imitators. The cheese goes on pizza, is baked with pasta and tomatoes, or is simply sliced with tomato and basil to make everyone's favorite light lunch, the *insalata caprese* (Capri salad). This dish is now eaten all over Italy, sometimes with arugula instead of basil, but nowhere is it better than in Campania.

The rest of southern Italy has eating traditions that

A fine stucco relief decorates the ceiling of a bathhouse in Pompeii, which was buried by the eruption of Vesuvius in A.D. 79.

At right: A wooden fishing boat awaits a day's work in Atrani on the Almafi Coast. The boat is named for Saint Andrew, one of the twelve apostles, who worked for a time as a fisherman.

Many visitors are drawn to southern Italy by its wealth of antiquities, such as the Temple of Apollo at Pompeii. These architectural splendors are reminders of the glorious heritage that is fundamental to the area.

differ substantially from Campania. In ancient times, the whole area was occupied and developed by the Greeks, but Campania later drew heavily from ancient Roman ways to form a distinct civilization. The region became more pleasure-seeking and flamboyant, characteristics that are expressed in its hedonistic delight in food. The rest of the south is more pastoral, and its food relies on fewer elements, most of which were raised by the Greeks: wheat, the olive, the grape, leafy vegetables, fava (broad) beans and the meat and milk of sheep. Onions, garlic and, later, hot chili pepper were the principal flavorings. Sweet peppers (capsicums), tomatoes and potatoes arrived in the rest of southern Italy after they were introduced into Campania, which came in the years after Columbus's travels to the Americas.

Wheat became the basis for pasta and large loaves of breads. Apulia (which produces 40 percent of Italy's wheat) and Calabria each have dozens of pasta shapes.

In the latter region, one of the bases on which a young woman is deemed marriageable is her ability to make a variety of pasta shapes. A dish of pasta is still the anchor of most southern Italian meals, and would customarily be followed by a vegetable dish or a piece of fruit and perhaps a slice of cheese. As the south has become more affluent, the only gesture to modernity is that the pasta may now be followed by a meat or fish course.

In the south, bread was sent along with shepherds as they headed for the pastures, and *mamma* always placed a loaf in the hands of her son as he set out to make his fortune in a faraway place. Some of the best breads in Italy come from Molise and Apulia. The former makes big, round dark loaves, while the latter has bread in all shapes and sizes.

Apulia is also Italy's leading producer of olive oil and wine, in quantity if not always in quality. In addition to being a cooking medium, olive oil is employed as a condiment to give flavor to soups, vegetables, fish and seafood, cheese and bread. This method of flavoring, also found in Liguria and central Italy, is now widespread and is one of the hallmarks of new Italian cooking.

The sheep is the principal source of protein in the south, except along the seafood-rich coasts. Lamb—grilled, braised, roasted, sautéed, baked—is ubiquitous in Abruzzo, Molise and the northern reaches of Apulia and Basilicata, and has been since Greek times. Sheep's milk is turned into cheese with the generic name of pecorino, but in fact there are innumerable cheeses in the south made from this milk, from the softest ricotta to long-aged cacio suitable only for grating.

All sorts of shellfish (except for lobster) are eaten raw and cooked in Apulia. With its bread, pasta, olive oil, wine, fish, seafood and vegetables, this region can make a strong claim to exemplify what is popularly called the Mediterranean diet, although the same could be said for Liguria in the northwest.

Basilicata and Calabria are among the least known of Italian regions, and their foods have made little impact beyond their borders. While this is unfortunate, it also means that they harbor secret treasures that food lovers should endeavor to discover. Basilicata is most famous for *lucanica,* a flavorful sausage made with pork or lamb.

The region also produces Aglianico, perhaps the finest red wine of southern Italy. The name derives from the word *Hellenic,* and the grape is one of the oldest in cultivation, having been planted by the ancient Greeks.

Calabria, next door, has a different culinary patrimony. While wine grapes came from the Greeks, the Arabs brought eggplants (aubergines) in the ninth century, and this vegetable has become the emblem of the Calabrese kitchen. Whether baked, fried or stuffed, eggplant appears at almost every meal. The region also has spectacular red onions that are prized throughout Italy, as well as fragrant citrus fruits. In addition, Calabria produces a wealth of chestnuts that are used for dessert pastes, for stuffing poultry or to make a flour used for pasta and bread. All of these ingredients are regularly wedded with pasta and chilies, and often with the tuna and swordfish caught nearby.

The legacy of privation dies hard, and while most southern Italians now dine in a way that is imitated in the north and throughout the world, the memory lingers of when food and money were scarce. So when *mamma* says that dinner is ready, everyone runs to the table.

One of the trulli, *the traditional limestone dwellings of Alberobello in Apulia. Each dome of a* trullo *corresponds to a room beneath it.*

Le Carni

A poultry-shop sign in Bologna beckons discriminating shoppers looking for the freshest, most flavorful chickens, turkeys and game birds.

Le Carni

MEATS, POULTRY AND GAME

Meat, especially red meat, is undergoing an identity crisis in Italy, as it has in much of the world. On the one hand, succulent beef is gratifying when grilled or broiled, as is famously done in Tuscany with *bistecca alla fiorentina,* or slow-cooked in Barolo as might be found in Piedmont or with local rich red wines in other regions. On the other hand, Italians express reservations about the heaviness of beef when compared to other sources of protein, and are concerned about its fat content. Yet in Italy, where image counts, serving a huge piece of beef (particularly in Tuscany and Piedmont) is thought to do honor to one's guests and oneself.

A bovine family grazes and feeds in a pasture in Sardinia. Meat is as important as fish to the island's diet.

For most Italians, beef has always been a luxury, so they have not had to worry about giving it up. For many, milk-fed veal from Lombardy is preferable. Boneless veal cutlets are ubiquitous throughout the country, but never better than in Milan, where they are dipped in egg and bread crumbs and fried in butter to make the sublime *cotoletta alla milanese.* In Friuli, slow-cooked veal shank (shin) is the perfect match for the red and white wines of that region. *Spezzatino* (veal chunks) cooked with peas is beloved in Romagna, and veal chops, once more popular in Italian restaurants abroad, now appear regularly on Italian tables. *Ossobuco* is Milan's famous veal shank, braised in white wine and other flavorings. In the Valle d'Aosta, cow's udder is boiled, cooled and sliced thin as an antipasto.

While cattle have always had a following among Italian chefs, the real stars in the Italian protein parade are traditionally the pig and the sheep. Italian cured meats are among the world's best. In the past, hams and sausages figured in main courses for those lucky enough to afford them, and now are a staple on many antipasto plates, in sandwich fillings and as snacks. Nowhere is the pig more venerated than Emilia-Romagna, which has given the world *prosciutto di Parma,* air-cured ham from the pig's hind leg. *Culatello,* from Zibello (near Parma), is the most silken prosciutto of all and the most

Previous pages: Clockwise from left: Beef Fillet Wrapped in Pancetta (recipe page 176); Chicken Cooked in Herbs (recipe page 198); Rabbit with Olives and Thyme (recipe page 183)

174

Each morning, this butcher advertises his specials. Because only the freshest meats, poultry and rabbits are offered, availability changes daily.

more succulent and has a crackling skin. In Lombardy, locals enjoy *nervetti* (boiled pig's feet) cooked with vegetables, chilled and tossed with oil and vinegar.

Lamb is the chief meat of southern Italy, where it is roasted, braised, grilled, put into stews, made into sausage or ground (minced) and used in pasta sauces. In Molise, the organ meats of lamb are as prized as the flesh, while the decadent Romans love not only those of lamb, but of cow and pig as well.

Open-minded and adventurous eaters that they are, Italians enjoy the meat of too many of God's creatures to name, but here are some: wild boar (Tuscany), horse (the Veneto), rabbit (Liguria and Sardinia), hare, goat, frog (Lombardy), snail (Liguria and Sardinia), deer (the Alps) and chamois (Valle d'Aosta).

Poultry is no less popular. Go to a good *rosticceria* (roasting store) and you will find chicken, capon, rooster, duck, turkey, goose, guinea fowl, squab, grouse, partridge, lark, thrush, sparrow and warbler. Small game birds are especially prized in Lombardy and the Veneto, where they are roasted three to a skewer.

The greatest triumph of Italian meat eating, though, is the *bollito misto,* a specialty of Lombardy, Emilia-Romagna and the Veneto. This is a cart of boiled meats and poultry that draws from many of the animals listed here. Slices of the meats are cut to order, served with great pride and garnished with *mostarda* (mixed fruit pickled with mustard seed) and numerous sauces. This gargantuan undertaking requires hours to prepare and is almost exclusively eaten in restaurants today, but is among the greatest expressions of the Italian love of food and dedication to cookery.

expensive. *Prosciutto cotto* (boiled ham) is at its best in Parma when it is served sliced transparently thin. The town of Felino, near Parma, produces what is generally thought to be the best salami in Italy. In Parma there is a saying about their native son and their favorite animal: "The music of Verdi is like the meat of a pig. It's all good and there is nothing to throw away."

Also in Emilia-Romagna, Modena makes *zampone,* stuffed pig's trotter that is traditionally served with lentils at New Year's to ensure good luck in the future. Bologna has given the world mortadella, which is to "bologna" what satin is to polyester. Mortadella is the only cold cut that tastes as good served in chunks as it does in slices; it is also now used as a filling for *polpettone,* rolled meat loaf. Ferrara makes *salama da sugo,* a delectable crumbly sausage served hot.

Other regions also use pork in memorable ways. Braised pork shank (shin) in Friuli is as popular as veal shank. The butchers of Norcia like to lace their sausages with black truffles, while elsewhere in Italy cheese and herbs are added. Neapolitans love *braciole alla pizzaiola,* pork chops cooked in a spicy tomato sauce. In the winter in northern Italy, a popular dish for Sunday lunch is boneless pork roast that has been slow-cooked in milk until it is tender and the milk turns pink; today it may also be done with veal. In Umbria and Lazio, *porchetta* is a decadently delicious roasted suckling pig flavored with garlic, rosemary and sage. In Sardinia, this pig is called *porceddu* and is made without those flavors, but is even

A wood carving of a hunter and his prey serves as the marker for the meat section in a specialty food store in Bologna.

ARROSTO DI VITELLO AL LATTE

Veal Roasted in Milk

In Lombardy, cooks consider the tastiest cut of veal the piece near the tail, what is called arrosto di codino, *"tail roast." It includes a little fat, which gives it extra flavor. Another appreciated cut is the deboned loin. Either one would work for this recipe. Traditionally, pork is cooked in milk, which helps to tenderize it, but in this updated dish, veal receives that classic treatment.*

1 boneless veal roast, 2 lb (1 kg)
4 cups (32 fl oz/1 l) milk, or to cover
2 fennel bulbs, thinly sliced
pinch of freshly grated nutmeg
2 bay leaves
salt and freshly ground pepper
1 tablespoon unsalted butter
1 tablespoon all-purpose (plain) flour

✍ Tie the roast with kitchen string and place in a nonmetal container. Add the milk to cover. Cover and refrigerate for about 12 hours, turning a couple of times. Remove the veal roast and place in a deep pan.

✍ Measure out 1 cup (8 fl oz/240 ml) of the milk used for the marinade and add it to the pan holding the roast. Reserve the remaining milk. Add the fennel, nutmeg, bay leaves, and salt and pepper to taste. Cover and bring to a simmer over low heat, then cook until tender, about 2 hours, turning every 45 minutes or so. Add more milk as needed to keep the cooking juices moist.

✍ Remove from the heat. Transfer the roast to a platter and place in a warm oven. Discard the bay leaves from the cooking liquid and pass the remainder through a sieve or food mill into a bowl, or purée in a food processor fitted with the metal blade.

✍ In a saucepan over low heat, melt the butter. Add the flour and stir for a minute or two until blended. Add the sieved mixture and stir to mix well. Cook gently, stirring often, until a smooth, slightly thickened sauce forms, about 3 minutes. If it is too thick, thin with a little of the reserved milk. Adjust the seasoning with salt and pepper.

✍ Slice the meat and arrange on a platter. Spoon the sauce over the top and serve at once.

SERVES 6

COSCIOTTO D'AGNELLO FARCITO

Stuffed Leg of Lamb

In Tuscany, cooks make deep slits in a leg of lamb and stuff the slits with a mixture of garlic, rosemary, sage, salt and pepper. I prefer to bone the leg (you can ask your butcher to bone it for you) because I think it looks more elegant. And since I have a variety of herbs in my garden, I vary the aromas as well, using mint, thyme, fennel and others. Each time it tastes like a new dish.

1 tablespoon unsalted butter
1 egg, lightly beaten
salt
1 boned leg of lamb, about 3½ lb (1.75 kg)

freshly ground pepper
2 large bunches wild fennel or fresh mint, finely chopped
3 cloves garlic, finely chopped
2 tablespoons extra-virgin olive oil
½ cup (4 fl oz/120 ml) dry white wine
¼ cup (2 fl oz/60 ml) water

✍ Preheat an oven to 350°F (180°C).

✍ In a small nonstick frying pan over medium heat, melt the butter. Add the egg and season to taste with salt. Cook the egg until it sets in a thin omelet, about 1 minute, then turn it out onto a plate. Set aside.

✍ On a work surface, slit open the leg of lamb so it lies flat, cutting from the center toward the edge to form a uniform thickness. Season to taste with salt and pepper. Place the omelet on top and sprinkle it with the fennel or mint and the garlic. Wrap both sides of the lamb around the stuffing and secure them in place with kitchen string. Drizzle the bottom of a roasting pan with the oil and place the lamb in it.

✍ Roast, moistening occasionally with the wine, until nicely browned and tender, about 1½ hours. Transfer to a warmed platter, snip the string and let stand for a few minutes.

✍ Meanwhile, using a large spoon, skim off any fat from the pan juices. Place the pan on the stove top over medium heat. Add the water and stir to dislodge any browned bits stuck to the pan bottom, forming a sauce. Taste and adjust the seasonings.

✍ Slice the lamb and arrange on a warmed platter. Serve the sauce with the lamb.

SERVES 6

FILETTO DI MANZO ALLA PANCETTA

Beef Fillet Wrapped in Pancetta

Substituting bacon for the pancetta will impart a slightly smoky flavor to the meat. A whole-grain French mustard with coarsely crushed seeds is best for coating the roast, although a smooth variety such as Dijon mustard works fine, too.

2 lb (1 kg) beef fillet
salt
3 tablespoons French whole-grain mustard
6 thin slices pancetta

✍ Preheat an oven to 400°F (200°C).

✍ Trim off any fat from the beef fillet. Rub the fillet with salt and then coat evenly with the mustard. Wrap the pancetta slices around the fillet, covering it completely and tying them in place with kitchen string. Place in a roasting pan.

✍ Roast for 20 minutes. Turn off the oven heat. Open the oven door to cool the interior for a few seconds and close again. Leave the fillet in the turned-off oven for another 20 minutes.

✍ Remove from the oven to a cutting board. Snip and remove the string and thickly slice the fillet. Arrange the slices on a platter and serve immediately.

SERVES 6   *Photograph pages 172–173*

Top to bottom: Veal Roasted in Milk; Stuffed Leg of Lamb

MOSAICO DI CARNE AI PEPERONI

Beef Stuffed with Peppers and Cheese

Rolled and stuffed meat dishes are popular all over Italy, from the traditional stuffed veal breast of Liguria to the little veal rolls known as saltimbocca *in Rome. Be sure to use Italian Fontina for this recipe, the mild cow's milk cheese of the Valle d'Aosta. Scandinavian Fontina is not a good substitute. This colorful meat roll can also be served cold as a buffet dish.*

1 piece rump steak, about 1⅓ lb (700 g)
3 oz (90 g) Fontina cheese, cut into 3 thin slices
1 red bell pepper (capsicum), seeded and cut into long, narrow strips
1 yellow bell pepper (capsicum), seeded and cut into long, narrow strips
6 oz (180 g) green beans, blanched in boiling water 2 minutes and drained
1 tablespoon unsalted butter
2 tablespoons extra-virgin olive oil
1 clove garlic, chopped
1 fresh rosemary sprig
salt and freshly ground pepper
½ cup (4 fl oz/120 ml) dry white wine

❧ Preheat an oven to 350°F (180°C).
❧ Gently flatten the meat with a meat pounder to an even thickness of ½ in (1 cm). Cover with the cheese slices and then with the pepper strips and the green beans. Carefully roll up the meat and tie securely with kitchen string.
❧ In a roasting pan, combine the butter, oil, garlic and rosemary and place in the oven until the butter melts and the oil is hot. Add the meat roll and season to taste with salt and pepper. Roast until tender when pierced, about 1½ hours, basting the meat roll occasionally with the white wine to keep it moist.
❧ Remove the pan from the oven and transfer the roll to a cutting board. Snip and remove the string, then slice the meat, arrange on a platter and serve.
SERVES 6

Campania

GENOVESE

Beef Stewed with Onions

Notwithstanding its name—Genovese means "from Genoa"—this dish is a specialty of Naples. Some say it is called this because of the sparse ingredients; Neapolitans historically considered the Genoese parsimonious. It is essentially an Italian version of pot roast. Use some of the sauce to dress 1¼ pounds (600 g) spaghetti or other dried pasta and serve as a first course. The remaining sauce is served on the meat.

Clockwise from left: Braised Beef with Savory Sauce; Beef Stewed with Onions; Beef Stuffed with Peppers and Cheese

2 lb (1 kg) beef top round
½ cup (4 fl oz/120 ml) extra-virgin olive oil
2 tablespoons unsalted butter
3 lb (1.5 kg) red (Spanish) onions, finely chopped
salt and freshly ground pepper
½ cup (4 fl oz/120 ml) dry white wine

❧ Place the meat in a deep, heavy pot with the oil, butter and onions. Season to taste with salt and pepper. Cover and place over medium heat. Bring to a simmer and cook, turning frequently, for 1½ hours.
❧ Uncover and raise the heat to high to brown the meat and onions, about 10 minutes. Add the wine a little at a time, allowing each addition to evaporate before adding more.
❧ Re-cover and continue to simmer until the meat is tender and the onions are creamy, about 1 hour longer, adding a little water to moisten, if necessary. The sauce should be thick and dark.
❧ To serve, remove the meat from the pot, slice it and arrange on a warmed platter. Spoon some of the onion sauce over the top.
SERVES 6

Campania

ARREGANATA

Braised Beef with Savory Sauce

While the cooking of Campania is renowned for its seafood, the Neapolitans do have a few favorite meat dishes. Like the dish Genovese (left), this classic Neapolitan recipe yields tender meat and a succulent sauce. Use some of the sauce to dress 1¼ pounds (600 g) spaghetti or other dried pasta and serve as a first course, if desired. Spoon the remaining sauce over the meat.

4 cloves garlic, chopped
2 oz (60 g) pancetta or bacon, chopped
¼ cup (2 oz/60 g) unsalted butter
⅓ cup (2½ fl oz/80 ml) extra-virgin olive oil
2 lb (1 kg) beef top round, cut into thick slices, each weighing about 3 oz (90 g)
2 lb (1 kg) ripe plum (Roma) tomatoes, peeled and coarsely chopped, or canned tomatoes, coarsely chopped
1 tablespoon dried oregano
salt and freshly ground pepper
½ cup (4 fl oz/120 ml) dry red wine

❧ In a deep, heavy frying pan over medium heat, combine the garlic, pancetta or bacon, butter and oil. When the butter melts, add the meat slices and cook, turning once, until they are lightly browned, about 10 minutes.
❧ Add the tomatoes, reduce the heat to low, cover and cook for about 15 minutes.
❧ Add the oregano, season to taste with salt and pepper, and turn over each beef slice. Cover partially and continue to cook over low heat until the sauce thickens, about 30 minutes.
❧ Uncover, raise the heat to medium, pour in the wine and cook until evaporated, about 5 minutes. Cover and simmer until the sauce is shiny and the meat can be cut with a fork, another 10 minutes.
❧ Arrange the meat slices on a platter, cover with some of the sauce and serve.
SERVES 6

Sardegna

SPEZZATINO D'AGNELLO AL FINOCCHIO

Lamb Stewed in Fennel

While many people think island cuisines are based on fish and shellfish, the Sardinians have only recently turned to the sea for their food. Historically, lamb has been their mainstay; here it is coupled with the flavor of fennel, an herb that grows wildly on the island. You can also prepare rabbit in this same way, but remember that it requires a little less cooking time.

6 tablespoons (3 fl oz/90 ml) extra-virgin olive oil
2 lb (1 kg) lamb cut from the leg, cut into 1-in (2.5-cm)
   pieces
½ cup (4 fl oz/120 ml) dry white wine
¼ cup (¾ oz/20 g) fennel seeds
salt and freshly ground pepper
3 fennel bulbs

In a large sauté pan over high heat, warm 3 tablespoons of the oil. Add the lamb and brown well on all sides, turning frequently, about 7 minutes. Add the wine and fennel seeds and season to taste with salt and pepper. Cover, reduce the heat to low and cook for about 30 minutes.

Meanwhile, cut off all the stalks and feathery leaves from the fennel bulbs (reserve for another use) and chop the bulbs. Pour the remaining 3 tablespoons oil into a saucepan and place over medium heat. When the oil is hot, add the chopped fennel and cook, stirring frequently, until tender, about 10 minutes, adding a little water if the fennel begins to scorch.

Add the fennel to the lamb after the lamb has cooked for 30 minutes, and moisten with a little water if necessary to prevent sticking. Mix well, re-cover and continue to simmer until the meat is tender, about 20 minutes longer. Taste and adjust the seasonings.

Transfer to a warmed platter and serve at once.

SERVES 6

Emilia-Romagna

NOCE DI VITELLO FARCITA

Stuffed Veal

This flavorful, slow-cooked dish should be accompanied by an assertive vegetable, such as cauliflower with prosciutto and olives (recipe on page 123).

1 veal rump steak, 2 lb (1 kg)
3 oz (90 g) thinly sliced prosciutto with fat, cut into long,
   narrow strips
¼ cup (1 oz/30 g) all-purpose (plain) flour
salt and freshly ground pepper
½ cup (4 fl oz/120 ml) extra-virgin olive oil
4 small yellow onions, sliced
4 celery stalks, thinly sliced
4 carrots, sliced
½ cup (4 fl oz/120 ml) dry white wine
½ cup (4 fl oz/120 ml) milk

Roll up the veal rump steak and tie with kitchen string. Using a sharp knife, make several shallow slits in the meat. Stuff the prosciutto into the slits. In a small bowl, stir together the flour and salt and pepper to taste and rub the mixture over the veal to coat evenly.

In a large, heavy pot over medium heat, warm the oil. Add the onions, celery and carrots and sauté until lightly browned, about 20 minutes. Add the meat and cook until brown on all sides, about 10 minutes. Pour in the wine and milk, cover, reduce the heat to low and simmer gently, turning occasionally, until tender, about 1½ hours, adding a little water as needed to keep the veal moist.

Transfer the meat to a warmed platter; snip the strings and keep warm. To make a sauce, pass the contents of the pot through a food mill placed over a saucepan. Or purée in a blender and force through a fine-mesh sieve. Place over medium heat and reheat to serving temperature, thinning with a little water, if necessary.

Cut the meat into slices and arrange on a warmed platter. Serve with the sauce.

SERVES 6

Clockwise from left: Lamb Stewed in Fennel; Veal Scallops in a Spicy Sauce; Stuffed Veal

COSTOLETTE DI VITELLO IN SALSA PICCANTE

Veal Scallops in a Spicy Sauce

Breaded, sautéed veal scallops—similar to the classic cotoletta alla milanese—are topped with a deeply flavored sauce for this elegant main course. It can be accompanied with puréed spinach and potatoes, served on a separate platter so they do not absorb the meat sauce.

1¼ lb (600 g) veal scallops, each about ½ in (1 cm) thick
2 eggs
salt and freshly ground pepper
2 cups (8 oz/240 g) fine dried bread crumbs
2 tablespoons unsalted butter
¼ cup (2 fl oz/60 ml) extra-virgin olive oil
1 cup (8 fl oz/240 ml) light meat stock (recipe on page 40)
2 teaspoons meat extract, such as Bovril
4 teaspoons Worcestershire sauce
juice of ½ lemon

Gently flatten the veal scallops with a meat pounder until ¼ in (.5 cm) thick. In a deep bowl, whisk the eggs with a pinch each of salt and pepper. Put the bread crumbs in another bowl. Coat the veal scallops well on both sides first with the egg and then with the bread crumbs. Pat the coating on with the palm of your hand.

In a deep frying pan over medium heat, melt the butter with the oil. Add the veal scallops and cook, turning once and browning well, until tender, about 2 minutes on each side. Transfer the veal scallops to a warmed platter; keep warm.

Pour off the fat from the frying pan. Add the stock, extract, Worcestershire sauce, lemon juice and pepper to taste to the pan and stir rapidly over medium heat to form a thick sauce. Pour the sauce over the veal scallops and serve.

SERVES 6

181

STINCO ALLE ERBE

Braised Veal Shank with Herbs

It is generally preferable to use fresh herbs, although thyme, marjoram and bay remain aromatic and flavorful even when dry, and can be used in place of the fresh in this recipe. If using dried thyme and marjoram, add 1 teaspoon of each. Because a whole veal shank can be difficult to locate, you may have to special order it from your butcher.

1 tablespoon unsalted butter
3 tablespoons extra-virgin olive oil
1 whole veal shank (shin), about 3½ lb (1.75 kg)
salt and freshly ground pepper
3 bay leaves
3 fresh sage leaves
5 juniper berries
1 tablespoon chopped fresh thyme
1 tablespoon chopped fresh marjoram
1 fresh rosemary sprig
¼ cup (2 fl oz/60 ml) Cognac or other good-quality brandy
1 cup (8 fl oz/240 ml) light meat stock (recipe on page 40)

🦎 Preheat an oven to 350°F (180°C).
🦎 In a large, heavy ovenproof pot over medium heat, melt the butter with the oil. Add the veal shank and brown on all sides, turning frequently, for about 15 minutes. Season to taste with salt and pepper. Pierce the meat with a large fork to help the marrow escape from the bone (which it will do anyway during the cooking) and flavor the cooking juices.
🦎 Add the bay leaves, sage leaves, juniper berries, thyme, marjoram, rosemary and the Cognac or other brandy. Raise the heat to high and allow the liquor to evaporate. Add the meat stock and cover the pot.
🦎 Place the pot in the oven and cook, turning the veal occasionally in its cooking juices, until very tender, about 3 hours. Transfer the veal to a warmed platter and serve.

SERVES 4

POLLO ARROSTO AL BALSAMICO

Roasted Chicken with Balsamic Vinegar

The way to roast chicken so that the skin is crisp and crackly is to cook it with abundant butter and olive oil, which are skimmed out of the pan and discarded at the finish. Balsamic vinegar, with its slightly sweet flavor, is ideal for deglazing meat or fruit sauces.

1 chicken, 3½ lb (1.75 kg)
salt and freshly ground pepper
12 bay leaves, preferably fresh
3 tablespoons unsalted butter, cut into small pieces
3 tablespoons extra-virgin olive oil

*Top to bottom: Roasted Chicken with Balsamic Vinegar;
Braised Veal Shank with Herbs*

½ cup (4 fl oz/120 ml) dry white wine
3 tablespoons balsamic vinegar

🦎 Preheat an oven to 350°F (180°C).
🦎 Rub the chicken with salt and pepper to taste. Place some of the bay leaves in the cavity and tuck the others under the breasts and wings. Truss the chicken with kitchen string, securing the wings and legs close to the body. Scatter the butter pieces in the bottom of a roasting pan, then drizzle the oil evenly over the bottom. Place the chicken breast side up in the pan. Roast, turning every 30 minutes or so, until nicely browned and the juices run clear when a thigh is pierced, about 1½ hours.
🦎 Remove the chicken from the oven and place on a warmed platter. Snip the strings and discard the bay leaves; cover loosely with aluminum foil to keep warm. Using a large spoon, skim off any fat from the pan juices. Place the pan on the stove top over medium heat. Add the wine and the vinegar and stir to dislodge any browned bits stuck to the pan bottom, forming a sauce.
🦎 Carve the chicken and arrange on a warmed platter. Serve with the pan sauce.

SERVES 6

CONIGLIO ALLE OLIVE E TIMO

Rabbit with Olives and Thyme

You can add a spicy touch to this classic Umbrian recipe by adding a pinch of red pepper flakes with the wine.

1 rabbit, about 3½ lb (1.75 kg)
¼ cup (2 fl oz/60 ml) extra-virgin olive oil
3 cloves garlic, unpeeled
salt
1 cup (8 fl oz/240 ml) dry white wine
1 cup (8 fl oz/240 ml) tomato purée
1 cup (5 oz/150 g) Gaeta or other Mediterranean-style small black olives
2 tablespoons fresh thyme leaves
freshly ground pepper

🦎 First, cut the rabbit into serving pieces: Using a sharp knife, cut the rabbit from the top of the breast to the cavity and open slightly to reveal the central cavity. Sever the front and rear legs from the rabbit by cutting through the joints. If you like, cut the rear legs and thighs apart. Cut the body in half crosswise, then cut each half in half again lengthwise, if desired.
🦎 In a frying pan large enough to hold the rabbit pieces in a single layer, warm the oil over medium heat. Add the rabbit and garlic and cook the rabbit, turning as needed, until lightly browned on all sides, about 5 minutes. Add salt to taste and ½ cup (4 fl oz/120 ml) of the wine. Raise the heat and cook until the wine evaporates, just a few minutes. Add the remaining ½ cup (4 fl oz/120 ml) wine and the tomato purée, cover, reduce the heat to low and simmer gently, stirring occasionally, until the rabbit is tender when pierced with a fork, about 50 minutes. About 10 minutes before the rabbit is done, stir in the olives and thyme.
🦎 Transfer the rabbit and sauce to a warmed platter. Season to taste with pepper and serve.

SERVES 6   *Photograph pages 172–173*

STUFATO AL RABARBARO
Beef Stewed in Rhubarb

This dish requires long braising, with a tender and flavorful stew the result. Rhubarb is botanically a vegetable, although most cooks more often treat it as if it were a fruit, sweetening its tartness with sugar. Be sure to remove any leaves from the stalks, as they are toxic.

¼ cup (2 oz/60 g) unsalted butter
1 yellow onion, finely chopped
1¼ lb (600 g) boneless beef stew meat, cut into 1-in
   (2.5-cm) pieces
salt and freshly ground pepper
1¼ lb (600 g) rhubarb stalks, cut into 2-in (5-cm) lengths
juice of 1 lemon

  In a large, heavy pot over medium heat, melt half of the butter. Add the onion and sauté until translucent, about 3 minutes. Add the meat and brown well on all sides, about 10 minutes. Add water to cover and season to taste with salt and pepper. Bring to a gentle boil and simmer until the meat is very tender when pierced with a fork, about 2 hours.

  Just before the beef is done, melt the remaining butter in a saucepan over medium heat. Add the rhubarb and a few spoonfuls of water and cook, stirring occasionally, until the rhubarb is almost tender, 5–7 minutes. Add the lemon juice and cook 3 minutes longer.

  Add the rhubarb to the pot holding the beef and continue to cook slowly for about 10 minutes to blend the flavors. Taste and adjust the seasonings. Transfer to a warmed serving dish and serve very hot.

SERVES 6

Emilia-Romagna

INVOLTINI DI VITELLO, SALVIA E PROSCIUTTO COTTO
Veal Rolls Stuffed with Sage and Ham

Veal rolls are popular throughout Italy and the most widely known recipe is the classic Roman saltimbocca. *These delicious little bundles feature a balsamic vinegar sauce and are easy to prepare. You must secure the rolls with both a toothpick and kitchen string to ensure that they maintain their shape during cooking.*

1 bunch fresh sage
2 tablespoons drained brine-cured capers
¼ lb (120 g) ham
12 green olives, pitted
freshly ground pepper
1⅔ lb (800 g) veal scallops
3 tablespoons extra-virgin olive oil
2 tablespoons balsamic vinegar

  Remove the sage leaves from their stems and chop the leaves along with the capers, ham and olives. Place the ingredients in a bowl, mix together well and season to taste with pepper. Spread an equal amount of the mixture over each veal slice. Then, starting at a narrow end, roll up each slice, secure in place with a toothpick and tie with kitchen string.

  In a large frying pan over medium heat, warm the oil for 1 minute. Add the veal rolls and brown well on all sides. Sprinkle with the vinegar, cover, reduce the heat to low and cook, turning once after 10 minutes, until tender, about 20 minutes in all.

  Remove from the heat, snip the strings and remove the toothpicks. Transfer to a warmed platter and serve.

SERVES 6

LOMBATINE DI MAIALE ALLE MELE
Pork Chops with Applesauce

I often vary the spice that I use to flavor the applesauce. Cinnamon or even curry powder is an interesting alternative to the cloves. Any full-flavored cooking apple will work here.

6 pork chops, about ½ lb (240 g) each
2 tablespoons unsalted butter
2 whole cloves

Clockwise from left: Pork Chops with Applesauce; Veal Rolls Stuffed with Sage and Ham; Beef Stewed in Rhubarb

2 apples, peeled, halved, cored and sliced
salt
2 tablespoons extra-virgin olive oil
freshly ground pepper
½ cup (4 fl oz/120 ml) dry white wine

❧ Trim off any fat from the pork chops and set aside.
❧ In a saucepan over low heat, melt 1 tablespoon of the butter. Add the cloves and apple slices, cover and cook until the apples are soft, about 10 minutes. Check occasionally to make sure the slices are not sticking and stir as needed. Remove from the heat and discard the cloves. Pass the apples through a sieve placed over a bowl, or mash them in the pan until smooth. Season lightly with salt and set the applesauce aside.

❧ In a frying pan over medium heat, melt the remaining 1 tablespoon butter with the oil. Add the pork chops, sprinkle to taste with salt and pepper and cook, turning once, until golden, about 3 minutes on each side. Pour off any fat from the pan and add the white wine. Cook until the wine is reduced by half, about 5 minutes.

❧ Add the applesauce and cook for a few minutes until the pork chops are cooked through and the flavors are blended. Transfer the chops and sauce to a warmed platter and serve at once.

SERVES 6

185

Toscana

COSTATA DI BUE AL CHIANTI

Steak Marinated in Chianti Wine

Normally a Tuscan steak is at least 1¼ inches (3 cm) thick. For this recipe, a steak one-third that thickness will suffice. Chianti Classico has been aged a minimum of three years, producing the full-bodied wine that this dish requires for its success.

3 T-bone steaks, about 1¼ lb (600 g) each
1 carrot, coarsely chopped
1 yellow onion, coarsely chopped
1 celery stalk, coarsely chopped
2 bay leaves
1 tablespoon juniper berries
1 bottle (24 fl oz/750 ml) Chianti Classico
2 tablespoons extra-virgin olive oil
salt and freshly ground pepper

🐇 Place the steaks in a single layer in a large nonmetal container. Add the carrot, onion, celery, bay leaves and juniper berries. Pour in the wine, cover and place in the refrigerator to marinate for about 12 hours.

🐇 Remove the steaks from the marinade and pat dry. Pour the marinade into a saucepan and place over medium heat. Bring to a simmer and cook until reduced by one-fourth, about 1 hour. Discard the bay leaves and put the rest of the reduced marinade through a food mill placed over a saucepan. Or purée in a blender and force through a fine-mesh sieve. Warm the resulting sauce over low heat.

🐇 Meanwhile, prepare a fire in a charcoal grill or preheat a broiler (griller).

🐇 Rub the steaks on both sides with the oil and salt and pepper and place on the grill rack or broiler pan (tray). Grill or broil, turning once, for about 1½ minutes on each side for medium-rare or longer according to taste. Transfer the steaks to a warmed platter, pour on the warm sauce and serve.

SERVES 6

Turkey in Tuna Sauce

Piemonte

TACCHINO TONNATO

Turkey in Tuna Sauce

A summer dish to be served with chilled white wine, this is an updated version of the classic vitello tonnato, *cold veal in tuna sauce. It is also a good choice for a buffet because it can be prepared a couple of hours before serving.*

8 cups (64 fl oz/2 l) water
salt
2 yellow onions
2 celery stalks, cut up
2 small carrots, cut up
3 peppercorns
½ turkey breast, about 2 lb (1 kg)
1 whole egg, plus 2 egg yolks
1 teaspoon Dijon mustard
1¼ cups (10 fl oz/300 ml) extra-virgin olive oil
2 teaspoons white wine vinegar
½ lb (240 g) olive oil–packed tuna, drained
2 olive oil–packed anchovy fillets
3 small sour pickles
1 tablespoon drained brine-cured capers, plus additional
    capers for garnish (optional)

🐇 In a large saucepan, bring the water to a boil. Add salt to taste, the onions, celery, carrots, peppercorns and the turkey breast. Bring back to a boil, reduce the heat to low and simmer, uncovered, until the breast is cooked through, about 30 minutes.

🐇 Meanwhile, prepare the sauce: In a blender or in a food processor fitted with the metal blade, combine the whole egg and egg yolks, mustard and salt to taste. Process to blend. With the motor running, add the oil in a slow, steady stream, blending until thickened. Add the vinegar and blend to mix. Add the tuna, anchovy fillets, pickles and 1 tablespoon capers. Process until smooth. Transfer to a bowl, cover and refrigerate.

🐇 When the turkey breast is cooked, drain and set aside to cool completely. Slice the breast thinly and arrange the slices on a platter. Pour the tuna sauce over the top, cover and refrigerate until ready to serve, or for up to 3 hours. Garnish with additional capers, if desired.

SERVES 6

Top to bottom: Porcini Mushrooms with Bay Leaves (recipe page 89);
Steak Marinated in Chianti Wine

Alto Adige

ARROSTO DI MAIALE ALLE PESCHE
Pork Roast with Peaches

In the northeastern region of Alto Adige, pork has traditionally been cooked with apples or plums. Now the restaurants there are trying new flavors, preparing it with peaches and apricots as well. The bones are roasted alongside the meat to give the sauce extra flavor.

1 pork loin, 3 lb (1.5 kg)
1 tablespoon extra-virgin olive oil
1 tablespoon unsalted butter, at room temperature
2 peaches
1 cup (8 fl oz/240 ml) dry white wine
salt and freshly ground pepper

✺ Preheat an oven to 350°F (180°C).
✺ Using a sharp knife, cut the bones from the pork loin. Grease a roasting pan with the oil and butter. Place the pork loin fat side up in the pan, turning it a couple of times to coat with the oil and butter. Add the bones to the pan as well. Roast until nicely browned and tender, about 1½ hours.
✺ Meanwhile, bring a saucepan of water to a boil. Add the peaches and blanch for 1 minute. Remove with a slotted spoon, immerse in cold water and slip off the skins. Cut in half, discard the pits and chop the flesh.
✺ Add the peaches to the roasting pan along with ½ cup (4 fl oz/120 ml) of the wine during the last 30 minutes of roasting. Season to taste with salt and pepper.
✺ When the pork is ready, remove the pan from the oven and discard the bones. Set the meat aside on a platter and keep warm.
✺ Using a large spoon, skim off any fat from the pan juices. Scoop out the peaches and cooking juices and pass them through a sieve. Return them to the roasting pan.
✺ Place the pan on the stove top over medium heat and add the remaining ½ cup (4 fl oz/120 ml) wine. Heat, stirring to dislodge any browned bits stuck to the pan bottom, until the sauce is reduced and thickened. Taste and adjust the seasonings.
✺ Slice the pork and arrange the slices on a warmed platter. Spoon the peach sauce over the top and serve at once.

SERVES 6

COSTOLETTE DI VITELLO AL CARTOCCIO
Veal Chops Baked in Foil

These veal chops, which should be cut from the saddle, are called nodini *in Italy. They have a short bone, almost in the center, and also include part of the tender fillet. In the past,* al cartoccio *described the wrapping of foods in oiled cooking paper (parchment), but the introduction of aluminum foil has made such dishes easier to prepare.*

1 tablespoon unsalted butter
6 veal chops (see note)
salt and freshly ground pepper
18 cherry tomatoes
1 fennel bulb, thinly sliced lengthwise

✺ Preheat an oven to 400°F (200°C).
✺ Using the butter, grease 6 pieces of aluminum foil, each large enough to wrap a veal chop. Place a chop on each piece of foil and season to taste with salt and pepper. Using a needle, prick each tomato and place 3 tomatoes on top of each chop. Scatter the fennel slices over the chops and wrap the chops in the foil, securing them closed.
✺ Bake until the chops are done, about 20 minutes. To check for doneness, open a corner of 1 packet and cut into the chop with a knife; it should be tender.
✺ To serve, slightly open the foil of each packet and transfer the packets to a platter. Serve immediately.

SERVES 6

Toscana

POLPETTE AL VINO ROSSO
Meat Patties in Red Wine

Meat patties are popular throughout Italy, but especially in Tuscany where they are often the centerpiece of a midday meal. They can be made with a combination of various red and/or white meats and are always cooked slowly in a small amount of liquid such as wine, milk, stock or tomato sauce.

½ lb (240 g) ground (minced) chicken
½ lb (240 g) ground (minced) veal
½ lb (240 g) ground (minced) pork
handful of coarse country bread, soaked in milk and squeezed dry
1 tablespoon dry mustard
2 tablespoons chopped fresh flat-leaf (Italian) parsley
1 clove garlic, chopped
2 eggs, lightly beaten
2 tablespoons grated Parmesan cheese
salt and freshly ground pepper
1 cup (4 oz/120 g) all-purpose (plain) flour
2 tablespoons unsalted butter
2 tablespoons extra-virgin olive oil
½ cup (4 fl oz/120 ml) dry red wine

✺ In a bowl, combine the meats, bread, mustard, parsley, garlic, eggs and Parmesan cheese. Season to taste with salt and pepper and mix well with your hands until all the ingredients are perfectly blended. Form the mixture into oval patties about 2 in (5 cm) long and dust with the flour, shaking off the excess.
✺ In a frying pan over medium heat, melt the butter with the oil. Add the patties and brown on both sides, turning them gently, about 5 minutes. Pour in the wine and bring to a boil. Cover, reduce the heat to low and continue to cook gently until the patties are tender and cooked through, another 20 minutes.
✺ Transfer the patties to a warmed platter and serve.

SERVES 6

Clockwise from left: Meat Patties in Red Wine; Pork Roast with Peaches; Veal Chops Baked in Foil

PROSCIUTTO COTTO AI FUNGHI

Ham with Mushrooms

In autumn, when mushrooms are plentiful in the mountains of the Veneto, they are used to prepare this tasty dish. Button mushrooms or shiitakes can be substituted for the porcini.

6 slices ham, about ¼ lb (120 g) each
1 cup (4 oz/120 g) all-purpose (plain) flour
2 tablespoons unsalted butter
2 tablespoons extra-virgin olive oil
10 oz (300 g) fresh porcini mushrooms, cut into thick slices
¼ cup (2 fl oz/60 ml) light meat stock (recipe on page 40)
¼ cup (2 fl oz/60 ml) Marsala wine
salt and freshly ground pepper

Dust the ham slices with flour, shaking off any excess. In a heavy pot over medium heat, melt the butter with the oil. Add the mushrooms and sauté until tender, about 5 minutes. Using a slotted spoon, transfer the mushrooms to a bowl; set aside.

Add the ham slices to the pot and brown on both sides, turning once, about 5 minutes. Pour in the stock. Cover and simmer for about 3 minutes. Add the Marsala, re-cover and continue to simmer for about 5 minutes to blend the flavors.

Return the mushrooms to the pot and continue to cook until blended, about 3 minutes. Season to taste with salt and pepper, transfer to a warmed platter and serve.

SERVES 6

OSSOBUCHI AL LIMONE

Stewed Veal Shanks with Lemon

This is my variation on the classic veal shank recipe served with gremolata, an aromatic mixture of lemon and parsley. This version is lighter and just as flavorful. Try serving it with fresh tagliatelle dressed with melted butter.

6 pieces veal shank (shin), each about 7 oz (210 g) and 1 in (2.5 cm) thick
1 cup (4 oz/120 g) all-purpose (plain) flour
3 tablespoons unsalted butter
3 tablespoons extra-virgin olive oil
1 cup (8 fl oz/240 ml) light meat stock (recipe on page 40)
salt and freshly ground pepper
2 tablespoons chopped fresh flat-leaf (Italian) parsley
juice of 2 lemons

Make several cuts along the edges of the veal pieces so that they will not curl during cooking. Dust well with flour on both sides, shaking off excess. In a large, heavy pot over high heat, melt the butter with the oil. Arrange the veal in the pot and brown, turning once, for about 10 minutes. Add about ¼ cup (2 fl oz/60 ml) of the stock. Reduce the heat to low, season to taste with salt and pepper, cover and simmer until tender, about 1 hour, occasionally adding a little more stock to keep the meat moist.

When the veal is done, add the parsley and lemon juice. Turn over the veal shanks to absorb the seasonings. Cover and continue to cook over low heat for another 5 minutes to blend the flavors. Transfer the veal shanks to a warmed platter, spoon the cooking juices over the top and serve hot.

SERVES 6

Left to right: Stewed Veal Shanks with Lemon; Ham with Mushrooms

SCALOPPINE DI POLLO ALL'ORIGANO

Chicken Scaloppine with Oregano

This is a very quick dish to prepare and tasty as well. Chicken breasts are a relatively new option to the veal used in scaloppine dishes. Of course, you can use turkey or veal scallops in place of the chicken.

6 boneless, skinless chicken breast halves
3 tablespoons all-purpose (plain) flour
1 tablespoon unsalted butter
2 tablespoons extra-virgin olive oil
1 teaspoon dried oregano
salt and freshly ground pepper
½ cup (4 fl oz/120 ml) dry white wine

Gently flatten the chicken breasts with a meat pounder until about ¼ in (.5 cm) thick. Dust with the flour, coating evenly and tapping off any excess.

In a large frying pan over medium heat, melt the butter with the oil. Add the chicken breasts and cook, turning once, until golden, about 3 minutes on each side. Sprinkle with the oregano, season to taste with salt and pepper and pour in the wine. Cook until most of the wine evaporates, about 2 minutes, leaving only a little of the cooking juices.

Transfer the chicken to a warmed platter and serve at once.

SERVES 6

POLLO CON POMODORO FRESCO

Chicken with Fresh Tomatoes

This is an updated variation on the traditional recipe called chicken alla cacciatora, "cooked the hunter's way." The hunter used lots of lard and oil and simmered tomatoes with the chicken. The contemporary cook lightens the dish by using small amounts of olive oil and butter and by adding diced fresh tomatoes near the end of cooking.

1 tablespoon unsalted butter
1 tablespoon extra-virgin olive oil
1 chicken, about 3½ lb (1.75 kg), cut into serving pieces
10 oz (300 g) small yellow onions, chopped
½ cup (4 fl oz/120 ml) dry white wine
salt and freshly ground pepper
6 ripe plum (Roma) tomatoes, peeled, seeded and diced
handful of fresh basil leaves

In a wide sauté pan over medium heat, melt the butter with the oil. Add the chicken pieces and cook, turning occasionally, until lightly browned on all sides, about 5 minutes.

Meanwhile, bring a saucepan filled with salted water to a boil. Add the onions and boil for about 5 minutes, then drain. Add the onions to the chicken, then pour in the wine. Season to taste with salt and pepper, cover, reduce the heat to low and simmer until the chicken is tender, about 40 minutes.

Add the tomatoes, raise the heat to medium and continue to cook for about 3 minutes. Sprinkle with the basil and mix well. Transfer to a warmed platter and serve.

SERVES 6

Left to right: Chicken Scaloppine with Oregano;
Chicken with Fresh Tomatoes

Grilled Marinated Game Hens

GALLETTI MARINATI ALLA GRIGLIA

Grilled Marinated Game Hens

In the old days, Tuscan farm wives would split young chickens in half and prepare them this way. Today you can find Cornish game hens in the markets, and they turn out perfectly when cooked in this old-fashioned manner.

3 Cornish game hens
salt and freshly ground pepper
juice of 1 lemon
3 cloves garlic, smashed
6 tablespoons (3 fl oz/90 ml) extra-virgin olive oil
1 fresh rosemary sprig

🌱 Cut each hen in half by splitting through the breastbone and then cutting along the backbone. Gently flatten the halves with a meat pounder. Place on a platter, season to taste with salt and pepper and add the lemon juice, garlic and oil. Turn the hen halves to coat evenly with the marinade. Cover and refrigerate for about 6 hours, turning occasionally.

🌱 Prepare a fire in a charcoal grill.

🌱 Remove the hen halves from the marinade, reserving the marinade. Place the hen halves on the grill rack over a hot fire and grill, turning once and brushing frequently with the rosemary sprig dipped into the reserved marinade, until the skin is crisp and nicely browned and the hens are tender, about 6 minutes on each side. Transfer to a warmed platter and serve.

SERVES 6

SCALOPPINE CON OLIVE VERDI

Veal Scaloppine with Green Olives

The pairing of olives and thyme often appears with rabbit in Liguria. Here it flavors a light veal dish that can be served with new potatoes, or on its own preceded by a first course of rice or pasta. Black olives can be used in place of the green.

1⅔ lb (800 g) veal from top round or eye of round,
   thinly sliced
2 tablespoons unsalted butter
3 tablespoons extra-virgin olive oil
¼ cup (2 fl oz/60 ml) dry white wine
30 green olives, pitted and finely chopped
salt and freshly ground pepper
1 tablespoon fresh thyme leaves

🌱 Gently flatten the veal slices with a meat pounder until ¼ in (.5 cm) thick. In a large frying pan over medium heat, melt the butter with the olive oil. Add the veal slices and cook, turning occasionally, until browned on both sides, about 5 minutes total.

🌱 Pour in the wine, cover and cook over low heat for 10 minutes, adding water if pan juices begin to cook away. Sprinkle on the olives, season to taste with salt and pepper and add the thyme leaves. Cover and cook for another 2 minutes to blend the flavors.

🌱 Transfer to a warmed platter and serve immediately.

SERVES 6

Veal Scaloppine with Green Olives

INVOLTINI DI TACCHINO
Stuffed Turkey Rolls

Turkey is very lean, which has made it a popular meat in the contemporary Italian diet. It can often be rather dry, however, a reputation that these tender rolls, stuffed with asparagus and cheese, put to rest. Caul fat, the lacy membrane of fat from a pig's stomach, is used to keep the roll moist as it cooks. It can be purchased, usually frozen, in a butcher's shop.

18 thin slices turkey breast, about 1¾ oz (50 g) each
¼ lb (120 g) Fontina cheese, cut into 18 thin slices
18 asparagus tips, parboiled in boiling water for 3 minutes and drained
18 pieces caul fat, each about 4 in (10 cm) square, soaked in cold water to cover for 30 minutes, drained and dried
salt and freshly ground pepper
1 tablespoon unsalted butter
2 tablespoons extra-virgin olive oil
½ cup (4 fl oz/120 ml) white wine
¼ cup (2 fl oz/60 ml) water

❧ Flatten the turkey slices with a meat pounder until very thin. Place a cheese slice and an asparagus tip on each turkey slice. Roll up the turkey slice to seal in the filling. Enclose each roll in a piece of caul fat and season with salt and pepper.

❧ In a saucepan over medium heat, melt the butter with the oil. Add the turkey rolls and sauté, turning as needed, until browned on all sides, about 10 minutes. Pour in the wine, reduce the heat to low and continue to cook until the liquid evaporates, about 2 minutes. Add the water and deglaze the pan, scraping up any browned bits. Turn the rolls over once in the sauce and then transfer them with a slotted spoon to a warmed dish. Pour the cooking juices over the rolls and serve at once.

SERVES 6

ROAST BEEF AL VINO ROSSO
Roast Beef in Red Wine

This easy recipe is an update of the way roast beef is traditionally prepared in Naples. The meat is cooked at high heat in order to sear it well on the outside, while the inside remains medium-rare. The sauce is simply the pan juices, skimmed of fat. Use a good-quality red wine for the best results.

2 lb (1 kg) lean beef roast, tied for roasting
2 tablespoons coarse salt
3 yellow onions, cut in half
⅓ cup (2½ fl oz/80 ml) extra-virgin olive oil
½ cup (4 fl oz/120 ml) dry red wine

❧ Preheat an oven to 400°F (200°C).

❧ Rub the beef with the salt so that the grains are embedded in the meat. Place in a roasting pan with the onions and oil.

❧ Roast for 20 minutes. Pour the wine into the pan and stir into the pan juices. Continue to roast for 10 minutes longer for medium-rare, or until done to your liking.

❧ Remove from the oven and transfer the beef to a cutting board. Let rest for a few minutes, then cut across the grain into thin slices. Arrange on a warmed platter with the onions.

❧ Meanwhile, using a large spoon, skim off any fat from the pan juices. Place the roasting pan on the stove top over medium heat and heat for a few minutes, scraping up any browned bits from the pan bottom. Pour the juices into a bowl and serve alongside the roast.

SERVES 6

Clockwise from left: Meat Roll with Mortadella (recipe page 198);
Stuffed Turkey Rolls; Roast Beef in Red Wine

Toscana

TACCHINO AL LIMONE E PREZZEMOLO

Turkey with Lemon and Parsley

*A perfect summer main course, this cold turkey dish is comple-
mented by zucchini and Parmesan cheese salad (recipe on page 86)
or grilled vegetables on skewers (recipe on page 111).*

½ small turkey breast, about 1⅓ lb (700 g)
1 yellow onion, cut in half
2 celery stalks, chopped
1 bay leaf
salt
juice of 1 lemon
2 tablespoons drained brine-cured capers
handful of fresh flat-leaf (Italian) parsley leaves, chopped
6 olive oil–packed anchovy fillets, drained and cut into
    pieces, or 3 salt-cured anchovies, rinsed, filleted and
    cut into pieces
6 tablespoons (3 fl oz/90 ml) extra-virgin olive oil

🐎 Place the turkey breast in a pot and add water to cover
along with the onion, celery, bay leaf and salt to taste. Bring to
a boil, reduce the heat to medium-low and simmer, uncovered, until tender, about 20 minutes. Drain the turkey and
let cool.

🐎 Cut the turkey across the grain into very thin slices and
arrange them on a deep platter. Sprinkle with the lemon juice,
cover and marinate, turning occasionally, for 8 hours in the
refrigerator.

🐎 Remove the turkey slices from the platter, draining well,
and arrange on a serving platter. Sprinkle with the capers,
parsley and anchovies and drizzle with the oil. Serve at room
temperature.

SERVES 6

Emilia-Romagna

POLPETTONE ALLA MORTADELLA

Meat Roll with Mortadella

*Meat rolls are popular in Italy, especially in Emilia-Romagna,
where every family has its own recipe. The secret is in the
seasoning and in using good-quality meat. Adding cheese and
kneading the mixture well will help hold the roll together while it
cooks. This dish is also good served cold the next day.*

1 lb (480 g) ground (minced) beef
handful of coarse country bread, soaked in milk and
    squeezed dry
1 tablespoon chopped fresh flat-leaf (Italian) parsley
1 tablespoon fresh thyme leaves
1 tablespoon chopped fresh rosemary
1 tablespoon grated Parmesan cheese
2 eggs
salt and freshly ground pepper
7 oz (210 g) mortadella, thinly sliced
1 tablespoon unsalted butter, cut into pieces
1 tablespoon extra-virgin olive oil
½ cup (4 fl oz/120 ml) dry white wine

🐎 Preheat an oven to 350°F (180°C).

🐎 Place the beef in a large bowl. Add the soaked bread,
parsley, thyme, rosemary and Parmesan cheese. Separate
1 egg and add the yolk plus the whole egg to the bowl. Set
the egg white aside. Season to taste with salt and pepper
and knead the mixture with your hands until all the ingredients are perfectly blended.

🐎 Transfer the mixture to a work surface and shape into
a rectangle about ¾ in (2 cm) thick. Place the mortadella
slices on top and, starting from a long side, roll up the meat
into a salamilike log. Pour the remaining egg white onto the
work surface and turn the roll in the egg white to coat
completely. Place the meat roll in a roasting pan with the
butter and oil.

🐎 Bake until the meat is cooked through, about 1½ hours,
adding half of the wine a little at a time. Remove the meat roll
from the oven and transfer it to a platter. Let cool slightly.
Slice the roll and arrange on a warmed platter. Keep warm.

🐎 Meanwhile, using a large spoon, skim off any fat from
the pan juices. Place the pan on the stove top over medium
heat. Add the remaining wine and some water if there is too
little liquid for a sauce. Stir to dislodge any browned bits
stuck to the pan bottom, forming a sauce. Taste and adjust
the seasonings. Strain the sauce through a fine-mesh sieve
onto the sliced meat roll and serve at once.

SERVES 6   *Photograph pages 196–197*

Lombardia

POLLO ALL'ORTO

Chicken Cooked in Herbs

*This is a simple, tasty and light way to cook chicken. When the
chicken is ready, it will have absorbed the flavors of the herbs.
Diced zucchini or peas can be substituted for the zucchini flowers.*

2 tablespoons extra-virgin olive oil
1 chicken, 3½ lb (1.75 kg), cut into serving pieces
1 tablespoon fresh marjoram leaves
6 fresh sage leaves
1 tablespoon fresh tarragon leaves
1 tablespoon fresh thyme leaves
2 tablespoons chopped fresh flat-leaf (Italian) parsley
¼ cup (2 fl oz/60 ml) light chicken stock (recipe on page 40)
6½ oz (200 g) zucchini flowers

🐎 Pour the oil into a large frying pan and arrange the chicken
pieces in it. Distribute the marjoram, sage, tarragon, thyme
and parsley evenly around the chicken and place over
medium heat. Cook, turning frequently, until the chicken is
tender, about 40 minutes, adding the chicken stock as necessary to keep the pan moist.

🐎 Several minutes before the chicken is ready, add the
zucchini flowers. Mix well to warm the flowers thoroughly.

🐎 Transfer the contents of the pan to a warmed platter
and serve.

SERVES 6   *Photograph pages 172–173*

Turkey with Lemon and Parsley

Le Grandi Isole

Le Grandi Isole

SICILIA, SARDEGNA

Because the names Sicily and Sardinia strike instant chords of recognition in many of us, we think we have a good sense of what these particular places are all about. After all, some of us may have encountered a Sicilian immigrant, and those of us who eat sardines may have guessed that the fish is named for the island. Yet in how many cases, when we think of other places, would a single frame of reference be sufficient to claim knowledge?

The first step to understanding Sicily and Sardinia—and their remarkable cooking—is to realize that the people of these two large islands consider themselves misunderstood. This lack of understanding, they believe, is not only the province of foreigners, but is omnipresent in the eighteen regions of the Italian peninsula. In addition, Sicilians and Sardinians would not even think of being viewed in tandem. Misconceptions and stereotypes depict these regions as backward and hidebound rather than custodians of grand traditions.

What they do have in common is that they are both islands. The Italian word for island is *isola,* and it is from this word that we derive the English "isolation" and "insular." Each gives an idea of part of what Sicily and Sardinia are about. But there is a key difference between the two islands: Sicily has been a landing stage for visitors and invaders from Europe and North Africa for more

Previous pages: Along the eastern shore of Sicily, the Greek Theater at Taormina, dating from the third century B.C., offers spectacular views of Mount Etna. At left: In the inland town of Piazza Armerina, the floors of the Roman villa, built at approximately the same time, are covered in colorful mosaics.

203

Young Sardinian girls in Arzachena enjoy gelato *(ice cream), but not everyone wants to partake.*

The concave facade of a building in Noto is an example of the "flexible baroque" architecture in this Sicilian town.

than three thousand years, while Sardinia was virtually impenetrable until the mid–twentieth century. This means that Sicilian cooking drew on the influences and traditions of all who arrived there, while Sardinia's table evolved and developed on its own, with relatively few influences from elsewhere.

Sicily's "visitors"—specifically Phoenicians, Greeks, Carthaginians, Romans, Byzantines, Arabs, Normans, Frenchmen, Spaniards and mainland Italians—reached the triangular island from every direction. Virtually all of the important cities and population centers of Sicily are at or near the coast: Palermo, its capital, sits in a zone on the northern edge of the island known as the Conca d'Oro, home to some of the most exquisite citrus fruit in the world: blood oranges, tangerines and lemons give color and tang to all Sicilian food.

On the eastern coast are the large cities of Messina, Catania and Syracuse, all of which have received visitors from the eastern Mediterranean since the dawn of time. Here, too, is Taormina, one of the most beautiful towns in Italy, and Mount Etna, an active volcano whose periodic eruptions threaten nearby cities but also make the terrain remarkably fertile. This is the most Greek area of Sicily, with heavy plantings of olives and grapes that produce oil, wine and raisins. All along this coast are abundant stocks of fish, with excellent tuna and swordfish being the chief catches.

Syracuse, the southernmost major city on the island, is a special place that draws from its Greek heritage (it was one of the most important cities in the Hellenic Era) and from its proximity to North Africa. The Arabs, who colonized much of southern and western Sicily in the ninth century, carried such foods as sugarcane, almonds, sesame, couscous, cinnamon, saffron and cloves. They also brought a special penchant for making ice-based sweets, with the result that the first ice cream as we

know it may have been invented near Syracuse and came only in very few local flavors: lemon, orange, mandarino (not unlike a Clementine orange), rose, mulberry and almond.

Western Sicily, which includes the cities of Agrigento and Trapani, is drier and less fertile than the rest of the island, and hot winds often blow up from Africa. Grapes are grown here to produce intense dessert wines such as Marsala. Trapani is also a major fishing port and produces sea salt of remarkable quality. The interior of Sicily is, by turns, lush and arid, and there are zones that are congenial to rice and wheat cultivation. Wheat arrived during the Roman occupation, and Sicily became the granary of the Empire. Not surprisingly, Sicily is one of the places where pasta making first occurred, and the island's breads are excellent.

A unifying phenomenon in Sicilian life and agriculture (and thus in its food) is the presence of the sun. The abundant light and heat produce fruits and vegetables of intense flavor, and are also used to dry foods such as grapes, figs, plums, tomatoes and fish, all of which are conserved and used year-round in the Sicilian kitchen.

Due to the island's incomparable flavor palette, and the influence of many foreign traditions, Sicilian food has long been considered one of the most exciting and varied in all of Italy. As the Sicilians gain affluence and spread their dishes to other parts of Italy, their classic flavors—capers, tuna, swordfish, citrus—are found in food preparations throughout the country, far more than the food of contemporary Italy affects Sicily.

While Sicily created a style of cooking by being fertile terrain for cultural and agricultural influences from throughout Europe, Sardinia remained isolated for most of its history. The lowlands near the seashore of this large rectangular island were infested with malaria-bearing mosquitoes until 1950, so that most Sardinians remained

A statue of the patron saint of Castelsardo, Sardinia, watches over the village's picturesque harbor.

inland. Only the cities of Cagliari, the region's capital, on the southern coast, and Alghero in the northwest have long histories as seaports, and thus ancient traditions of eating seafood. For example, the people of Alghero have enjoyed lobster for centuries, long before it was known elsewhere in Italy. Splendid isolation indeed!

Citrus trees in Taormina, Sicily, infuse the air with their fragrance and the local dishes with the essence of their fruit.

Beginning in 1353, Alghero belonged to Catalonia, giving the city's dialect, architecture and food a distinct accent, with preferences for ingredients such as rice and saffron. The latter finds its way into thumbnail-sized gnocchi called *malloreddus*. Cagliari has had periodic visitors throughout the centuries, ranging from the Phoenicians to mainland Italians, but the city has remained fundamentally Sardinian, drawing its food products—lamb, cheese, honey, vegetables—from the island's interior.

Aside from its two coastal cities, Sardinia is indisputably a place that has looked inward. Cities such as Nuoro, Sassari and Macomer can seem somewhat stern and unforgiving, the result of a culture that until recently turned its back on the rest of the world. When Sardinians talk about mainland Italy, which Sardinia joined when the nation was unified in the 1860s, they refer to it as *il continente*. Inland Sardinia has devoted itself largely to raising sheep, which provide meat, the milk for making the many types of pecorino cheese for which the island is renowned and wool for warmth (the mountainous interior can get very cold). There are 2.5 sheep for every resident of Sardinia.

Because sheepherding can take men and boys away from towns for extended periods, the social structure of Sardinia is often created by women. They gather in town squares, raise children and run households and businesses. As Sardinian shepherds tend to prefer foods they can travel with, such as cheeses, sausages and bread, a man considering a prospective bride will assess her ability to bake bread. A classic of Sardinia is *pane carasau*, a dry bread that shepherds soften with hot water or

A cheese maker in Sardinia, announces the availability of the "optimum" pecorino, as well as fresh and salted ricotta.

broth and serve with tomato sauce, grated cheese and perhaps a fried egg.

When shepherds return to towns, great feasting occurs, typically with *porceddu,* wonderfully tender suckling pig, and dishes made with lamb. With the wealth of meat and cheese consumed in Sardinia, one would never think this is the food of an island in the middle of the Mediterranean! All of this is washed down with some of the many formidable local wines, such as Vermentino (white) and Cannonau (red). Sardinian desserts are justifiably famous. Typically they are made with almonds, honey, dried fruits and candied orange peel.

There remains a mystery, a separateness about Sardinia that is hard for outsiders to comprehend. Unlike the Sicilians, who are more accustomed to strangers in their midst, the Sardinians seem awkward and unsure in the presence of someone they don't know. This should not be interpreted as hostility, but merely bespeaks the legacy of isolation that this island knew for so long. The mystery of Sardinia is in its strange cylindrical stone structures known as the *nuraghi.* These are said to date to the early Bronze Age and are thought to have been sites of veneration for ancient deities or perhaps forms of shelter during inclement weather. What the *nuraghi* tell us is that these proud, if shy, people have roots that stretch back to antiquity, and the flavors they know, of meat and bread, honey and myrtle, are the flavors of Sardinian history, as vibrant and consequential today as they were two thousand years ago.

The varied coastline and undulating bays and headlands of the Costa Smeralda in northeastern Sardinia have made it an enormously popular holiday destination.

Pani e
Dolci

Blood oranges, known in Italian as tarocchi *or* sanguigni, *are rushed to market by a local grower in southern Italy.*

Pani e Dolci

BREADS AND DESSERTS

In small towns in much of Italy one can still sometimes find *il vecchio forno,* the old oven that once occupied a central place of importance. The origin of these ovens can be traced to Etruscan and Roman times (one was found in the ruins of Pompeii). Throughout the centuries, many houses in coastal areas and in southern Italy were built without chimneys, so there was no way for the smoke from baking to exit the roof. This explains, in part, the long-standing Italian tendency to prepare foods over small open flames. It also tells us why a communal oven in a town would occupy a place of honor.

The oven, usually wood burning, was used to bake breads, tarts, vegetable pies, pizzas and focaccia. In some towns it was also used to bake pasta and vegetable dishes. Gradually there was an evolution in which talented entrepreneurs learned baking skills, built ovens, bought flour and other ingredients and set up businesses. There were bread bakers selling their wares in much of northern Italy in the Renaissance, while in parts of rural southern Italy communal ovens were still working full blast as recently as 1965.

In Liguria, Campania and Sicily, stores selling focaccia, pizza and other breads have always been prevalent. Breads topped with cheese, herbs, vegetables, fish or meat have been the standard "fast food" for centuries, although these are of such unsurpassed quality that they bear little relation to what is now called fast food.

Pizza, of course, is probably the most famous Italian bread. It is a citizen of Naples, and nowhere does it taste better. This is because Neapolitans use simple but excellent ingredients, but also because they have been making pizza for twenty-five hundred years. At first pizzas were flat breads dressed with oil, salt, herbs and occasionally cheese. Tomatoes were added in the early nineteenth century. Typically, the dough is made a day ahead, and only a little yeast is used. The pie is very thin, baked at a high temperature in a wood-burning oven and served crisp and hot. The thick, chewy pizza that is weighted down with toppings—found around the world and in Italy, too—has very little to do with the crisp, light perfection that is a Neapolitan pie.

Crispiness is also central to the *grissino* (breadstick). If pizza inevitably brings Naples to mind, real *grissini* are linked with the city of Turin. They were thought to be invented there in 1679, by a baker named Antonio Brunero, and they were much loved by Duke Vittorio Amedeo II. He asked the baker for a *ghersa,* a thin, oblong loaf of bread. It came out much thinner and crispier and was given the diminutive name *ghersino,* which gradually evolved to *grissino.* In most of Italy, *grissini* are thin and bland; in the south they are short, stubby and encrusted

Previous pages: Top to bottom: Flat Bread with Herbs (recipe page 221); Orange Cake (recipe page 239); Lemon Marmalade Tart (recipe page 231)

210

with sesame seeds. In Piedmont, though, they are often the length of a small table, and when people dine, a batch of them is placed in the center and diners break off large pieces. Breadsticks may be flavored with herbs, onion, spices or certain vegetables. They are the complete antithesis of the big, crusty loaves of bread found in much of Italy, but are no less gratifying.

Italians absorbed the best of the baking traditions of their longtime foreign rulers and created sweet desserts of their own. The ninth-century Arab occupation of Sicily brought sugarcane, almonds and certain fruits. (The Arabs also brought sherbet, which Sicilians later adapted to create *gelato,* the world's favorite dessert.) The French occupation of Milan, much of northern Italy and Naples introduced a more delicate style of baking that now informs many of the flavors and textures of breads and desserts in those cities. Sponge cake, though, was invented in Genoa, and the French stole it and called it *génoise.* The Austrians occupied much of north-eastern Italy, bringing the use of spices, nuts, nut creams and fruit. Apple strudel is common in Trentino–Alto Adige (which was and still is the chief source of apples for Vienna); a contemporary version using pears comes from Trieste. Nut and spice cakes with names such as *gubana, pinza, presnitz* and *putizza* are consumed with great passion in Friuli–Venezia Giulia.

But until quite recently, an Italian meal ended not with a *dolce* such as this, but simply with *la frutta.* Italians are discerning about their fruit and select them at the peak of ripeness and fragrance. In warm months a bowl of ice water is brought to the table, the fruit is immersed in it and then devoured with great enthusiasm. In the winter, *sanguigni,* wonderful Sicilian blood oranges, are consumed throughout Italy.

Nowadays, the influence of other nations has made Italians think about concluding meals with the *crostate* (jam tarts), nut cakes, baked fruit tarts, ice cream and custard-based desserts that in the past were eaten away from mealtime, typically with afternoon tea or coffee. Of course, ice cream and *granita* (fruit- or coffee-flavored

Crusty loaves prove irresistible when placed in the window of a bread baker's shop in Cannobio, on Lake Maggiore near the Swiss border.

ice) are still eaten all day in Italy, and no excuse is necessary to want them.

As with all other Italian cooks, the genius of Italian dessert makers has been to take the best ingredients and methods from home and abroad to create new delicacies using a combination of inspiration, perspiration and levitation.

New strains of seedless watermelon are showing up at market in Milan.

PIZZA ALL'AGLIO
Roasted Garlic Pizza

Roasted garlic is an ingredient not commonly used in Italian cooking. I have enjoyed its flavor in my travels, however, and have brought the idea home to use in pasta sauces, as a dressing for crostini and as a topping for pizza. This pizza can be offered as a first course for four or as a main course for two.

FOR THE DOUGH:

1 package (2½ teaspoons) active dry yeast
¾ cup (6 fl oz/180 ml) plus 2 tablespoons lukewarm water (105°–115°F/42–46°C)
3 cups (12 oz/360 g) all-purpose (plain) flour, plus additional flour for working
salt
olive oil for oiling bowl

FOR THE TOPPING:

1 lb (480 g) garlic heads
6 olive oil–packed anchovy fillets, drained and cut in half lengthwise
1 red or yellow bell pepper (capsicum), seeded and cut into long, narrow strips
salt and freshly ground pepper
1 tablespoon extra-virgin olive oil

To make the dough, in a large bowl, sprinkle the yeast over the lukewarm water and let stand until dissolved and foamy, about 10 minutes. Add the flour and salt to taste and, using your fingers, mix until the water is fully absorbed. Continue to work the mixture with your hands until it comes together to form a dough. Transfer the dough to a floured work surface and knead until smooth and elastic, about 10 minutes. Shape the dough into a ball, place in an oiled bowl, cover tightly with plastic wrap and let rise until the dough has doubled in size, about 1 hour.

Meanwhile, make the topping: Preheat an oven to 350°F (180°C). Place the garlic heads in a baking dish and bake until soft when pressed between your fingertips, about 40 minutes. Remove from the oven and set aside. Increase the oven temperature to 400°F (200°C).

Transfer the risen dough to the floured work surface. Punch it down and, using your hands, gradually and gently press it out, lifting and stretching it as you work, into a round 12 in (30 cm) in diameter and about ¼ in (.5 cm) thick. Using your fingertips, form a slightly raised rim on the round, then transfer it to a floured baking sheet (tray). Let rise in a draft-free place for about 20 minutes.

Squeeze out the garlic from its papery sheaths onto the surface of the pizza, distributing it evenly. Cover evenly with the anchovies and bell pepper. Season to taste with salt and pepper. Bake until lightly golden, about 30 minutes. Remove from the oven and drizzle with the oil. Cut into wedges and serve.

SERVES 4

FOCACCIA AL FORMAGGIO
Flat Bread with Cheese

Flat bread has different names, sizes and flavors in different regions of Italy, but Liguria has the greatest variety. Most of them are savory and some are sweet, and they are usually eaten as a snack. This one goes well with an aperitif or as part of an antipasto.

1 cup (8 fl oz/240 ml) lukewarm water (105°–115°F/42°–46°C)
1 oz (30 g) fresh cake yeast or 2 packages (2½ teaspoons each) active dry yeast

3 cups (12 oz/360 g) bread flour, plus ¼ cup (1 oz/30 g) for working
olive oil for oiling bowl, plus 3 tablespoons extra-virgin olive oil
2 oz (60 g) Fontina cheese, thinly sliced
generous pinch of salt

Place the lukewarm water in a small bowl, sprinkle the yeast over the top and let stand until dissolved and foamy, about 10 minutes.

Top to bottom: Pizza with Pancetta, Tomatoes, Olives and Oregano (recipe page 214); Roasted Garlic Pizza; Flat Bread with Cheese

In a large bowl, heap the 3 cups (12 oz/360 g) flour into a mound. Make a well in the center, then gradually add the yeast mixture, stirring with a fork in a circular motion until a dough forms.

Lightly flour a work surface and turn out the dough onto it. Knead until smooth and elastic, about 10 minutes. Shape the dough into a ball. Place the dough in a large oiled bowl, cover tightly with plastic wrap and let rise until doubled in size, about 1 hour.

Brush a 10-in (25-cm) tart pan with about half of the extra-virgin olive oil. Turn out the dough onto a lightly floured work surface and punch it down. Roll out into a round to fit the bottom of the tart pan. Lightly press the cheese slices into the surface of the dough. Transfer the dough round to the prepared pan and let rise for 20 minutes. (You may also bake the round on an oiled baking sheet [tray]).

Preheat an oven to 400°F (200°C).

Brush the focaccia with the remaining oil and sprinkle with the salt. Bake until lightly golden, about 30 minutes. Remove from the oven. Let cool on a wire rack before serving.

MAKES ONE 10-IN (25-CM) ROUND; SERVES 6

TRECCE AL COMINO

Braided Bread with Cumin Seeds

Even though the dough for this bread will be a little sticky, do not add more flour. Just work quickly as you are rolling it out. These braids look particularly lovely on a buffet table.

1 cup (8 fl oz/240 ml) milk, heated to lukewarm
    (105°–115°F/42°–46°C)
1 oz (30 g) fresh cake yeast or 2 packages (2½ teaspoons
    each) active dry yeast
3 cups (12 oz/360 g) all-purpose (plain) flour, plus
    2 tablespoons for working and dusting bowl
1½ teaspoons sugar
pinch of salt
¼ cup (2 oz/60 g) unsalted butter, at room temperature,
    cut into pieces
1 tablespoon cumin seeds
1 egg yolk, lightly beaten with a little water to thin

✎ Place the lukewarm milk in a small bowl, sprinkle the yeast over the top and let stand until dissolved and foamy, about 10 minutes.

✎ In a large bowl, stir together the 3 cups (12 oz/360 g) flour, sugar and salt. Heap the flour mixture into a mound and form a well in the center. Add the butter to the well, then gradually add the yeast mixture, stirring with a fork in a circular motion until a soft dough forms. Lightly flour a work surface and turn out the dough onto it. Sprinkle the dough with the cumin seeds and knead until smooth and elastic, about 10 minutes. Shape the dough into a ball. Lightly flour a large bowl. Place the dough in it, cover tightly with plastic wrap and let rise until doubled in size, about 1 hour.

✎ Turn out the dough onto a lightly floured work surface and punch it down. Divide into 6 equal portions. Using your palms, roll each portion into a rope ½ in (1 cm) in diameter and 12 in (30 cm) long. Using 2 ropes for each plait, braid the ropes together, forming 3 plaits in all. Then bring the ends of each plait around to form a circle and pinch together. Set on a floured surface and let rise for 20 minutes.

✎ Preheat an oven to 400°F (200°C). Flour a baking sheet (tray).

✎ Transfer the 3 rounds to the prepared baking sheet and brush with the egg yolk. Bake until golden, about 40 minutes. Remove from the oven and let cool on a wire rack.

MAKES 3 LOAVES; SERVES 2 EACH   *Photograph pages 218–219*

PIZZA MEDITERRANEA

Pizza with Pancetta, Tomatoes, Olives and Oregano

This pizza should come out thin and crunchy, so be careful not to overload it with topping. You should be able to taste the dough and distinguish the various Mediterranean flavors that crown it. Serve as a first course for four or a main course for two.

FOR THE DOUGH:

1 package (2½ teaspoons) active dry yeast
¾ cup (6 fl oz/180 ml) plus 2 tablespoons lukewarm water
    (105°–115°F/42–46°C)
3 cups (12 oz/360 g) all-purpose (plain) flour, plus additional
    flour for working
salt
olive oil for oiling bowl

FOR THE TOPPING:

2 oz (60 g) pancetta, thinly sliced
6 plum (Roma) tomatoes, peeled and cut in half lengthwise
9 Gaeta or other Mediterranean-style small black olives,
    pitted and halved
salt and freshly ground pepper
1½ teaspoons dried oregano
1 tablespoon extra-virgin olive oil

✎ To make the dough, in a large bowl, sprinkle the yeast over the lukewarm water and let stand until dissolved and foamy, about 10 minutes. Add the flour and salt to taste and, using your fingers, mix until the water is fully absorbed. Continue to work the mixture with your hands until it comes together to form a dough. Transfer the dough to a floured work surface and knead until smooth and elastic, about 10 minutes. Shape the dough into a ball, place in an oiled bowl, cover tightly with plastic wrap and let rise until the dough has doubled in size, about 1 hour.

✎ Transfer the risen dough to the floured work surface. Punch it down and, using your hands, gradually and gently press it out, lifting and stretching it as you work, into a round 12 in (30 cm) in diameter and about ¼ in (.5 cm) thick. Using your fingertips, form a slightly raised rim on the round, then transfer it to a floured baking sheet (tray). Let rise in a draft-free place for about 20 minutes.

✎ Preheat an oven to 400°F (200°C).

✎ To make the topping: Cover the dough with the pancetta slices and then place the tomatoes on top, cut side up. Arrange the olives around the tomatoes. Sprinkle the pizza with salt and pepper to taste and the oregano.

✎ Bake until the crust is golden and crunchy, about 30 minutes. Remove from the oven and drizzle with the oil. Cut into wedges and serve immediately.

SERVES 4   *Photograph pages 212–213*

PIZZA DI CIPOLLA E GORGONZOLA

Onion and Gorgonzola Pizza

When I am in a hurry, I use thick slices of coarse country bread toasted in the oven until golden for the pizza base. Fontina cheese, cut into thin slices, can be substituted for the Gorgonzola. This pizza may be served as a main course for two or a first course for four.

FOR THE DOUGH:

1 package (2½ teaspoons) active dry yeast
¾ cup (6 fl oz/180 ml) plus 2 tablespoons lukewarm water
    (105°–115°F/42–46°C)
3 cups (12 oz/360 g) all-purpose (plain) flour, plus additional
    flour for working
salt
olive oil for oiling the bowl

FOR THE TOPPING:

¼ cup (2 fl oz/60 ml) extra-virgin olive oil
2 yellow onions, thinly sliced
5 oz (150 g) Gorgonzola cheese, crumbled
freshly ground pepper
pinch of freshly grated nutmeg

✎ To make the dough, in a large bowl, sprinkle the yeast over the lukewarm water and let stand until dissolved and foamy, about 10 minutes. Add the flour and salt to taste and, using your fingers, mix until the water is fully absorbed. Continue to work the mixture with your hands until it comes

Onion and Gorgonzola Pizza

together to form a dough. Transfer the dough to a floured work surface and knead until smooth and elastic, about 10 minutes. Shape the dough into a ball, place in an oiled bowl, cover tightly with plastic wrap and let rise until the dough has doubled in size, about 1 hour.

⌥ While the dough is rising, make the topping: In a sauté pan over low heat, warm the oil. Add the onions and cook, stirring often, until soft and translucent, about 20 minutes. Do not allow them to take on color. If necessary, add a little water to prevent scorching. Set aside.

⌥ Transfer the risen dough to the floured work surface.

Punch it down and, using your hands, gradually and gently press it out, lifting and stretching it as you work, into a round about 12 in (30 cm) in diameter and about ¼ in (.5 cm) thick. Using your fingertips, form a slightly raised rim on the round, then transfer it to a floured baking sheet (tray). Let rise in a draft-free place for about 20 minutes. Preheat an oven to 400°F (200°C).

⌥ Scatter the cheese and sautéed onions evenly over the round and sprinkle with pepper to taste and the nutmeg. Bake until the top is lightly golden and the crust is browned, about 20 minutes. Cut into wedges and serve immediately.

SERVES 4

215

Clockwise from top: Sicilian Fig Bread; Corn Rolls; Sweet Raisin Bread

PANDOLCE ALL'UVETTA
Sweet Raisin Bread

In the past, whole-wheat bread was common in Italy, but white bread carried more status. Today, Italians are turning again to whole-wheat doughs. You can also make this loaf with ½ cup (2 oz/60 g) walnuts or equal amounts of raisins and walnuts.

1 cup (8 fl oz/240 ml) lukewarm water
  (105°–115°F/42°–46°C)
1 oz (30 g) fresh cake yeast or 2 packages (2½ teaspoons each) active dry yeast
3 cups (12 oz/360 g) whole-wheat (wholemeal) flour, plus ¼ cup (1 oz/30 g) for working
2 tablespoons sugar
pinch of salt
¼ cup (2 fl oz/60 ml) extra-virgin olive oil, plus extra for oiling bowl
½ cup (3 oz/90 g) raisins, soaked in water to cover for 30 minutes and drained

🖝 Place the lukewarm water in a small bowl, sprinkle the yeast over the top and let stand until dissolved and foamy, about 10 minutes. In a large bowl, combine the 3 cups (12 oz/360 g) flour, sugar and salt. Heap the flour mixture into a mound and form a well in the center. Add the ¼ cup (2 fl oz/60 ml) oil to the well, then gradually add the yeast mixture, stirring with a fork in a circular motion until a firm dough forms.

🖝 Lightly flour a work surface and turn out the dough onto it. Knead until smooth and elastic, about 10 minutes, then incorporate the raisins. Shape the dough into a ball. Lightly oil a large bowl. Place the dough in it, cover tightly with plastic wrap and let rise until doubled in size, about 1 hour.

🖝 Turn out the dough onto a lightly floured work surface and punch it down. Shape into a log about 12 in (30 cm) long. Let rise on the floured surface for about 20 minutes.

🖝 Preheat an oven to 400°F (200°C). Flour a baking sheet (tray) and transfer the loaf to it. Bake until lightly golden, about 40 minutes. Remove from the oven and let cool on a wire rack.

MAKES 1 LOAF; SERVES 6

PANE AI FICHI
Sicilian Fig Bread

Sicilian baking is widely appreciated as among the best in Italy. Enjoy this bread at breakfast or during a midmorning break accompanied with coffee. Other dried fruits can be substituted for the figs; apricots are particularly good. When dicing dried fruit, it is a good idea to oil the knife first to keep the fruit from sticking.

1 cup (8 fl oz/240 ml) lukewarm water
  (105°–115°F/42°–46°C)
1 oz (30 g) fresh cake yeast or 2 packages (2½ teaspoons each) active dry yeast
3 cups (12 oz/360 g) all-purpose (plain) flour, plus ¼ cup (1 oz/30 g) for working
1½ teaspoons sugar
pinch of salt
¼ cup (2 fl oz/60 ml) extra-virgin olive oil, plus extra for oiling bowl
1 cup (6 oz/180 g) dried figs, diced

🖝 Place the lukewarm water in a small bowl, sprinkle the yeast over the top and let stand until dissolved and foamy, about 10 minutes.

🖝 In a large bowl, stir together the 3 cups (12 oz/360 g) flour, the sugar and the salt. Heap the flour mixture into a mound and form a well in the center. Pour the ¼ cup (2 fl oz/60 ml) oil into the well, then gradually add the yeast mixture, stirring with a fork in a circular motion until all of the flour is absorbed and a dough forms.

🖝 Lightly flour a work surface and turn out the dough onto it. Knead until smooth and elastic, about 10 minutes, then incorporate the figs. Shape the dough into a ball. Lightly oil a large bowl. Place the dough in it, cover tightly with plastic wrap and let rise until doubled in size, about 1 hour.

🖝 Turn out the dough onto a lightly floured work surface and punch it down. Shape into a log about 12 in (30 cm) long. Let rise on the floured surface for 20 minutes.

🖝 Preheat an oven to 400°F (200°C). Flour a baking sheet (tray) and transfer the loaf to it. Bake until lightly golden, about 40 minutes. Remove from the oven and let cool on a wire rack.

MAKES 1 BREAD WHEEL; SERVES 6

PANE DI MAIS
Corn Rolls

Try to find stone-ground golden cornmeal or polenta, which has a pleasantly gritty texture. Because these rolls are slightly sweet, they can be served on their own or with a variety of sweet and savory dishes.

1 cup (8 fl oz/240 ml) lukewarm water
  (105°–115°F/42°–46°C)
1 oz (30 g) fresh cake yeast or 2 packages (2½ teaspoons each) active dry yeast
1 cup (4 oz/120 g) bread flour, plus additional flour for working
2 cups (10 oz/300 g) cornmeal or polenta
1 tablespoon sugar, plus ¼ cup (2 oz/60 g) for sprinkling
pinch of salt
olive oil for oiling bowl

🖝 Place the lukewarm water in a small bowl, sprinkle the yeast over the top and let stand until dissolved and foamy, about 10 minutes.

🖝 In a large bowl, stir together the bread flour, cornmeal or polenta, 1 tablespoon sugar and salt. Heap the flour mixture into a mound and form a well in the center. Gradually add the yeast mixture, stirring with a fork in a circular motion until a dough forms.

🖝 Lightly flour a work surface and turn out the dough onto it. Knead until smooth and elastic, about 10 minutes. Shape the dough into a ball. Lightly oil a large bowl. Place the dough in it, cover tightly with plastic wrap and let rise until doubled in size, about 1 hour.

🖝 Preheat an oven to 400°F (200°C).

🖝 Turn out the dough onto a lightly floured work surface and punch it down. Divide into 6 equal portions and shape each portion into a ball. Flatten each ball a little with your palm and, using the blunt side of a knife blade, mark a cross on the surface without cutting into the rolls.

🖝 Flour a baking sheet (tray) and transfer the rolls to it. Bake until golden, about 40 minutes. Remove from the oven and, while still hot, sprinkle evenly with the ¼ cup (2 oz/60 g) sugar. Let cool on a wire rack.

MAKES 6 ROLLS

BISCOTTI SALATI AL SESAMO
Crackers with Sesame Seeds

Set out a plate of these crackers with a white wine aperitif. They keep well in a tightly closed tin for up to two weeks, so I usually make a double batch.

¾ cup (6 fl oz/180 ml) plus 2 tablespoons lukewarm water (105°–115°F/42°–46°C)
1 oz (30 g) fresh cake yeast or 2 packages (2½ teaspoons each) active dry yeast
3 cups (12 oz/360 g) all-purpose (plain) flour, plus ¼ cup (1 oz/30 g) for working
1 teaspoon salt, plus extra for sprinkling
6 tablespoons (3 fl oz/90 ml) extra-virgin olive oil, plus extra for oiling bowl and pan
3 tablespoons sesame seeds

Place the lukewarm water in a small bowl, sprinkle the yeast over the top and let stand until dissolved and foamy, about 10 minutes.

In a large bowl, stir together the 3 cups (12 oz/360 g) flour and the 1 teaspoon salt. Heap the flour into a mound and form a well in the center. Pour 4 tablespoons (2 fl oz/60 ml) of oil into the well, then gradually add the yeast mixture, stirring with a fork in a circular motion until all of the flour is absorbed and a dough forms.

Lightly flour a work surface and turn out the dough onto it. Knead until smooth and elastic, about 10 minutes. Shape the dough into a ball. Lightly oil a large bowl. Place the dough in it, cover tightly with plastic wrap and let rise until doubled in size, about 1 hour.

Preheat an oven to 400°F (200°C). Brush a baking sheet (tray) with oil.

Turn out the dough onto a lightly floured work surface and punch it down. Roll out the dough into a rectangle about 12 by 16 in (30 by 40 cm).

Transfer the dough to the prepared baking sheet and, with the dull edge of a knife blade, mark the rectangle into 1¼-in (3-cm) squares. Brush the top of the dough with the remaining 2 tablespoons oil and sprinkle with a little salt and the sesame seeds.

Bake for 10 minutes. Remove from the oven and, using a sharp knife, cut the squares all the way through and separate them slightly. Return to the oven and bake until crisp, about 5 minutes longer. Remove from the oven, transfer to a wire rack and let cool completely before serving.

MAKES ABOUT 60 CRACKERS

Campania

CORONA DI PANE
ALLA SCAMORZA
Cheese Bread Crown

Scamorza is a cow's milk cheese from southern Italy. It can be bought fresh or smoked, is shaped like a pear and is soft and creamy, yet dry. This decorative bread is perfect for a buffet table.

FOR THE DOUGH:

½ cup (4 fl oz/120 ml) lukewarm water (105°–115°F/42°–46°C)
½ cup (4 fl oz/120 ml) milk, heated to lukewarm (105°–115°F/42°–46°C)
1 oz (30 g) fresh cake yeast or 2 packages (2½ teaspoons each) active dry yeast

3 cups (12 oz/360 g) all-purpose (plain) flour, plus ¼ cup (1 oz/30 g) for working and dusting bowl
2 tablespoons unsalted butter, at room temperature
1½ teaspoons sugar
1 tablespoon salt

FOR THE FILLING:

7 oz (210 g) scamorza cheese, roughly sliced
3 oz (90 g) pancetta

To make the bread, place the lukewarm water and milk in a small bowl. Sprinkle the yeast over the top and let stand until dissolved and foamy, about 10 minutes.

In a food processor fitted with the plastic blade, combine

Clockwise from top: Braided Bread with Cumin Seeds (recipe page 214); Cheese Bread Crown; Rosemary Breadsticks (recipe page 221); Crackers with Sesame Seeds

the 3 cups (12 oz/360 g) flour, the butter, sugar and salt. Process a couple of seconds and add the yeast mixture. Continue to process until a dough forms. (Alternatively, combine the flour, sugar and salt in a large bowl and stir together. Heap the flour mixture into a mound, make a well in the center and add the remaining ingredients to the well. Stir with a fork to form a dough.)

Lightly flour a work surface and turn out the dough onto it. Knead until smooth and elastic, about 5 minutes. Shape the dough into a ball. Lightly flour a large bowl and place the dough in it, cover tightly with plastic wrap and let rise until doubled in size, about 1 hour.

To make the filling, fit the food processor with the metal blade. Place the cheese and pancetta in the processor and process

until roughly chopped, about 30 seconds.

When the dough is ready, turn it out onto a floured work surface and punch it down. Flatten it with a rolling pin into a rectangle about 8 by 12 in (20 by 30 cm). Cover the dough evenly with the cheese-pancetta mixture. Starting from a long side, roll it up to enclose the filling. Bring the ends around to form a circle and pinch together. Flour a baking sheet (tray) and transfer the circle to it. Let rise again for 20 minutes.

Preheat an oven to 400°F (200°C). Bake until lightly golden, about 40 minutes. Remove from the oven and let cool on a wire rack before serving.

SERVES 6

GRISSINI AL ROSMARINO
Rosemary Breadsticks

Although grissini are a specialty of the Piedmont, the addition of herbs is a contemporary innovation. You can use other herbs such as finely chopped fresh sage or thyme in place of the rosemary.

¾ cup (6 fl oz/180 ml) plus 2 tablespoons lukewarm water
  (105°–115°F/42°–46°C)
1 oz (30 g) fresh cake yeast or 2 packages (2½ teaspoons
  each) active dry yeast
1 cup (4 oz/120 g) bread flour
1½ cups (6 oz/180 g) coarse semolina flour
1 teaspoon salt
2 tablespoons extra-virgin olive oil, plus extra for oiling bowl
3 tablespoons finely chopped fresh rosemary

☞ Place the lukewarm water in a small bowl, sprinkle the yeast over the top and let stand until dissolved and foamy, about 10 minutes.

☞ In a large bowl, stir together the bread flour, 1 cup (4 oz/ 120 g) of the semolina flour and the salt. Heap the flour mixture into a mound and form a well in the center. Pour the 2 tablespoons oil into the well, then gradually add the yeast mixture, stirring with a fork in a circular motion until all of the flour is absorbed and a dough forms.

☞ Lightly sprinkle a work surface with half of the remaining semolina flour and turn out the dough onto it. Knead until smooth and elastic, about 10 minutes. Shape into a ball.

☞ Lightly oil a large bowl. Place the dough in it, cover with plastic wrap and let rise until doubled in size, about 2 hours.

☞ Sprinkle the work surface with the remaining semolina flour and half of the rosemary. Turn out the dough onto it and punch it down. Roll out the dough into a rectangle about 8 in (20 cm) long by 4 in (10 cm) wide. Working from the short side, cut the dough into 16 strips about ½ in (1 cm) wide. Using your palms, gently roll the strips into long, thin breadsticks.

☞ Sprinkle a baking sheet (tray) with the remaining rosemary and arrange the breadsticks on it, spacing them about 1 in (2.5 cm) apart. Cover with a kitchen towel and let rise for about 20 minutes.

☞ Preheat an oven to 400°F (200°C). Bake on the middle rack of the oven until lightly golden and crisp, about 20 minutes. Remove from the oven and transfer the breadsticks to a wire rack to cool before serving.

MAKES 16 BREADSTICKS   *Photograph pages 218–219*

SCHIACCIATA ALLE ERBE
Flat Bread with Herbs

In Tuscany, this flat bread is traditionally flavored with a single herb, usually rosemary or sage. In autumn, it is often made with freshly harvested wine grapes. Here, I have suggested a mixture of herbs. You can assemble your own combinations. A blend of sage, rosemary, thyme, oregano and chives is particularly pleasing.

1 cup (8 fl oz/240 ml) lukewarm water
  (105°–115°F/42°–46°C)
1 oz (30 g) fresh cake yeast or 2 packages (2½ teaspoons
  each) active dry yeast
3 cups (12 oz/360 g) bread flour, plus ¼ cup (1 oz/30 g)
  for working
3 tablespoons finely chopped mixed fresh herbs (see note)
olive oil for oiling bowl and pan, plus 3 tablespoons
  extra-virgin olive oil
generous pinch of coarse salt

☞ Place the lukewarm water in a small bowl, sprinkle the yeast over the top and let stand until dissolved and foamy, about 10 minutes.

☞ In a large bowl, heap the 3 cups (12 oz/360 g) flour into a mound. Make a well in the center and gradually add the yeast mixture, stirring with a fork in a circular motion until a dough forms.

☞ Lightly flour a work surface and turn out the dough onto it. Knead until smooth and elastic, about 10 minutes, then incorporate the herbs. Shape the dough into a ball. Lightly oil a large bowl. Place the dough in it, cover tightly with plastic wrap and let rise until doubled in size, about 1 hour.

☞ Brush a 10-in (25-cm) tart pan with oil. Turn out the dough onto a lightly floured work surface and punch it down. Roll out into a round to fit the bottom of the tart pan. Transfer the dough round to the prepared pan. Or, if desired, pat the dough into a rectangle or an oval and transfer to an oiled baking sheet (tray). With 2 fingers, gently make evenly spaced depressions all over the surface of the dough to dimple it. Let rise for 20 minutes.

☞ Preheat an oven to 400°F (200°C). Brush the dough round with the extra-virgin olive oil and sprinkle with the salt. Bake until lightly golden, about 30 minutes. Let cool on a wire rack before serving.

SERVES 6   *Photograph pages 208–209*

PESCHE RIPIENE DI UVETTA
Peaches Filled with Raisins

Cooks in Genoa make this dessert, and they often fill the fruits with pieces of candied orange, lemon or pumpkin. The peaches are also good served cold.

7 ripe but firm peaches
⅔ cup (4 oz/120 g) raisins, soaked in light rum to cover for
  about 1 hour and drained
3 tablespoons sugar
½ cup (4 fl oz/120 ml) dry white wine

☞ Preheat an oven to 350°F (180°C).

☞ Cut the peaches in half and remove and discard the pits. Peel 1 peach and pass it through a food mill set over a bowl. Add the raisins to the peach purée, mixing well.

☞ Fill the hole left by the pit in the peach halves with the peach-raisin mixture. Put the halves back together and place the "whole" peaches in a baking dish. Sprinkle with the sugar and moisten with the wine.

☞ Bake until tender when pierced with the tip of a knife, about 30 minutes, moistening occasionally with the cooking liquid. Remove from the oven and arrange the peaches on a platter. Spoon the liquid from the baking dish over the top and serve.

SERVES 6

Trentino

MOUSSE DI MELE MERINGATA

Apple Mousse Meringue

Apples grow abundantly in Trentino, where they are used to flavor many dishes, both sweet and savory. This dessert is healthful and simple to make.

unsalted butter for preparing baking dishes
3 lb (1.5 kg) cooking apples, halved, cored, peeled and
    sliced
½ cup (4 oz/120 g) sugar
3 egg whites

🐿 Preheat an oven to 350°F (180°C). Butter a baking dish large enough to accommodate the apple slices.

🐿 Place the apple slices in the prepared dish and bake until tender when pierced with a fork, about 30 minutes.

🐿 Remove from the oven, let cool slightly and then, working in batches, place in a blender with half of the sugar and purée until smooth. Increase the oven temperature to 400°F (200°C).

🐿 Grease a separate round baking dish 10 in (25 cm) in diameter with butter and spread the apple purée on the bottom. Place the egg whites in a bowl and beat until foamy. Add the remaining sugar, a little at a time, and beat until stiff peaks form. Spoon the egg whites on top of the apple purée, distributing them evenly.

🐿 Bake until the meringue is lightly golden and the apple purée is still soft, not more than 10 minutes. Remove from the oven and serve.

SERVES 6   *Photograph pages 234–235*

Sicilia

SOFFIATO DI ARANCE

Orange Soufflé

French-style soufflés have been adapted by Italian cooks to suit the national taste. Here, you can use either Sicily's celebrated blood oranges or regular oranges. This is an anxiety-free soufflé. Since it is served "seated," that is, cold, the top will have already settled so you won't have to worry about it "falling" in front of your guests.

6 tablespoons (3 oz/90 g) unsalted butter
1 tablespoon all-purpose (plain) flour
2 cups (16 fl oz/480 ml) milk
unsalted butter and flour for preparing dish
6 tablespoons (3 fl oz/90 ml) fresh blood-orange juice or
    other fresh orange juice
zest of 2 blood oranges or other oranges
4 egg yolks, beaten until blended
5 egg whites
⅓ cup (3 oz/90 g) granulated sugar
1 tablespoon confectioners' (icing) sugar

🐿 In a deep saucepan over medium heat, melt the butter. Add the flour and stir until well blended. Pour in the milk a little at a time, stirring constantly, then continue to stir until the mixture thickens, about 10 minutes. Remove from the heat and let cool completely. Stir occasionally to prevent a film from forming on top.

🐿 Preheat an oven to 400°F (200°C). Butter a round baking dish 9 in (23 cm) in diameter or a 1½-qt (1.5-l) soufflé dish and dust with flour; tap out excess flour.

🐿 Add the orange juice and zest and the egg yolks to the cooled milk mixture and stir well. In a bowl, beat the egg whites until soft peaks form; then beat in the granulated sugar, a little at a time, until the mixture holds stiff peaks. Stir about one-fourth of the egg whites into the yolk mixture to lighten it, then gently fold in the remaining whites until no white streaks remain. Do not overmix. Pour into the prepared dish.

🐿 Bake until doubled in height, about 30 minutes. Remove from the oven and let cool completely. Sift the confectioners' sugar over the top just before serving.

SERVES 6

ANANAS ALLE NOCI IN FORNO

Baked Pineapple with Walnuts

When you can't find a pineapple to make this elegant dessert, use three large oranges peeled and cut into thick slices and caramelize strips of peel for decoration.

4 tablespoons (2 oz/60 g) unsalted butter, at room temperature
1 pineapple
10 walnut halves
½ cup (4 oz/120 g) granulated sugar
2 eggs, separated
1 tablespoon baking powder
¾ cup (3 oz/90 g) all-purpose (plain) flour
1 tablespoon confectioners' (icing) sugar (optional)

🐿 Preheat an oven to 350°F (180°C). Butter a 9-in or 21-cm springform pan with 1 tablespoon of the butter.

🐿 Trim the peel from the pineapple, capturing any juice. Cut crosswise into slices ½ in (1 cm) thick. Cut out the tough core section from the center of each slice and discard. Arrange the pineapple slices in the bottom of the prepared pan. Place the walnut halves amid the slices, slipping them between the slices and in their centers; if necessary, break the walnuts into smaller pieces. Sprinkle the pineapple slices with 3 tablespoons of the granulated sugar.

🐿 In a bowl, whisk together the egg yolks, the remaining granulated sugar, the baking powder, the flour and the remaining 3 tablespoons butter. Dilute with 2 tablespoons of the captured pineapple juice. Beat until blended.

🐿 In another bowl, beat the egg whites until stiff peaks form. Gently fold the whites into the yolk mixture, mixing only until no white streaks remain. Pour over the pineapple slices.

🐿 Bake until the top is golden, about 40 minutes. Remove from the oven and let cool on a wire rack. Release and remove the pan sides and invert it onto a serving plate so the pineapples and nuts face up. Sift the confectioners' sugar over the top, if desired, and serve.

SERVES 6

Top to bottom: Orange Soufflé; Baked Pineapple with Walnuts

AMARETTI

Bitter Almond Cookies

The most well-known commercially produced amaretti are made in the city of Saronno in the region of Lombardy. Traditionally, however, these tasty cookies come from the Piedmont and are different from the industrial Saronno product. You can usually find bitter almonds in health-food stores or in pastry shops. Sweet almond refers to the common nut.

1½ teaspoons unsalted butter
1 tablespoon all-purpose (plain) flour
¾ cup (6 oz/180 g) granulated sugar
¾ cup (4 oz/120 g) blanched sweet almonds
⅔ cup (3 oz/90 g) blanched bitter almonds
4 egg whites
1 tablespoon confectioners' (icing) sugar

❧ Grease a baking sheet (tray) with the butter and dust with the flour; tap out excess flour. In a blender, combine the granulated sugar and the sweet and bitter almonds and grind to a powder. Transfer to a bowl. In another bowl, beat the egg whites until they hold soft peaks. Fold the egg whites into the almond mixture. Using a wooden spoon, stir for about 10 minutes until smooth.

❧ Pack the mixture into a pastry (piping) bag fitted with a plain tip. Squeeze out 1-in (2.5-cm) mounds of the almond mixture onto the prepared baking sheet, spacing them about 1 in (2.5 cm) apart. Set aside at room temperature to expand for about 3 hours.

❧ Preheat an oven to 350°F (180°C).

❧ Sift the confectioners' sugar evenly over the cookies. Bake until golden and crunchy, about 20 minutes. Let cool completely on a wire rack before serving. Store for up to 2 weeks in an airtight container at room temperature.

MAKES ABOUT 2 DOZEN COOKIES

GELATO AL CROCCANTE DI NOCCIOLE

Hazelnut Crunch Ice Cream

You can use some of the hazelnut crunch as a garnish. Cut the crunch into thin strips while it is still soft. When it hardens, break it into pieces and arrange them on the servings of ice cream. For best flavor, use almond oil to make the crunch; if unavailable, use a mild-flavored vegetable oil such as peanut.

FOR THE ICE CREAM BASE:

4 egg yolks
½ cup (4 oz/120 g) sugar
1¼ cups (10 fl oz/300 ml) milk

FOR THE CRUNCH:

¾ lb (360 g) hazelnuts (filberts)
1⅓ cups (11 oz/330 g) sugar
juice of ½ lemon
1 tablespoon almond oil

❧ To make the ice cream base, in the top pan of a double boiler, using a wooden spoon, stir together the egg yolks and sugar until fully blended. Continuing to stir constantly, add the milk a little at a time. Place the pan over the lower pan of simmering water and cook, stirring constantly, until the mixture thickens enough to coat a spoon, about 5 minutes. Remove from over the bottom pan and set aside to cool. Stir occasionally to prevent a film from forming on top.

❧ To make the crunch, preheat an oven to 400°F (200°C). Spread the hazelnuts on a baking sheet (tray) and toast until golden and fragrant and the skins have begun to flake off, about 10 minutes. Remove from the oven and, while still hot, place in a towel and rub between your palms to remove the skins.

❧ Place the hazelnuts and sugar in a saucepan over medium heat. Mix well and cook without stirring, shaking the pan occasionally to coat the nuts with sugar, until caramelized, about 10 minutes. Add the lemon juice and mix well.

❧ Spread the oil in a large, sided baking sheet (tray) and pour the contents of the saucepan onto it. Smooth out about ½ in (1 cm) thick. When it has hardened, after about 10 minutes, break into small pieces using a nut hammer or other similar tool.

❧ Fold the hazelnut pieces into the ice cream base. Transfer to an ice cream maker and freeze according to the manufacturer's directions.

MAKES ABOUT 2½ CUPS (20 FL OZ/600 ML); SERVES 6

MOUSSE DI CIOCCOLATA AL RUM

Chocolate Rum Mousse

This mousse should be prepared at least 6 hours before serving, so that it will be very cold and firm.

½ cup (4 oz/120 g) sugar
2 tablespoons water
¾ cup (6 fl oz/180 ml) heavy (double) cream
3 egg yolks
3 tablespoons dark rum
6½ oz (200 g) bitter chocolate
⅓ cup (2 oz/60 g) almonds, toasted and roughly chopped

❧ In a saucepan over medium heat, combine half of the sugar and the 2 tablespoons water. Heat, stirring, until the sugar dissolves, about 3 minutes. Remove from the heat and let cool.

❧ In a bowl, whip the cream until stiff peaks form. In a separate bowl, beat together the egg yolks and the remaining sugar with a wooden spoon until the mixture falls from the spoon in a ribbon, about 5 minutes. (Alternatively, use an electric mixer on high speed.) Add the rum and the cooled sugar syrup and mix well. Gently fold in the whipped cream.

❧ In a small saucepan, melt the chocolate over low heat and remove from the heat. Allow to cool slightly and then add to the egg-cream mixture. Stir in the chopped almonds. Spoon the mousse into individual glasses or bowls, dividing it evenly. Cover and chill for at least 6 hours or for up to 12 hours before serving.

SERVES 6

TORTA ALLE BANANE E NOCI
Banana Walnut Pie

The "pastry" for this pie is made with semolina flour, the durum wheat flour also used to make some gnocchi and fresh pastas. You must stir vigorously to make sure that the semolina does not form lumps when you add it to the milk.

4 bananas
¼ cup (2 fl oz/60 ml) dark rum
½ cup (4 oz/120 g) sugar
4½ cups (36 fl oz/1.1 l) milk
1 teaspoon salt
1¾ cups (7 oz/210 g) coarse semolina flour
4 tablespoons unsalted butter, plus extra for preparing pan
grated zest of 1 lemon
4 eggs
1 tablespoon fine dried bread crumbs
generous 1½ cups (6½ oz/200 g) walnuts, finely chopped

🐚 Peel and slice the bananas. Place them in a bowl and add the rum and 2 tablespoons of the sugar. Let stand for about 2 hours.

🐚 In a saucepan over medium heat, combine the milk and salt and bring to a boil. Add the semolina flour in a slow, steady stream, whisking constantly. Reduce the heat to low and simmer, stirring continuously with a wooden spoon, until thick, about 20 minutes.

🐚 Remove from the heat and stir in the butter, the remaining sugar and the lemon zest. When the mixture has cooled a little, add the eggs one at a time, beating well after each addition.

🐚 Preheat an oven to 350°F (180°C). Grease a 9-in (23-cm) tart pan with butter and dust the bottom and sides with the bread crumbs.

🐚 Scatter about one-third of the nuts over the bottom of the prepared pan and then top with one-third of the semolina mixture in a smooth layer. Drain the banana slices and top the semolina with a layer of one-third of the banana slices. Top with half of the remaining semolina and then half of the remaining banana slices and nuts. Finish with a semolina layer, then the remaining banana and nuts.

🐚 Place the tart pan inside a baking pan and add hot water to the baking pan to a depth of ¾ in (2 cm). Bake until firm, about 1 hour. Transfer to a wire rack and serve warm or at room temperature.

MAKES ONE 9-IN (23-CM) PIE; SERVES 6

Sardegna

CROSTATA DI FRUTTA SECCA
Dried-Fruit Tart

Because dried fruits have a high sugar content, the dough for this tart is made without sugar and should be rolled out very thin. Cannonau, a medium-bodied red wine, is one of the finest wines produced in Sardinia. You can soak the dried fruits in any dry red wine or dessert wine or in rum diluted with water in place of the Cannonau.

FOR THE FILLING:

½ cup (3 oz/90 g) raisins
½ cup (3 oz/90 g) dried apricots
½ cup (3 oz/90 g) pitted prunes
1 cup (8 fl oz/240 ml) Cannonau wine (see note)

FOR THE PASTRY:

2 cups (8 oz/240 g) all-purpose (plain) flour, plus extra for
   dusting pan and working

½ cup (4 oz/120 g) unsalted butter, chilled, cut into small
   pieces, plus extra for greasing pan
pinch of salt
2 tablespoons water

3 tablespoons apricot or peach jam
¼ cup (1 oz/30 g) chopped walnuts
¼ cup (1¼ oz/35 g) chopped almonds

🐚 To make the filling, in a bowl, combine the raisins, apricots and prunes. Pour in the Cannonau and let stand for at least 2 hours or for up to 6 hours. Stir occasionally.

🐚 Meanwhile, make the pastry: Heap the 2 cups (8 oz/ 240 g) flour into a mound on a work surface. Make a well in the center and add the ½ cup (4 oz/120 g) butter and the salt to it. Using your fingertips, work the ingredients together until the mixture is the consistency of large crumbs. Add the water and form quickly into a ball. Cover with plastic wrap and refrigerate for about 1 hour.

🐚 Preheat an oven to 350°F (180°C). Butter a 10-in (25-cm) tart pan with removable bottom and dust evenly with flour; tap out excess. On a lightly floured board, roll out the dough into a very thin round large enough to line the bottom and sides of the prepared pan. Carefully transfer it to the pan and press gently against the bottom and sides. Trim the dough even with the rim of the tart pan. Prick the bottom of the pastry all over with a fork.

🐚 Bake until lightly golden, about 30 minutes. If the pastry pops up in places as it bakes, press it down with your palm when you remove it from the oven. Transfer to a wire rack and let cool completely. Remove the sides from the tart pan and slide the pastry shell onto a platter.

🐚 To fill the tart shell, spread the jam evenly over the bottom. Drain the dried fruit and place it in the pastry shell, spreading it evenly. Sprinkle with the walnuts and almonds and serve.

MAKES ONE 10-IN (25-CM) TART; SERVES 6–8

Piemonte

TORTA GLASSATA AL CIOCCOLATO
Chocolate Apricot Cake

To cut this cake into layers, place it on a flat surface and slice horizontally through the middle with a serrated knife; cut gently so you do not crumble the cake. You can decorate the finished cake with whipped cream, or serve it with plain cream or a fruit sauce. Offer it at the end of a special dinner.

FOR THE CAKE:

unsalted butter for greasing pan
5 oz (150 g) bitter chocolate
2 tablespoons water
6 eggs, separated
⅔ cup (5 oz/150 g) plus 2 tablespoons sugar
⅔ cup (5 oz/150 g) unsalted butter, at room temperature,
   cut into pieces
¾ cup (4 oz/120 g) fine dried bread crumbs
6 tablespoons (3½ oz/100 g) apricot jam

FOR THE ICING:

4 oz (120 g) bittersweet chocolate
1 tablespoon water

🐚 Preheat an oven to 350°F (180°C). Butter a 9-in or 21-cm springform pan.

Clockwise from left: Banana Walnut Pie; Chocolate Apricot Cake; Dried-Fruit Tart

To make the cake, in a saucepan over low heat, melt the bitter chocolate with the water, stirring occasionally. Remove from the heat and let cool. In a bowl, combine the egg yolks, sugar, butter, bread crumbs and melted chocolate. Using a wooden spoon, beat until creamy, about 5 minutes.

In a bowl, beat the egg whites until stiff peaks form. Stir about one-fourth of the egg whites into the chocolate mixture to lighten it, then gently fold in the remaining whites just until no white streaks remain; do not overmix. Pour the mixture into the prepared pan.

Bake until firm to the touch, about 50 minutes. Remove from the oven and release and remove the pan sides. Transfer to a wire rack and let cool.

When the cake is cool, slice it horizontally in half to form 2 layers. Spread half of the apricot jam on each cut side and then sandwich the halves together on a serving plate.

To make the icing, in a saucepan over low heat, melt the bittersweet chocolate with the water, stirring occasionally. Remove from the heat and let cool. Using a metal spatula, spread the cooled chocolate over the top and sides of the cake, then serve.

MAKES ONE 9-IN OR 21-CM CAKE; SERVES 6

DOLCE DI PERE E MORE

Pear and Blackberry Dessert

I serve this dessert toward the end of summer, when blackberries are juicy and ripe. Out of season, you can use blackberry jam diluted with a little dessert wine and heated to form a sauce. The best pears for poaching are elongated, tender-firm Bosc pears. Comice and Anjou work well, too.

6 firm Bosc pears or other dessert pears
½ cup (4 fl oz/120 ml) sweet red wine
6 tablespoons (3 oz/90 g) sugar
10 oz (300 g) blackberries
juice of 1 lemon

Halve, core and peel the pears. Place in a wide saucepan, hollow sides down in a single layer. Add the wine and 5 tablespoons (2½ oz/80 g) of the sugar, cover and cook over low heat, turning once, until tender, about 10 minutes. Using a slotted spoon, remove the pear halves to a plate to cool.

Clockwise from top: Lemon and Pepper Sorbet; Pear and Blackberry Dessert; Zabaione Ice Cream

Veneto

GELATO ALLO ZABAIONE

Zabaione Ice Cream

This is a wonderful way to experience the flavors of the traditional warm egg-and-Marsala pudding known as zabaione *(also spelled* zabaglione*). For a delicious dessert, top this ice cream with wild strawberries or raisins soaked in Marsala wine, or crown it with melted chocolate as they often do in the Veneto.*

6 egg yolks
¾ cup (6 oz/180 g) sugar
1 cup (8 fl oz/240 ml) Marsala wine
1 cup (8 fl oz/240 ml) heavy (double) cream

In the top of a double boiler, stir the egg yolks and sugar together with a wooden spoon until soft and foamy. Gradually add the Marsala, stirring constantly. Place the pan over the lower pan of simmering water and cook, whisking constantly, until the mixture thickens and coats the spoon, about 5 minutes. Do not allow the mixture to overheat or the eggs will set. Remove from the heat and let cool. Stir occasionally to prevent a film from forming on top.

In a bowl, whip the cream until stiff peaks form. Fold the cream into the cooled Marsala mixture. Transfer to an ice cream maker and freeze according to the manufacturer's directions. Serve in chilled bowls or cups.

MAKES ABOUT 3½ CUPS (28 FL OZ/870 ML); SERVES 6

SORBETTO AL LIMONE E PEPE

Lemon and Pepper Sorbet

Aromatic green pepper gives this sorbet a pleasing fragrance. Green peppercorns are harvested before they turn black and hard; therefore they are milder than black peppercorns. To achieve the right balance, add the pepper and lemon juice a little at a time and taste as you go along.

1 cup (8 fl oz/240 ml) water
1⅓ cups (11 oz/330 g) sugar
about 3 cups (24 fl oz/750 ml) strained fresh lemon juice
ground green pepper
1 egg white

In a saucepan, combine the water and sugar and bring to a boil while stirring. Boil for a couple of minutes until the sugar is fully dissolved. Remove from the heat and add the lemon juice and green pepper to taste. Mix well and let cool. Pour into a container, cover and place in the freezer until frozen, about 2 hours, stirring with a fork 2 or 3 times at regular intervals to break up the mixture.

About 30 minutes before serving, place the sorbet in a blender, working in batches if necessary. Add the egg white and blend until the mixture resembles snow. Return to the container and place in the freezer for 30 minutes before serving. Scoop into chilled bowls or glasses.

SERVES 8

Meanwhile, place the blackberries in a bowl, sprinkle with the remaining 1 tablespoon sugar and add the lemon juice. Toss gently, cover and refrigerate until needed.

Using a sharp knife, cut several slices into the thickest part of each pear half, but do not cut all the way through. Arrange 2 halves on each individual plate, fanning the slices slightly. Surround with the blackberries and refrigerate until chilled, then serve.

SERVES 6

PERE RIPIENE DI SPUMA DI RICOTTA
Pears Filled with Ricotta Mousse

Select ripe yet firm pears. Use a good-quality white wine, either dry or sweet, depending upon your preference. In summertime, it is a nice touch to serve the pears on a chilled platter. Ground espresso-roast coffee beans can be substituted for the cocoa.

½ cup (4 fl oz/120 ml) good-quality white wine
6 tablespoons (3 oz/90 g) sugar
6 firm Bosc pears or other dessert pears, halved, cored and peeled
1¼ cups (10 oz/300 g) ricotta cheese
1 tablespoon semisweet cocoa powder

In a wide saucepan large enough to hold the pear halves in a single layer, combine the wine and half of the sugar and bring to a boil over low heat, stirring to dissolve the sugar. Boil for 2 minutes. Add the pear halves hollow sides down and continue to cook over low heat, turning once, until tender when pierced with a fork, about 10 minutes longer. Using a slotted spoon, transfer the pears to a plate and let cool. Reserve the liquid in the pan.

In a bowl, stir together the ricotta, the remaining sugar and the cocoa powder until well mixed.

Arrange the pear halves on a platter hollow sides up. Spoon an equal amount of the ricotta mixture atop each half. Pour the reserved liquid over the top and serve.

SERVES 6

Sicilia

ARANCE ALLA CREMA
Oranges in Pastry Cream

You can prepare this pleasing dessert ahead of time, but keep the oranges and cream separate, combining them just before serving. Adding potato starch before cooking the cream helps to keep it from curdling but it adds a slightly floury taste, so it is optional. Try slipping it under a very hot broiler (griller) for a couple of minutes to scorch the cream.

6 oranges
2 cups (16 fl oz/480 ml) milk
4 egg yolks
½ cup (4 oz/120 g) sugar
1 teaspoon potato flour (optional)

Remove the zest of 1 orange in large pieces and place in a heavy saucepan with the milk. Place over medium heat and bring to a boil. Remove from the heat and let cool.

In the top pan of a double broiler, beat together the egg yolks and sugar with a wooden spoon until the mixture falls from the spoon in a ribbon, about 10 minutes. (Alternatively, use an electric mixer on high speed.) If using the potato flour, sift it directly into the yolk mixture and stir well. Pour the cooled milk a little at a time through a fine-mesh sieve into the yolk mixture, stirring constantly. Place the pan over the lower pan of simmering water. Cook, stirring constantly,

until the cream coats a spoon, about 10 minutes. Do not allow it to boil. Remove from the heat and pour into a bowl. Set aside to cool, stirring occasionally to prevent a film from forming on top.

Peel the 6 oranges, being careful to remove all the white pith and membrane. Slice the oranges crosswise, remove any seeds and arrange the slices in a bowl. Pour the cream over the slices and serve.

SERVES 6

CROSTATA ALLA MARMELLATA DI LIMONE
Lemon Marmalade Tart

This is a perfect dessert to conclude a rich meal, as lemons aid digestion. It can also be made with oranges. Try to find lemons with peels that have not been sprayed. If only sprayed lemons are available, prick their skins with a pin and boil them in three changes of water before slicing.

FOR THE PASTRY:

2⅔ cups (11 oz/330 g) all-purpose (plain) flour
3 egg yolks
½ cup (4 oz/120 g) sugar
6 tablespoons (3 oz/90 g) unsalted butter, chilled, cut into small pieces
pinch of salt

FOR THE MARMALADE:

¾ cup (6 oz/180 g) sugar
¼ cup (2 fl oz/60 ml) water
¾ lb (360 g) lemons, thinly sliced crosswise and hard area around stems discarded

unsalted butter and all-purpose (plain) flour for preparing pan

To make the pastry, heap the flour into a mound on a work surface. Make a well in the center and add the egg yolks, sugar, butter and salt. Using your hands, combine all the ingredients, mixing well to form a dough. Then knead the dough until smooth and elastic, about 15 minutes. Shape the dough into a ball, wrap in plastic wrap and refrigerate for 1 hour.

To make the marmalade, place the sugar and water in a saucepan over medium heat. Cook without stirring, shaking the pan occasionally, until the sugar darkens and caramelizes, about 10 minutes. Add the lemon slices and continue to cook for 1 minute. Remove from the heat and set aside.

Preheat an oven to 350°F (180°C). Butter a 9-in (23-cm) tart pan and dust with flour; tap out excess.

Roll out two-thirds of the dough into a round large enough to line the bottom and sides of the pan. Carefully transfer the dough round to the prepared pan and press it gently against the bottom and sides. Trim the dough even with the rim of the tart pan. Or, if desired, roll the dough into an oval or a rectangle about 10 in (25 cm) long and transfer the dough to a buttered and floured baking sheet (tray). Gently pinch the edge of the dough to create a slight lip.

Spread the lemon marmalade evenly over the prepared tart dough.

Roll out the remaining dough thinly and cut into narrow strips. Lay across the top of the tart in a lattice pattern.

Bake until the pastry turns a deep gold, about 40 minutes. Transfer to a rack and let cool completely before serving.

MAKES ONE 9-IN (23-CM) TART; SERVES 6
Photograph pages 208–209

Left to right: Oranges in Pastry Cream; Pears Filled with Ricotta Mousse

Veneto

TORTA DI PANE AL CIOCCOLATO

Chocolate Bread Cake

This is a traditional way cooks use up stale bread in the Veneto. Like many Italian dolci, it is meant to be served at teatime rather than as a finish to a meal.

10 oz (300 g) coarse country bread, at least 3 days old, broken into pieces
2 cups (16 fl oz/480 ml) milk
unsalted butter and all-purpose (plain) flour for preparing pan
4 eggs
¾ cup (6 oz/180 g) sugar
⅓ cup (3 oz/90 g) unsalted butter, at room temperature, cut into small pieces
6 oz (180 g) bittersweet chocolate, finely grated
¼ cup (2 fl oz/60 ml) light rum

➤ In a bowl, combine the bread and milk and let soak for about 10 minutes.
➤ Preheat an oven to 350°F (180°C). Butter a 9-in (23-cm) tart pan and dust with flour; tap out excess flour.
➤ In a bowl, stir together the eggs and sugar until blended. Add the ⅓ cup (3 oz/90 g) butter, the chocolate and rum. Squeeze the bread to remove the excess milk and add to the egg-sugar mixture; mix well. Spread the bread mixture over the bottom of the prepared pan and smooth the surface with the back of a knife.
➤ Bake until a knife inserted into the center comes out clean, about 1 hour. Remove from the oven. Run a knife around the edges of the pan to loosen the cake and transfer to a platter. Serve warm.

MAKES ONE 9-IN (23-CM) CAKE; SERVES 6

Campania

FAGOTTINI DI FICHI

Figs in Sweet Pastry

In the area around Salerno between the months of June and September, there is an abundance of fresh figs. They are dried, made into jam and used in various desserts. This recipe is a family favorite.

unsalted butter for preparing pan
30 ripe figs, peeled
¼ cup (2 oz/60 g) sugar
¼ cup (2 fl oz/60 ml) Cognac or other good-quality brandy
pastry dough for lemon marmalade tart (recipe on page 231)

➤ Preheat an oven to 350°F (180°C). Butter a baking sheet (tray).
➤ Place the figs in a bowl and mash with a fork. Add the sugar and Cognac and mix well.
➤ Flatten the pastry dough into a disk and place between 2 sheets of parchment (greaseproof) paper. Roll out about ⅛ in (2 mm) thick.
➤ Peel away the top sheet of parchment paper and cut the pastry into 4-in (10-cm) squares. You should have about 30 squares in all. Place an equal amount of the fig mixture on each square and fold the corners to the center to form packets, enclosing the filling completely. Pinch to seal well. Arrange the packets on the prepared baking sheet.
➤ Bake until golden, about 30 minutes. Remove from the oven and let cool completely on a wire rack before serving.

MAKES 30 PASTRIES; SERVES 10

Alto Adige

TORTA DI MELE

Apple Cake

As in neighboring Trentino, bakers in Alto Adige have devised many uses for the local apples. Easy and quick to prepare, this cake can also be baked in a ring mold. If the top browns too quickly, you can cover it with parchment.

Clockwise from top left: Apple Cake; Chocolate Bread Cake;
Figs in Sweet Pastry

unsalted butter for preparing pan
3 tablespoons fine dried bread crumbs
2 lb (1 kg) cooking apples, halved, cored, peeled and
    thinly sliced
½ cup (4 oz/120 g) unsalted butter
2 eggs, lightly beaten
½ cup (4 oz/120 g) sugar
1 cup (4 oz/120 g) all-purpose (plain) flour
1 tablespoon baking powder
pinch of salt

☞ Preheat an oven to 350°F (180°C). Generously butter a 9-in or 21-cm springform pan and dust with the bread crumbs; tap out excess crumbs.

☞ Place the apples in a large bowl. In a deep saucepan over very low heat, melt the butter. Remove from the heat. Add the eggs, sugar, flour, baking powder, salt and melted butter to the apples and stir well to form a smooth mixture. Pour the apple mixture into the prepared pan.

☞ Bake until set, about 1 hour. Transfer to a wire rack to cool completely. Release the pan sides and transfer to a serving plate.

MAKES ONE 9-IN OR 21-CM CAKE; SERVES 6

TORTA DI SAVOIARDI

Ladyfinger Cake

The baking of the Piedmont was heavily influenced by the French tradition through the dynastic House of Savoy, which ruled the area for centuries and gave its name to this now-classic cake. It is important to dip the ladyfingers in the rum only briefly, so they do not become soggy.

7 eggs
6 tablespoons (3 oz/90 g) unsalted butter, at room
    temperature
1 cup (8 oz/240 g) plus 2 tablespoons sugar
1 cup (8 fl oz/240 ml) water
¼ cup (2 fl oz/60 ml) dark rum
10 oz (300 g) ladyfingers

☙ Bring a saucepan three-fourths full of water to a boil. Carefully slip the eggs into the water, reduce the heat so the water does not boil hard and cook for 7 minutes. Remove from the heat and transfer the eggs to cold water. Let cool completely, then peel and separate the yolks from the whites.

234

stand even with the pan rim. Pour in the egg yolk–butter mixture and cover the top with the remaining lady fingers.

Cover with parchment paper and refrigerate for 3 hours. Remove the paper and release and remove the pan sides. Slide the cake onto a serving plate to serve.

SERVES 6

Venezia Giulia

STRUDEL DI PERE
Pear Strudel

This is a variation from Trieste on the celebrated Austrian dessert. The pears, which are standing in for the more common apples, should be very firm and not too juicy.

FOR THE PASTRY:

2 cups (8 oz/240 g) plus 2 tablespoons all-purpose (plain) flour
1 egg
3 tablespoons unsalted butter, at room temperature
1 tablespoon extra-virgin olive oil
3 tablespoons warm water
1 tablespoon sugar
pinch of salt
unsalted butter for preparing dish

FOR THE FILLING:

2 lb (1 kg) ripe but firm Bosc pears or other
    dessert pears
grated zest of 1 lemon
juice of ½ lemon
¾ cup (6 oz/180 g) granulated sugar
all-purpose (plain) flour for dusting
¼ cup (2 oz/60 g) unsalted butter
⅓ cup (2 oz/60 g) pine nuts
2 tablespoons fine dried bread crumbs
1 tablespoon confectioners' (icing) sugar

To make the pastry, heap the flour into a mound on a work surface. Make a well in the center and add the egg, butter, oil, warm water, sugar and salt. Using your hands, combine all the ingredients, mixing well to form a dough. Then knead the dough until smooth and elastic, about 15 minutes. Shape the dough into a ball. Cover with a bowl and set aside to rest for about 30 minutes.

Preheat an oven to 340°F (170°C). Butter a large baking sheet (tray).

To make the filling, halve, core, peel and thinly slice the pears. Place in a large bowl. Add the lemon zest, lemon juice and granulated sugar and mix well.

Cover a work surface with a kitchen towel. Dust the towel with flour. Transfer the dough to the towel and roll out very thinly into an 12-by-18-in (30-by-46-cm) rectangle; work as quickly as possible so that it does not dry out.

Melt the butter in a saucepan over low heat and brush the dough with some of the melted butter. Carefully arrange the pear slices on the pastry, leaving an uncovered border on one long side to make the rolling of the strudel easier. Sprinkle evenly with the pine nuts and brush the pears with more of the melted butter. Sprinkle evenly with the bread crumbs.

Holding onto the edge of the towel on the side with the uncovered border, carefully roll up the pastry. Place the roll in the prepared baking sheet and shape it into a circle, horseshoe or as you wish.

Bake until golden, about 1 hour, brushing occasionally with the remaining melted butter. Transfer to a serving platter. Serve the strudel warm, sifting the confectioners' sugar over the top just before slicing.

SERVES 6

Clockwise from top: Ladyfinger Cake; Pear Strudel; Apple Mousse Meringue (recipe page 222)

Pass the yolks through a sieve into a bowl; discard the whites or reserve for another use. Add the butter and 1 cup (8 oz/ 240 g) of the sugar and beat well with a mixer until fluffy. In a saucepan, combine the water and the 2 tablespoons sugar and bring to a boil, stirring to dissolve the sugar. Boil for 10 minutes until a light syrup forms. Remove from the heat and stir in the rum. Let cool.

Line the bottom and sides of an 8-in (20-cm) springform pan with parchment (greaseproof) paper. Working with one at a time, briefly dip the ladyfingers into the rum mixture and line the bottom and sides of the prepared pan with them, cutting off the bottoms, if necessary, so that the ladyfingers

Campania

CREMA DI LIMONE CON BACCHE

Lemon Custard with Berries

Serve this attractive dessert for a summer snack or as a refreshing finish to a light lunch. Accompany it with glasses of the traditional lemon liqueur of the Amalfi coast, limoncello. The tart liqueur is always served well chilled.

4 egg yolks
½ cup (2 oz/60 g) all-purpose (plain) flour
¼ cup (2 oz/60 g) sugar
4 cups (32 fl oz/1 l) milk
zest of 2 lemons, in large strips
1 lb (480 g) raspberries or sliced small strawberries

☙ In a saucepan, using a wooden spoon, stir together the egg yolks, flour and sugar until fully blended. Continuing to stir constantly, add the milk a little at a time. Place the pan over medium heat and cook, stirring constantly, until the mixture comes to a boil and thickens, about 10 minutes. Remove from the heat and stir in the lemon zest. Set aside to cool. Stir occasionally to prevent a film from forming on top.
☙ When cool, remove and discard the lemon zest. Pour the cream onto a deep platter and spoon the berries over the top, covering completely. Cover and refrigerate for about 2 hours before serving.

SERVES 6

Top to bottom: Watermelon and Pineapple with Sambuca; Apricot and Raisin Dessert

Lazio

ANGURIA E ANANAS ALLA SAMBUCA

Watermelon and Pineapple with Sambuca

This delicious dessert contains sambuca, a licorice-flavored liqueur made from elderberries that comes from Civitavecchia near Rome. The recipe can be prepared in just a few minutes.

½ small watermelon
1 pineapple
1 pt (480 ml) vanilla ice cream
6 tablespoons (3 fl oz/90 ml) sambuca

☙ Slice the watermelon into 6 rounds, each about ½ in (1 cm) thick. Eliminate the rind and seeds. Trim the peel from the pineapple, capturing any juice. Cut crosswise into 6 slices ½ in (1 cm) thick. Cut out the tough core section from the center of each slice and discard.
☙ On each of 6 individual plates, arrange the watermelon slices. Top them with the pineapple slices. In the center of each stack of fruit slices, place a spoonful of vanilla ice cream. Pour any captured pineapple juice and the sambuca over the tops and serve.

SERVES 6

DOLCE DI ALBICOCCHE E UVETTA

Apricot and Raisin Dessert

Here is a typical Italian dessert. The most common way to finish a meal in Italy is with fresh fruit. This is an easy-to-prepare elaboration of that longtime tradition. Top with a spoonful of whipped cream and a dusting of cinnamon, if desired.

3 tablespoons unsalted butter
4 lb (2 kg) apricots, pitted, peeled and cut into small pieces
generous 1 cup (6 oz/180 g) raisins, soaked in water to
    cover for 30 minutes and drained
7 tablespoons (3½ oz/100 g) sugar
2 tablespoons ground cinnamon

☙ Preheat an oven to 265°F (130°C). Butter a mold about 9 in (23 cm) square with 1 tablespoon of the butter.
☙ Place a layer of apricots on the bottom of the prepared mold and cover with a handful of raisins, a spoonful of sugar and a sprinkling of cinnamon. Repeat the layers in this way until the mold is filled, reserving a little sugar and cinnamon and some raisins for the top. Press the layers down well. Cut the remaining 2 tablespoons butter into small pieces and use to dot the top of the mold. Sprinkle with the reserved sugar, raisins and cinnamon.
☙ Bake until firm, about 3 hours. Remove from the oven and let cool. Invert onto a plate, lift off the mold and cut into squares to serve.

SERVES 6

Lemon Custard with Berries

Veneto

GALANI DI CARNEVALE

Sweet Fritters

Sweet fried pastries are typically eaten during the festivities of Carnevale, the period before Lent. Each region has its own fritters in different shapes and with different names. Galani are the Venetian version.

3 cups (12 oz/360 g) all-purpose (plain) flour, plus additional flour for working
2 whole eggs, plus 1 egg yolk
1 tablespoon sugar
pinch of salt
2 tablespoons unsalted butter
¾ cup (6 fl oz/180 ml) dry white wine
4 cups (32 fl oz/1 l) olive oil for deep-frying
½ cup (2 oz/60 g) confectioners' (icing) sugar

✑ Heap the flour into a mound on a work surface. Make a well in the center. Place the whole eggs, the egg yolk, sugar, salt, butter and wine in the well. Using your hands, combine all the ingredients, mixing well to form a dough. Then knead the dough until smooth and elastic, about 15 minutes. Shape the dough into a ball. Cover with a bowl and set aside to rest for about 30 minutes.

✑ On a lightly floured work surface, roll out the dough into a very thin sheet. Cut into strips 4 in (10 cm) long and ¾ in (2 cm) wide.

✑ Pour the oil into a large, deep frying pan and heat to 340°F (170°C). Working in batches of 5 dough strips, drop in the strips and turn them rapidly in the oil. As soon as they are golden and crisp on both sides, after about 3 minutes, transfer with a slotted spoon to paper towels to drain.

✑ Layer the hot fritters on a platter in a pyramid shape, sifting a generous amount of confectioners' sugar over each layer. Serve hot.

SERVES 12

Toscana

BISCOTTI ALLE MANDORLE

Almond Cookies

While all sorts of new flavors are appearing in biscotti elsewhere, in Tuscany, they are still made mainly with nuts. You can substitute chopped hazelnuts (filberts) for the almonds, or even leave the nuts out, if you prefer. Serve your guests glasses of Vin Santo for dunking these cookies.

2¼ cups (9 oz/270 g) unbleached all-purpose (plain) flour, plus ¼ cup (1 oz/30 g) flour for working and dusting pan
pinch of salt
½ cup (4 oz/120 g) sugar
1½ teaspoons baking powder
2 whole eggs, plus 1 egg yolk

Top to bottom: Sweet Fritters; Almond Cookies

⅔ cup (3½ oz/100 g) chopped blanched almonds (optional)
1 egg yolk lightly beaten with 1 teaspoon milk for glaze

✑ Preheat an oven to 350°F (180°C).

✑ In a large bowl, using a wooden spoon, stir together the 2¼ cups (9 oz/270 g) flour, salt, sugar, baking powder, whole eggs and egg yolk. Transfer to a lightly floured work surface and knead until a smooth dough forms, about 10 minutes. Incorporate the almonds, if using, distributing them evenly. Divide the dough into 4 equal portions and form each portion into a cigar-shaped strip about 8 in (20 cm) long. Brush the strips with the glaze. Flour a baking sheet (tray) and arrange the strips on it, spacing them well apart.

✑ Bake until golden, about 12 minutes. Remove from the oven and let cool slightly. Then while the strips are still soft, cut them into slices about 1 in (2.5 cm) wide. Place the slices flat on the baking sheet, separating them so they are not touching. Return the baking sheet to the oven and bake until the cookies are golden and dry, 12–15 minutes longer.

✑ Transfer to a wire rack to cool. Store in an airtight container for up to 2 weeks.

MAKES ABOUT 32 COOKIES

TORTA ALL'ARANCIA

Orange Cake

For a complementary sauce that can be put together with ease, heat some orange marmalade thinned with a little sweet dessert wine. Pass the sauce with the cake. You can also garnish each slice with a little mascarpone.

1 large orange
2 cups (16 fl oz/480 ml) water
1 tablespoon unsalted butter for preparing dish
5 eggs, separated
1 cup (8 oz/240 g) sugar
1 teaspoon light or dark rum
1⅓ cups (8 oz/240 g) blanched almonds, finely chopped
confectioners' (icing) sugar (optional)

✑ In a saucepan over medium heat, combine the orange with the water. Bring to a boil. Reduce the heat to low and cook, uncovered, until only about ½ cup (4 fl oz/120 ml) syrupy liquid remains, about 1 hour. Remove from the heat.

✑ When cool enough to handle, remove the orange, cut in half and remove and discard the seeds. Put the orange halves (with peels intact) and ¼ cup (2 fl oz/60 ml) of the syrupy cooking liquid into a blender or a food processor fitted with the metal blade and purée until smooth.

✑ Preheat an oven to 350°F (180°C). Butter a 9-in or 21-cm springform pan.

✑ In a bowl, beat together the egg yolks and sugar with a wooden spoon until the mixture falls from the spoon in a ribbon, about 5 minutes. (Alternatively, beat with an electric mixer.) Add the rum, orange purée and chopped almonds and mix well. In a bowl, beat the egg whites until stiff peaks form. Stir about one-fourth of the whites into the yolk mixture to lighten it, then gently fold in the remaining whites just until no white streaks remain; do not overmix. Pour into prepared pan.

✑ Bake until set, about 1 hour. Remove from the oven and let cool completely in the pan. Release and remove the pan sides and transfer the cake to a serving plate. Sift confectioners' sugar over the top, if desired.

MAKES ONE 9-IN OR 21-CM CAKE; SERVES 6
Photograph pages 208–209

TORTA DI ALBICOCCHE E MANDORLE
Apricot and Almond Cake

Apricots flourish in climates that are not too hot, so the mountainous slopes of Abruzzo are ideal terrain. You can substitute sliced pears for the apricots.

unsalted butter for preparing pan
1 cup (8 oz/240 g) sugar
¾ cup (6 oz/180 g) unsalted butter, at room temperature
2 whole eggs, plus 3 egg yolks
3 oz (90 g) crumbled amaretti (see glossary)
½ cup (2 oz/60 g) all-purpose (plain) flour
1 tablespoon baking powder
⅓ cup (2 oz/60 g) chopped blanched almonds
2 lb (1 kg) apricots, halved and pitted
confectioners' (icing) sugar (optional)

✎ Preheat an oven to 350°F (180°C). Butter a 9-in or 21-cm springform pan.

✎ In a bowl, using a wooden spoon, beat together the sugar and butter until light and creamy, about 3 minutes. Add the whole eggs and egg yolks, the crumbled amaretti, the flour and the baking powder and mix well.

✎ Scatter the almonds evenly over the bottom of the prepared pan. Pour in one-third of the butter mixture, spreading it evenly. Cover with half of the apricots, hollow sides down. Top with half of the remaining butter mixture and then all of the remaining apricots, hollow sides down. Spread the remaining butter mixture evenly over the top.

✎ Bake until set, about 40 minutes. Remove from the oven and let cool completely on a wire rack. Release and remove the pan sides and slide the cake onto a serving plate. Sift confectioners' sugar over the top, if desired.

MAKES ONE 9-IN OR 21-CM CAKE; SERVES 6

Left to right: Figs in Honey; Apricot and Almond Cake

TORTA DI CIOCCOLATO
Chocolate Cake

This dense cake goes perfectly with freshly brewed coffee. The rich flavor is nicely accented by serving it with a dollop of mascarpone or whipped cream and fragoline di bosco *(wild strawberries) or small sweet cultivated berries.*

1 tablespoon unsalted butter for preparing pan
5 egg yolks
1 cup (8 oz/240 g) plus 2 tablespoons sugar
½ cup (2 oz/60 g) all-purpose (plain) flour
1 teaspoon baking powder
5 oz (150 g) bitter chocolate
⅔ cup (5 oz/150 g) unsalted butter, at room temperature
2 egg whites

✎ Preheat an oven to 350°F (180°C). Butter a 9-in or 21-cm springform pan.

✎ In a bowl, combine the egg yolks and sugar and beat with a wooden spoon until light and creamy, about 3 minutes. Combine the flour and baking powder in a small bowl and stir to mix well. Add the flour mixture to the yolk mixture in a slow, steady stream while beating constantly.

✎ In a small, heavy pan, combine the chocolate and butter and melt over low heat just until creamy, stirring occasionally. Stir the chocolate into the egg-flour mixture.

✎ In a bowl, beat the egg whites until stiff peaks form. Stir about one-fourth of the egg whites into the chocolate mixture to lighten it, then gently fold in the remaining whites just until no white streaks remain; do not overmix. Pour the mixture into the prepared pan.

✎ Bake until a toothpick inserted into the center comes out dry, about 50 minutes. Remove from the oven and release and remove the pan sides. Slide onto a serving plate and let cool before serving.

MAKES ONE 9-IN OR 21-CM CAKE; SERVES 6

FICHI AL MIELE
Figs in Honey

The best figs in Italy, called dottati, *are small, white and have a sweet liquid "drop" at their center. Calabrian cooks also lightly brush figs with honey, cover them with chestnut leaves and bake them until soft. Use a good-quality white wine, either sweet or dry, depending upon your taste.*

2 lb (1 kg) firm white figs
1 cup (8 fl oz/240 ml) good-quality white wine
1 cup (12 oz/360 g) honey

✎ Stand the figs upright side by side in a flameproof earthenware dish. Pour the wine over the figs and place the dish over medium heat. When the wine begins to boil, add the honey, cover, reduce the heat to very low and simmer until the liquid is reduced and thickened and the figs are soft when pierced, about 1 hour.

✎ Remove from the heat and let cool. Serve directly from the cooking dish.

SERVES 6

Chocolate Cake

Glossary

AGNOLOTTI see *fresh pasta.*

AGRODOLCE means "sour and sweet" and is used to describe the sweet-and-sour sauces popular in parts of Italy.

AL DENTE, literally "to the tooth," is used to describe the correct consistency of cooked pasta—that is, just cooked through but still firm and slightly chewy. To cook pasta al dente, you must taste it as you near the end of the cooking time indicated on the package. Each brand and each shape can have a slightly different cooking time.

ALL'ONDA means "wavy" and is used to indicate the correct consistency for a cooked **risotto**—that is, still liquid enough to move in waves in the bowl.

ALMOND OIL, a fragrant oil expressed from almonds, is found in the kitchens of Italy, France, Spain and Portugal. Almond oil produced elsewhere is generally milder in flavor. Look for almond oil in shops specializing in southern European foods and in some health-food stores. Refrigerate the oil to preserve its delicate flavor.

ALMONDS are widely used in Italian recipes, especially for **biscotti** and pastries. Called *mandorle* in Italian, they have a mild, sweet flavor and are high in nutrition. To blanch almonds, drop into boiling water and cook for 2 minutes. Drain and let cool slightly, then squeeze each nut between your fingers to pop the meat from the skin.

AMARETTI are crisp macaroon cookies made with bitter almonds (*amaro* means "bitter"). They will keep for long periods, and the best-known brand is Lazzaroni di Saronno, packed in elegant red tins. A recipe for homemade amaretti appears on page 225.

ANCHOVIES are preserved in oil in cans or jars, or in salt, usually in cans. Oil-packed anchovies come already filleted; if working with salt-packed anchovies, brush off all visible salt, pull the fillets off each side of the bone and rinse briefly before using. Anchovies in oil (preferably olive oil) can be found in food markets; anchovies in salt are available at well-stocked Italian shops.

ANTIPASTO literally translates as "before the meal." In the past, this was typically a small appetizer of vegetables (raw or packed in oil or vinegar), cured meats (salami, **mortadella** or boiled or air-cured ham) or cooked seafood salad that came before a first course of either pasta, risotto or soup. Now the antipasto, although still a small portion meant to prepare the palate for the meal, may be any of the foods typically served, as well as cheese tarts, savory pies, cooked vegetables, thin slices of goose or duck breast or just about anything else that fires the imagination of an inspired chef. Ideally, the flavors of the antipasto complement those of the course that follows.

ARBORIO RICE see *rice.*

ARTICHOKE, native to the Mediterranean, is grown for its flower, which is picked before it blooms. The flower, or head, is globelike, with thick, firm, thorn-topped leaves surrounding a tender heart and a prickly, inedible choke. The more mature the artichoke, the more developed the choke. Artichokes range in size from tiny buds of no more than 1 or 2 ounces (30 or 60 g), which can be eaten whole after light trimming, to large globes up to 5 inches (13 cm) in diameter. Most artichokes grown in Italy are tinged a beautiful purple at the leaf tips.

ARUGULA, also known as rocket, is a leafy green with slender, multiple-lobed leaves and a peppery flavor. It is called *rucola* in Italy and is often used raw in antipasti and salads. In certain regions, a wild variety known as *rucola selvatica* can be found; it has more jagged edges and a stronger flavor.

ASIAGO, a cow's milk cheese from the hills above Vicenza in the Veneto, is creamy and compact when young, making it a good dessert cheese. When aged *(stagionato),* it becomes granular and is suitable for eating or grating, much as **Parmesan cheese** might be.

BACCALÀ see *salted cod.*

BALSAMIC VINEGAR *(aceto balsamico)* is an extraordinary ingredient made with great care and patience in Modena and Reggio Emilia in Emilia-Romagna. You should only use *aceto balsamico tradizionale* that has either API MO (from Modena) or API RE (Reggio Emilia) on the label. The traditional method for making balsamic vinegar has not changed for more than 1,000 years. Each fall Trebbiano grapes are dried slightly to concentrate their sweetness. They are pressed and their juice is simmered to concentrate them further and to caramelize the sugars in the juice. The liquid is then placed in an oak barrel to age for a year. In succeeding years it ages in ever-smaller barrels made of chestnut, cherrywood, ash and mulberry. Each wood imparts its own characteristics, which combine to make the end product distinct. The vinegar is further aged for many years (typically a minimum of 12), creating an intense and concentrated flavor, so that only a little bit is required for a dish. Balsamic vinegar should be thought of as a condiment rather than as a traditional vinegar that might be used to dress salads. It is excellent on simple ingredients (Parmigiano-Reggiano cheese; poached fish; steamed potatoes; fresh strawberries) or may be used in cooking to give intense flavor to sautéed chicken, to meats or to many other foods. If traditionally aged balsamic is unavailable, commercial balsamic vinegar (often called *industriale*) can be used, as long as it comes from Modena or Reggio Emilia. It may be somewhat more acidic, although it does have some of the sweet and woody qualities of traditional balsamic vinegar.

BASIL, or *basilico,* in Italian, is the distinctive herb of Liguria. The basis of the classic sauce known as **pesto**, it is also found in recipes up and down the peninsula. The aromatic, flavorful leaf can be used whole, torn or chopped.

BAY LEAVES are whole leaves of the bay laurel tree, usually used dried, although recipes can be made with fresh bay leaves if one has access to an unsprayed tree. The Mediterranean variety, available in specialty-food shops, has a milder, sweeter flavor than California bay. Remove the leaves from a dish before serving.

BEANS form the basis of many Italian dishes. *Cannellini* are the classic Tuscan white beans. These thin-skinned, kidney-shaped legumes are at their best at the end of summer, when they are eaten fresh, and they can be found in Italian shops and well-stocked food stores dried or in cans. White kidney beans, Great Northern beans (which are slightly smaller and rounder) or white haricot beans (which are slightly larger and rounder) can be substituted. *Borlotti* beans, also known as cranberry beans, are pale beige, oval beans with reddish mottling. They, too, are eaten fresh at summer's end, as well as dried, and are easily found dried in many food stores. *Fave,* known as fava beans or broad beans in English, are encased in flat green pods that range from about 4 inches (10 cm) up to 12 inches (30 cm) or so in length. It is traditional to eat fresh fava beans on the first day of May. Only the very youngest favas may be eaten pod and all; older, larger pods must be discarded. Each moist, flat green bean is covered with a sturdy skin that should be removed by blanching the beans for 30 seconds and then slipping off the skin. The beans are also available dried. *Ceci,* known as chick-peas or garbanzo beans, are round and beige and have a mild, nutty flavor. They are available dried and canned (tinned), and are commonly used in central Italy, especially in Tuscany and Umbria.

BEETS (beetroots) are a much-used vegetable that require lengthy cooking, either by boiling or baking. Nowadays beets are cooked commercially and canned or sold in airtight packs. The greens can also be cooked and served as a vegetable dish or used as a stuffing for pasta.

BELGIAN ENDIVE (chicory/witloof) is a member of the chicory family and thus a cousin of **radicchio**. Its slightly bitter, spear-shaped leaves are generally white to pale yellow-green, although a variety with pale red leaf tips is sometimes seen. While not common in the classical Italian diet, its availability today is a sign of the migration of ingredients throughout Europe.

BISCOTTI is a wide-ranging term in Italy. These are biscuits, cookies or crackers and may be salty, sweet or dry. The salted type may be made with cheese, herbs or salt and can accompany vegetables and alcoholic drinks. Sweet biscotti may be made with chocolate, nuts or fruit flavors

and are served with ice cream, coffee or tea. Twice-baked almond biscotti from Prato in Tuscany are called *cantuccini* and are traditionally dipped into **Vin Santo**, a sweet dessert wine, before eating.

BLOOD ORANGES have an intense red interior and a sweet yet acidic juice that has hints of raspberry flavor. Grown on Sicily's northern coast, they are called *tarocchi* or *sanguigni* and are prized throughout Italy for eating, for juice or for making sauces.

BORLOTTI see *beans.*

BREAD CRUMBS are produced by drying out stale bread in the oven and grinding it in a food processor (or otherwise crushing it) until it is like coarse sand. The Italian name, *pangrattato,* derives from the fact that the bread used to be grated to produce the crumbs. Italian bread crumbs are now sold in transparent packs and are also exported.

BROCCOLI RABE, also known in Italian as *rapini, rape* and *cima di rape,* is a variety of foliage turnip that does not produce an enlarged base, hence its other common English name, turnip tops. It has dark green leaves on sturdy stalks topped with small flower clusters. A local variety known as *friarielli* is grown in some southern areas.

BRODO means "broth" or "stock." In Italy, a very light stock is made by simply putting a large piece of boneless beef or a chicken in a deep pot with a carrot, onion, celery, zucchini, parsley, a bay leaf, a pinch of salt and pepper and an abundant amount of water and leaving the mixture to simmer for a couple of hours (recipe on page 40). Unlike the French method, no roasted bones or marrow bones are added. The stock is light, not fatty, and has a very fresh flavor. Herbs such as thyme and basil may be added.

BRUSCHETTA is a popular dish traditionally made by toasting slices of **country bread** over hot coals and then liberally dressing them with **extra-virgin olive oil**. Bruschetta is generally served as an **antipasto**.

BUCATINI see *dried pasta.*

BUTTER in Italy is never salted.

CABBAGES are large round or elongated heads of compact leaves that are generally green, red or white. Red cabbage, called *cavolo nero* (black cabbage), has very long, dark leaves and is especially used in Tuscany. *Cavolo cappuccio* (another name for red cabbage) is especially popular in Trentino–Alto Adige. The name means "hooded cabbage" because of the shape of the leaves.

CABBAGE, SAVOY, is a variety of cabbage with green, curly leaves and a pronounced, full flavor. It takes its name from the House of Savoy (*Savoia* in Italian, *Savoie* in French), a Western European dynasty that ruled parts of Italy until 1946.

CACIOCAVALLO is a hard, white cow's milk cheese from southern Italy. It is a bulk cheese with a rather strong taste and light rind that gives it good storage properties.

CALAMARI are squid. They are called *calamaretti* if they are small. *Seppie* are cuttlefish. See also *squid* and *cuttlefish*.

CANNELLINI see *beans*.

CAPERS are the unopened flower buds of a shrub native to the Mediterranean. The buds, which range in size from very tiny to about the size of a pea, are preserved in vinegar in jars (called brine-cured) or packed in salt in wooden boxes. Capers in vinegar are readily found on the shelves of food stores; capers in salt are available in Italian shops. If working with the latter, rinse them briefly in cold water before using.

CARDOON, a vegetable popular especially in central Italy and Piedmont, is related to the artichoke and looks somewhat like an overgrown celery plant. The tenderest cardoons (*cardi* in Italian) are those that have been wrapped in paper as they grow, to produce white stalks. Green cardoons are tougher and their flavor is less delicate.

CARPACCIO is generally a cold dish of raw meat that has been sliced paper-thin and dressed with olive oil and lemon juice. Various seasonings may be added, such as flakes of **Parmesan cheese**, chopped lemon zest or parsley. It was named after the famous Venetian painter by the proprietor of Harry's Bar in Venice, but its origin is definitely Piedmontese. The term is now being applied to other dishes made of raw fish or vegetables dressed with similar ingredients.

CAUL FAT is the fat-ribbed transparent membrane that holds the organs of the abdominal cavity of mammals in place. It is used as a wrapping for meats to keep them moist as they cook. Caul fat can sometimes be found fresh, but more often frozen, in better meat markets and butcher shops.

CECI see *beans*.

CELERIAC (celery root) is called either *sedano rapa* (celery root) or *sedano di Verona* (Verona celery), the latter because it was traditionally grown near that Veneto city. This large, knobby root vegetable was cultivated from wild celery; a separate plant is grown for the crisp stalks. The intriguing, refreshing flavor of celeriac makes it a favorite in salads, but it can also be cooked as a side dish or puréed into soups.

CHIANTI is the name of an area that lies between Siena and Florence and is also the name of the wine produced there. Chianti Classico, one of the finest wines in Italy, is a DOCG wine (*Denominazione d'Origine Controllata e Garantita*), meaning that it complies with the strictest regulations set by the government concerning grape variety, geographic origin, aging requirements and so on. It is produced in the heartland of the Chianti region and is aged not less than 12 months according to the new rule instituted in 1996. Chianti Classico Riserva is a higher-quality Chianti Classico and must be aged not less than 2 years. Chianti wine is principally made from the Sangiovese grape, usually with the addition of Canaiolo, Trebbiano or other grapes; the exact proportions of the varieties depend upon the type of Chianti being bottled. Any good-quality, full-bodied, dry red wine may be substituted.

COARSE-GRAINED CORNMEAL is most commonly eaten in Italy in the form of **polenta**, a thick, hot porridge that can also be cooled, sliced and fried or grilled. (Polenta can also be made from other ingredients, including barley or chestnuts). Look for coarse-grained yellow cornmeal sold under the name polenta or *granturco* in Italian food stores and well-stocked food markets. If unavailable, use any coarsely ground cornmeal, yellow or white.

COGNAC is a spirit distilled from wine produced in the Cognac region of France. It is sometimes used to flavor Italian desserts or sauces. Other good-quality dry wine–based brandies can be substituted.

CONCHIGLIE see *dried pasta*.

COOKING UTENSILS are described in Italian in different ways. More important than the terminology is the material: different types are suitable for different methods of cooking. *Tegame,* a round, wide, shallow pan usually of terra-cotta, is used for cooking sauces, braising meats and stewing vegetables. Terra-cotta pans diffuse the heat particularly well. *Padella* is a frying pan, usually of cast iron, used above all for deep-frying and for sautéing sliced meat or vegetables. *Teglia,* a round, wide, shallow pan of copper, aluminum or stainless steel, has two handles and is suitable for braising or roasting meat and vegetables. *Casseruola* is a saucepan with tall sides. Italians cook in heavy aluminum when the object is for the food (usually meat) to stick to the bottom of the pan, so that browned bits can then be scraped up by stirring in stock or wine at the end of cooking to form a sauce or gravy, a process known as deglazing. Stainless steel is used for **risotto***,* soups, stocks, tomato sauce, and for boiling pasta, meat or fish. Often, the cooking utensil appears as part of the recipe name, as in *teglia di patate al formaggio.*

CORNMEAL see *coarse-grained cornmeal.*

COSTATA is a large T-bone steak. Cut from young beef, it is a famous Florentine specialty. Everywhere except in Tuscany it is called *bistecca alla fiorentina.*

COSTOLETTE (cutlets) are thick slices of meat cut from the bony part of the animal, particularly the ribs (hence the name, *costolette,* from *costole,* or "ribs"). The meat close to the bone is always tastier and more tender. Cutlets are normally cooked in butter or oil after they have been dipped in egg and coated with bread crumbs.

COUNTRY BREAD should be coarse-textured, dense and chewy, with a crunchy crust. Throughout Italy, the wonderful tradition of local baking has yielded endless versions of good bread.

CRANBERRY BEANS see *beans.*

CREAM in Italy is of only one kind. It is not a thickened cream and is always used fresh.

CROSTATA is the term used to describe a tart made with a buttery crust and topped with a sweet filling, typically apricot, cherry, plum jam or marmalade.

CROSTONI are a popular antipasto. They are large slices of bread that have been toasted in a broiler (griller) or over a charcoal fire, or fried, then spread with a topping. If the bread slices are small, they are called *crostini.*

CUTTLEFISH is a marine mollusk that looks very much like a **squid** but with a broader, thicker oval body. It has prominent eyes on a wide head, ten tentacles and an ink sac. Cleaned and cooked in much the same way as squid, cuttlefish are enjoyed in Italy, Spain, Greece and many Asian countries. Look for cuttlefish in fish markets that cater to Asian or southern European communities.

DRAGONCELLO see *tarragon.*

DRIED MUSHROOMS in Italy always means dried **porcini** mushrooms, which grow wild in chestnut or oak woods.

DRIED PASTA, made from water and hard-wheat durum flour, comes in infinite varieties in Italy, known by infinite names according to region. Found particularly in the south, dried pasta takes oil-based sauces, often with tomato, vegetables or fish. The definitions below describe the shapes used in recipes in this book; many other shapes can be substituted.

Dried pasta must be cooked until **al dente**, and as soon as it is drained the prepared sauce should be mixed with it. *Bucatini,* also known as *perciatelli,* are hollow, spaghettilike rods. *Conchiglie* are medium-sized, shell-shaped pasta. *Farfalle* derive their name from the butterflies they are made to resemble (also called bow ties). *Farfalline* are small butterfly-shaped pasta that are often served in soups. *Lasagne* are squares of fresh or dried pasta that are boiled in water, then drained and layered with various sauces. *Linguine,* meaning "small tongues," are long, narrow ribbons of pasta that are slightly rounded on one side with the other side flat; also available fresh. *Tagliatelle,* also called *fettuccine,* are long, narrow, flat ribbons that are available fresh as well. *Orecchiette* are slightly concave pasta shapes made by forming balls of dough with the hands and pressing a hollow into the center of each to form a "little ear." Today this pasta is more often available dried. *Penne* means "quills," and these tubes of pasta have angled ends resembling pen nibs. They are available smooth or ridged *(rigate). Pennette* are small penne pasta. *Spaghetti* may be the most common

dried pasta shape. These thin strands derive their name from the word *spago* (string). A very thin spaghetti, called *spaghettini,* is also available. *Vermicelli* are very thin strands of pasta (the name means "little worms"). Dried *capelli d'angelo* (angel's hair) pasta can be substituted when vermicelli are called for.

EGGPLANTS (aubergines) are called *melanzane* in Italy and are usually elongated ovals and not too large. In other areas, look for small- to medium-sized globe eggplants with firm, glossy skin, or use slender (Asian) eggplants.

EGGS, HARD-COOKED, are made by placing eggs in a saucepan with cold water to cover by 1 inch (2.5 cm). Bring to a boil, then remove from the heat. Cover the pan and let stand for about 10 minutes. Transfer the eggs to cold water until cool, then peel.

EMMENTALER is a type of Swiss cheese that is also used in some contemporary Italian dishes. Good for grating and shredding, this dense cheese can also be cut into matchstick-sized pieces and tossed in salads. It has a nutty flavor and small- to medium-sized holes. Often called Swiss cheese in the United States.

ESCAROLE, also known as Batavian endive, is a variety of chicory with refreshingly bitter leaves. *Scarola* (the Italian name) is used raw in salads or is cooked and used in *torte* (savory tarts) and other vegetable dishes.

EXTRA-VIRGIN OLIVE OIL *(olio extravergine d'oliva)* is made from the first-pressing of olives that are hand-picked to avoid bruising. It is the purest type of olive oil and cannot exceed 1 percent acidity. Oil from Tuscany is the most famous and it is delicious, but superb oils also come from Liguria, Lake Garda (Lombardy and the Veneto), Umbria, the Marches and Lazio. Apulia produces more oil than any Italian region, and much of it is now of high quality. See also *frantoio.*

FARFALLE see *dried pasta.*

FARFALLINE see *dried pasta.*

FARRO see *spelt.*

FAVA BEANS see *beans.*

FENNEL, known in Italian as *finocchio* and sometimes in English as Florence fennel, is a crisp bulb with an anise flavor that is eaten raw in salads or cooked in vegetable dishes, sauces, stews and soups. The rounder male bulb, with its milder flavor and more tender texture, is preferred for salads; the more elongated female bulb is usually cooked. For fennel to be white, the plant must be continuously covered with earth as it grows. *Finocchio selvatico,* or wild fennel, is an herb that grows spontaneously in parts of Italy, but is at its best in Sicily, where it is an essential ingredient in *pasta con le sarde,* pasta served with a sauce of fennel, fresh sardines, raisins and almonds.

FENNEL SEEDS are small, greenish brown seeds from a variety of fennel known as common fennel, a close relative of Florence fennel (see *fennel*). Used as a spice, they add a mild anise flavor. They are often used to flavor mild Italian sausage.

FIGS are prized throughout the Mediterranean and are one of the world's oldest cultivated fruits. Both white and purple figs are eaten in Italy. The "white" one is actually pale green in color. *Fichi,* as they are called in Italian, are found in various regions from June until September. As a deliciously simple antipasto, serve peeled, halved fresh figs with slices of **prosciutto.**

FINOCCHIO see *fennel*.

FOCACCIA is the delicious crunchy bread of Liguria, made with flour, water, yeast, olive oil and salt. Additional ingredients may be added to focaccia, including sage, rosemary, onions or olives. Traditional *focaccia col formaggio* is somewhat different: soft cheese is baked between two sheets of dough. An updated version, with cheese placed on top, can be found on page 212.

FONTINA CHEESE is the pride of the Valle d'Aosta. This cow's milk cheese has a nutty flavor and wonderful melting properties, making it ideal for fondue. Fontina is at its peak at 3 months old, and cheese made in the summer months is particularly prized because the cows have grazed on Alpine grass rather than hay. A cheese produced in Scandinavia called Fontina has little resemblance to the genuine article and is not an acceptable substitute.

FRANTOIO is a mill where olives are pressed as soon as possible after picking. To make extra-virgin olive oil, the olives are pressed between two huge granite grindstones. The oil flows into a special bath and is then passed through a paper filter to rid it of any impurities.

FRESH PASTA is worth making at home. Although commercially made fresh pasta is available, the quality of homemade pasta is always preferable. It is most easily made with a hand-cranked pasta machine that rolls out the dough into very thin sheets for cutting into noodles of any width or for forming stuffed pastas. (Electric machines work well, too, but are expensive; manual ones, in contrast, are quite reasonably priced.) You will need to feed the dough, a small piece at a time, through the machine's rollers, beginning with the rollers set at their widest opening and gradually adjusting them to narrower settings until the desired thickness is achieved. At each degree of thickness, the dough should be put through the rollers until it is smooth and elastic, dusting it lightly with flour whenever it becomes sticky. Once you have a thin sheet of pasta, the machine blades may be adjusted to the noodle width desired. Tagliolini, for example, would probably require the narrowest setting, while tagliatelle would call for a setting of slightly less than ¼ inch (.5 cm) wide. Rolling out pasta dough by hand is difficult for all but the most experienced cooks, as it is a challenge to produce a very thin, very even

sheet. If, however, no pasta machine is available, the dough can be rolled out on a lightly floured work surface. To make fresh pasta, follow the recipe below and cut it into the desired width.

FRESH PASTA

3 cups (12 oz/360 g) all-purpose (plain) flour, plus additional flour for working
3 extra-large eggs

✒ Heap the flour in a mound on a work surface. Make a well in the center and break the eggs into it. Beat the eggs lightly with a fork, then gradually work the flour into the eggs until a loose ball of dough forms. Knead the dough on a lightly floured work surface until smooth and elastic, about 5 minutes, adding more flour to the work surface as necessary to prevent sticking.
✒ Cut the dough into 4–6 equal portions. Using a pasta machine, roll out each portion into a very thin sheet. Feed the dough sheets through the cutters on the machine, using the wide cutters for tagliatelle and the narrow cutters for tagliolini. Lift a handful of noodles at a time, roll it into a little nest and place on a lightly floured kitchen towel to dry.
✒ To roll out the pasta by hand, dust a clean work surface generously with flour. Flatten the ball of dough with the palm of your hand and, using a rolling pin, roll it out thinly and evenly, always rolling away from you and rotating the round to keep it from sticking. Lightly sprinkle a kitchen towel with flour, transfer the dough round to the towel and leave to dry for about 10 minutes, or less if the air is very dry; it should be neither sticky nor dry.
✒ To cut the pasta, roll up the round into a cylinder, flatten the top lightly and, using a sharp knife, cut across the roll into strips ¼ in (.5 cm) wide for tagliatelle, and ⅛ in (2 mm) wide for tagliolini.
✒ Dry as indicated above. Cook the pasta as directed in the recipe.

MAKES ABOUT 1¼ LB (600 G) FRESH EGG PASTA; SERVES 6

Agnolotti are stuffed fresh pastas most typical of Piedmont but found in other versions in much of northern Italy. They vary in size from thumbnail to postage stamp to the dimension of a small handkerchief. Other filled pastas that are folded are known variously as *tortelli, tortellini, ravioli, anolini, anvein, marubini, casonsei* and *cappelletti,* depending on their size, shape, filling and place of origin. *Fettuccine,* a specialty of Rome, are slightly wider than tagliatelle (see below). *Lasagne* are pasta squares (also available dried) that are boiled in water, then drained and layered with various sauces. *Tagliatelle,* very thin fresh pasta strands cut about ¼ inch (.5 cm) wide, are a specialty of Emilia-Romagna. *Tagliolini* are very fine strands of fresh pasta cut from fresh dough passed through the finest cutters on the pasta machine.

FRITTATA, essentially an Italian omelet, is a dish of eggs cooked with other ingredients such as vegetables, cheese or even leftover pasta. A frittata is always cooked in a heavy cast-iron or nonstick frying pan, never in the oven. A similar mixture cooked in the oven becomes a **tortino**, which is drier in the center. A good Italian frittata must be *bavosa*—"liquid in the center."

FRITTURA can be deep-fried vegetables, meat, fish or sweet pastries, preferably cooked in olive oil.

GAETA OLIVES are small, salt-cured olives with wrinkled black skins. Small, black Greek or Spanish olives may be substituted.

GAMBERONI and GAMBERETTI are both names for shrimp (prawns). *Gamberoni* are large and *gamberetti* are small. *Gamberoni* are delicious grilled or cooked in fish stews. *Gamberetti* are perfect for pasta sauces or **risotto**.

GARBANZO BEANS see *beans.*

GELATO (ice cream) is one of Italy's most popular foods and one of the few that is eaten at almost any time of the day or night. It has less butterfat and a more concentrated flavor than ice cream from most other countries. The resulting sensation in the mouth is at once lighter but more immediate. The first gelato is thought to have been made in Sicily more than a millennium ago, an adaptation of the sherbet that was brought by the Arabs from North Africa. Sicilians added milk and local flavors such as citrus or almonds. In modern times, gelato flavors are divided into two categories: *crema* (made with either nuts, chocolate, coffee or cream with flavorings such as egg, vanilla or spices) or *frutta* (made with any one of a vast variety of fruits). In combining flavors, an Italian tends to have only *crema* or *frutta* flavors in his or her cup, although chocolate, vanilla or cinnamon ice cream is often paired with one or more fruit flavors.

GNOCCHI is a generic term for small dumplings served as a first course. They are made of potatoes, **ricotta** and spinach, cornmeal or **semolina**. Potato gnocchi are generally turned against the prongs of a fork to give them their characteristic ridges. *Gnocchetti* are small gnocchi.

GOAT'S MILK CHEESE is known by the generic name *caprino* in Italy. It is found in various regions around the country, although it tends not to be as popular as cow's or sheep's milk cheese. Goat's milk cheese is much prized in Piedmont and Valle d'Aosta, two of the three Italian regions that border on France, which eats much more chèvre than Italians eat caprino. Typically, goat's milk cheese is eaten young and soft, although in Piedmont it is often combined with either cow's or sheep's milk to make cheeses generically called *tome,* which are aged for several months.

GORGONZOLA, a full-fat cheese with green mold veins, was first made in a small town of the same name near Milan. Now most of it is produced in Novara in Piedmont. Both mild and strong varieties are available.

GRAPPA, a by-product of the wine-making process, was once a lowly, generic firewater made of grape skins that served to keep the poor warm during the cold months. In recent years, grappa has been transformed into a superb postprandial distillate, as producers have carefully selected the finest grape skins and handled them with great care to make a fragrant, intensely flavored drink. As often as not in Italy today, a grappa will be made with skins of one type of grape (Refosco or Picolit, for example) and will be called a *monovitigno* grappa. The best grappas come from northeastern Italy: Friuli–Venezia Giulia, the Veneto, Trentino–Alto Adige.

GREEN PEPPERCORNS are unripened berries from a vine that have been pickled in brine or dried. Originally found in French recipes, they appear occasionally in Italian dishes. Bottled or canned (tinned) peppercorns should be rinsed before using. Dried green peppercorns are used like white or black pepper to season dishes.

IN UMIDO is used to describe foods that are braised, stewed or sometimes steamed. Typically, when meat or seafood is cooked *in umido,* a small amount of liquid remains at the bottom of the pan that is used as a gravy. When greens or potatoes are cooked *in umido,* they are steamed or braised until tender.

JUNIPER BERRIES are the fruit of the evergreen shrub of the same name. The pungent, small, hard berries, which are a deep blue-black, are used to make gin and to flavor game and other meat dishes. They can be found bottled in the spice section of most supermarkets.

KALAMATA OLIVES are brine-cured black Greek olives packed in vinegar. They are a good choice if black Italian olives are unavailable.

LASAGNE see *dried pasta* and *fresh pasta.*

LEEKS are a member of the onion family. Known as *porri* in Italian, they are long and cylindrical with a pale white root end and dark green leaves. Always clean leeks thoroughly before use to rid them of grit and sand.

LENTILS *(lenticchie)* are small, disk-shaped dried brown, red or green legumes that are prized for their rich, earthy flavor when cooked. The best are said to come from the towns of Castelluccio in Umbria and Capracotta in Molise. Cooked lentils appear in soups, salads and as a side dish; they are delicious hot or cold.

LIMONCELLO is one of the most popular postmeal drinks in Italy today. It is made by infusing grain alcohol with lemon peels from Campania (especially Amalfi, Capri and Ischia) and then combining with sugar and water. Genuine limoncello has no added colorants, deriving its color and delightful flavor entirely from lemons.

LINGUINE see *dried pasta.*

MARJORAM, or *maggiorana,* is an aromatic herb very similar in flavor to oregano and used to season meats, sauces and soups. Crushing dried marjoram in the palm of your hand releases its flavor.

MARSALA WINE is a rich, amber, fortified wine produced in the Sicilian provinces of Trapani, Agrigento and Palermo. Its flavor can range from sweet to dry, and it is prized as an aperitif and a dessert wine as well as an ingredient in desserts. Any well-stocked wine shop will carry a selection of Sicilian Marsalas.

MASCARPONE is a creamy, rich, cow's milk cheese from Lombardy and Emilia-Romagna that resembles sweet butter but has a slightly brown rather than yellow tint. It is combined with ladyfingers or sponge cake, espresso and chocolate in tiramisù, but also makes a delicious dessert when a little Cognac or brandy is stirred into it. Because it is very delicate and highly perishable, genuine mascarpone (as opposed to commercial brands packed in plastic containers for supermarkets) is not produced in hot months.

MELONS in Italy are generally round, with a slightly lined skin and a pale orange color. They are very fragrant and are only to be found in late summer. Melon is often served with **prosciutto** as a first course.

MINESTRA is a soup with chopped vegetables, often with rice or the special small pasta made for soups. It may also be chicken or vegetable stock in which these small pasta shapes *(pastina)* are cooked.

MINT is a refreshing herb used to flavor sweet and savory dishes, especially in Lazio. Romans like to combine the flavors of mint and tomato, while other Italians combine mint with shrimp (prawns) and a touch of olive oil. It is used in various vegetable dishes today as well.

MORTADELLA is among the most popular of all Italian sausages, in Italy as well as abroad. Its distinctive pattern comes from the mixing of finely ground (minced) pork with coarsely diced pork fat. The slowly cooked sausage, which usually measures about 6 inches (15 cm) in diameter, is a popular sandwich meat and is sold at most delicatessens.

MOZZARELLA is a rindless white cheese traditionally made from water buffalo's milk. It is much sought after and becoming increasingly difficult to find. The only areas producing it are Salerno and Caserta. Mozzarella is now also commercially produced using cow's milk, but it has much less flavor.

MUSSELS are known as *cozze* in many areas, and in others as *muscoli* or *peoci*. A similar mollusk is called *dattero di mare,* or "date mussel"; highly prized and having an elongated light brown shell, it is found in the area around the Ligurian port city of La Spezia. To clean a mussel, scrub the shell under cold running water with a stiff brush. Grasp the beard—the cluster of fibers at the side of each shell—and pull it off swiftly.

OLIVE OIL see *extra-virgin olive oil.*

OLIVES are best packed in brine (a mixture of water and salt) or preserved in oil. Less delicate in taste are the olives preserved in vinegar. The black ones have the strongest flavor. In general, Italian olives are rather small. See also *Gaeta* and *Kalamata.*

ORECCHIETTE see *dried pasta.*

OSSOBUCO, braised veal shank (shin), is a specialty of Milan. Traditionally, it is served with *gremolata,* a mixture of lemon zest and parsley. The Milanese also love to eat the marrow from the bone. The name literally translates as "bone hole," a sign of how important this feature is.

PANCETTA is Italian bacon, usually a tightly rolled slab that is sliced crosswise to form spirals of meat and fat. In its most common form, pancetta is salt-cured pork belly, although a *pancetta affumicata* (smoked pancetta) is also made. Pancetta can be purchased in Italian shops and in most markets specializing in European foods. If unsmoked pancetta is unavailable, unsmoked bacon may be substituted.

PANZANELLA is a salad originally invented to use up stale bread. In the classic version, the dampened bread is mixed with tomatoes and onion and dressed with olive oil and a little vinegar. Occasionally tuna fish, capers and cucumbers are added.

PARMESAN CHEESE, which is made from cow's milk, is a hard cheese with a granular texture and a pleasantly sharp flavor. It is used in cooking and as a condiment, especially on pastas. True Italian Parmesan is produced between April 1 and November 11 in a region that stretches from Parma Province to Mantua Province on one side and Bologna on the other. The best is Parmigiano-Reggiano, marked clearly on the rind. A great deal of Parmesan is also made in the United States, Argentina, Australia and other countries with large populations of Italian descent. Parmigiano-Reggiano is quite expensive and other high-quality Parmesan cheese can be substituted, although it will not have the same flavor. Never purchase pregrated Parmesan cheese and do not grate the cheese until you are ready to use it, as the flavor of the cheese is at its peak immediately upon grating.

PARMIGIANO-REGGIANO see *Parmesan cheese.*

PARSLEY is available in two varieties, curly leaf and flat leaf (also known as Italian parsley). Although the former is more easily found in markets outside of Italy, the latter, which has a more pungent flavor, is preferred for the recipes in this book. The Italian name for parsley is *prezzemolo.*

PECORINO is the generic term for any sheep's milk cheese. It is popular in several Italian regions, but particularly in Tuscany, Umbria, Lazio, Abruzzo, Molise and Sardinia. The Tuscans like softer pecorino;

the freshest one is marzolino (made in *marzo*—March). The best Tuscan pecorino cheese comes from Pienza, near Siena. In Lazio there is pecorino romano, an aged sheep's milk cheese used for grating. Much of the pecorino romano actually comes from Sardinia, but they are easy to distinguish. The Lazio cheese has a slight greenish tinge because it is aged in tufa caves; the Sardinian cheese is whiter. These cheeses can be either nutty or sharp, and are ideal for pasta. Umbria, Abruzzo, Molise and Sardinia also have a great variety of shepherd's cheeses made with sheep's milk.

PENNE see *dried pasta.*

PENNETTE see *dried pasta.*

PEPPERS, SWEET (capsicums), are a sweet-fleshed vegetable that came to Italy by way of the New World. Unripe green and ripened red or yellow varieties are most common. Italian peppers are slightly sweeter and more slender than bell pepper varieties.

PESTO is the glorious sauce made from **basil**, pine nuts, olive oil, garlic and a mixture of **Parmigiano-Reggiano** and **pecorino** cheese. Pesto is the touchstone taste of Liguria, although it is now consumed throughout Italy. The word comes from the action of pounding ingredients with a mortar in a pestle. Although it refers specifically to this sauce, a pesto can be made with other ingredients as long as the name explains what is used. For example, *pesto di rucola* is made with arugula and *pesto di pesce* is made with fish.

PINE NUTS are small, ivory seeds, extracted from the cones of a species of pine tree, with a rich, slightly resinous flavor. The Italian name is *pinoli.*

PINZIMONIO refers to a way of presenting raw vegetables that involves dipping them in bowls filled with **extra-virgin olive oil**, salt and pepper. The Piedmontese version is *bagna cauda,* a cooked sauce made up of half butter and half olive oil, with a few fillets of anchovy and some chopped garlic blended in. A Neapolitan version—*acciugata*—features anchovies, olive oil and capers.

PIZZA is a bread from Naples that has been made in that city since antiquity. The dough is made with flour, water and a little yeast and is allowed to sit overnight before baking in a very hot wood-burning oven. It was traditionally made with cheese, oil and herbs. The tomato was only added in the early nineteenth century. Neapolitan pizza has a thin, crunchy crust that bears little resemblance to the thick, chewy pizza found elsewhere in Italy and in much of the world.

PLUM TOMATOES, also known as egg, Roma or pear tomatoes, are oval and are particularly suitable for making sauces because of their meaty flesh. If fresh, flavorful plum tomatoes are unavailable, canned ones may be substituted. Look for cans that contain whole, peeled plum tomatoes imported from Italy, as the Italian tomatoes have the finest, fullest flavor.

POLENTA is a typical northern dish made from **coarse-grained cornmeal** that is sprinkled into boiling water and stirred as it cooks. It must not be too firm when done, and is often served simply with fried sage leaves, melted butter and grated Parmesan. Or it may be served with meat, fish or vegetable sauces, or as an accompaniment to grilled sausages, small birds and the like. It can also be cooled, sliced and grilled or fried. Typically it is made with yellow cornmeal, but sometimes the Venetians use more finely ground white cornmeal.

POLPETTE are traditionally meatballs made of ground (minced) meat seasoned with herbs and cooked in tomato sauce, but the term can also be applied to other mixtures, such as cooked vegetables bound with eggs and rolled into balls. *Polpettone* is a meat loaf, and in Italy the center is generally filled with **hard-cooked eggs**, slices of **mortadella** or thin omelet strips.

POMEGRANATES are an ancient fruit of the Middle East that are a symbol of fertility and abundance. While not traditionally used in Italian cooking, they are found in some contemporary recipes. To seed a pomegranate, cut it in half, then, holding the fruit under water in a bowl, break it apart, separating the seeds from the rind. The seeds will sink to the bottom of the bowl. Discard the rind.

PORCINI is the common name of *Boletus edulis,* the most sought-after wild mushrooms in Italy. They come up in early autumn after the first rain, when, as the local farmers say, "the earth boils." The stalks are broad and pale and the caps thick and dark—the darker the cap, the better the mushroom. When buying them, make sure the stalks are firm. In autumn, porcini are thinly sliced and dried for use when out of season. Good-quality dried slices usually measure about 2 inches (5 cm) long.

PROSCIUTTO is raw, salt-cured ham that has been aged to produce moist, lightly veined, intense pink meat with an edge of fat. Imported Italian prosciutto is quite costly (the best is from Parma), but many domestic products are of good quality and can be used. Avoid prosciutto that tastes too salty, and buy only what is needed, as once cut, it dries out rapidly. Prosciutto can be found in Italian shops, delicatessens and many well-stocked food stores. If unavailable, substitute another raw, salt-cured ham, such as French Bayonne or German Westphalian; do not use a smoked ham.

PROVOLONE is a butter-colored cow's milk cheese found throughout southern Italy. It is often shaped like a bell or, more amusingly, shaped to look like a piglet. It is hung to age for several months to a year. It is a bit chewy and salty, and is delicious as an integral part of an antipasto. *Provola* is a smaller version of a provolone; when smoked, it is called *provola affumicata.*

RADICCHIO is a generic term for leafy vegetables that vary according to their place of cultivation. In Liguria and Friuli, they are a delicate green leaf lettuce with a slightly peppery taste. More commonly known outside Italy, however, is radicchio from the Veneto, which has red-and-white leaves and a sweet-strong taste. It is delicious in salads or grilled. *Radicchio di Treviso* is the most sought after. It is much whiter than other Veneto radicchio because it is whitened in a cellar under sand or compost. It has elongated leaves with long, soft white ribs and a dark red color just at the leaf tips. The more common type of Veneto radicchio is from Castelfranco Veneto (small and round like a ball, with wrinkly leaves and a rather bitter taste) and from Chioggia (very similar, but lighter red).

RAPINI see *broccoli rabe.*

RED PEPPER FLAKES come from coarsely ground dried red chilies. They are very hot. Traditionally, in Italy, a whole dried pepper pod or a crumbled dried pepper would be used to flavor oils or sauces, but red pepper flakes are more widely available.

RAVIOLI are small, stuffed pastas. Depending upon the region, ravioli can take different shapes, but generally they are small squares or rounds with crimped edges.

RICE cultivation occurs in the Po River Valley in an area stretching from Vercelli and Novara in Piedmont through Pavia and Mantua in Lombardy through Verona and Rovigo in the Veneto. Not surprisingly, this is also the part of Italy where rice is eaten most frequently: **risotto** is the classic *primo* in this zone. Different types of rice are grown here. Arborio is a popular short-grain white variety. It has stubby kernels that absorb a remarkable amount of liquid as they cook, resulting in round, plump grains that, because of their high starch content, become quite creamy when tender. Other varieties, with subtle differences in shape and starch content, are Baldo, Carnaroli and Vialone Nano (which is perhaps the most prized because it is relatively scarce).

RICOTTA is a very light cheese made from whey that has been cooked twice (*ricotta* means "recooked"). Traditional ricotta is made from pure sheep's milk; it is still found in Tuscany, Lazio and Sardinia. A far less tasty ricotta made from cow's milk is found in other Italian regions.

RISOTTO is a dish made from **rice** cooked in stock that is added gradually, so the rice remains just covered with liquid throughout cooking. The most suitable type of rice has an oval-shaped grain, with Arborio rice being the most commonly available. If Arborio rice is unavailable, substitute short-grain white rice. When cooked, risotto must be creamy but still firm to the bite and the consistency should be **all'onda**—that is, wavy—with some liquid remaining. From the time the stock is added, a risotto must be stirred constantly; also, it is not possible to stop the cooking and finish the dish at a later time.

ROMANO CHEESE see *pecorino.*

ROSEMARY, a hearty shrub that belongs to the mint family, has needlelike leaves, blue flowers and a strong, woodsy scent. Italian cooks regularly use it with roasted or grilled meats such as pork, lamb and chicken. It can be found dried in bottles on supermarket spice shelves or fresh in many vegetable sections. It is also easily grown in the home garden. The Italian name is *rosmarino.*

SAFFRON comes from the stigmas of the crocus, a flower that grows around L'Aquila in the Abruzzo region and is cultivated there specifically for saffron. Crocuses need rather cold winters and hot summers for their development. The most expensive saffron is sold in the form of dried whole stigmas, sometimes labeled "threads"; the less valuable powdered kind is more generally available. Spanish saffron can be used.

SAGE, called *salvia* in Italian, has gray-green leaves and a potent flavor. Tuscans like to add the coarse-textured, oval leaves to bean dishes and meats. Better food markets stock fresh sage year-round; dried sage is also available.

SALTED COD is cod that has been preserved by first salting and then drying. It is available both boneless and with bones and is most commonly found in Italian, Portuguese, French, Spanish, Greek and Caribbean markets. Sometimes salted cod is sold packed in small wooden boxes that hold about 1 pound (500 g); other times large pieces are stacked in a heap and you select the one you want. Before cooking salted cod, it should be soaked in cold water to cover for 24 hours, changing the water three or four times, to soften it and rid it of excess salt. (In Italy, where it is called *baccalà,* it is often sold presoaked.)

SAUSAGE, or *salsiccia* in Italy, goes by various names. In Lombardy and the Veneto, for example, it is called *luganega.* In northern and central Italy, as a general rule sausage is not spicy; ground (minced) pork is simply seasoned with salt and pepper and then packed into a sausage casing. Sweet pork sausage is a good substitute. In the south, sausage is often very hot. It may be thick or thin, long without links tied off, or fatter and divided into short lengths. The sausages of Tuscany are famous, particularly those produced in the Chianti area. They are fried and presented on a bed of beans cooked with tomato, oil, garlic and abundant fresh sage. See also sweet Italian sausage.

SCAMORZA is a pear-shaped, white, cow's milk cheese with a smooth, thin rind.

SCAMPI, also called langoustines or Dublin Bay prawns, are actually small lobsters found in Mediterranean and Adriatic waters. While these scampi may be hard to locate outside of those regions, widely available large shrimp (prawns) can be substituted.

SCHIACCIATA is a flat bread, about ½ inch (1 cm) thick, sprinkled with olive oil and salt. It is sometimes flavored with herbs, or in Tuscany, covered with wine grapes.

SEMOLINA is coarse-grained, gold durum-wheat flour. It is an essential ingredient in certain Italian breads, and also in **dried pasta** and certain **fresh pastas**. Some bakers sprinkle semolina on baking stones to prevent dough from sticking.

SMOKED PROVOLA CHEESE see *provolone.*

SPAGHETTI see *dried pasta.*

SPELT (emmer), called *farro* in Italian, is an ancient variety of wheat with small, reddish brown grains. The early Romans made a dish called *puls,* which was something like a **polenta**, made of ground spelt. Spelt is still popular in Lazio and Umbria but above all in the Garfagnana, an area of Lucchesia. It is sold in well-stocked Italian shops and some health-food stores.

SPIEDINI, which are similar to kabobs, are made from pieces of meat, sausage, bread or vegetables such as eggplants (aubergines) and peppers (capsicums). They are nearly always cooked over the embers of a wood fire. Butchers in Italy sell meat kabobs already prepared, especially in autumn and winter when fires are lit in the open hearths.

SPRINGFORM PANS are high, round, straight-sided baking pans with removable sides held in place by a clamp. They are used primarily for baking cakes and tortes. Because diameter widths vary from manufacturer to manufacturer, a recipe calling for a 9-inch springform pan should be made in a 21-centimeter pan outside the United States.

SQUID are mollusks with a thin, transparent cuttlebone running down the middle of the body. They contain an ink sac that releases its contents as a defense mechanism; it is this dark ink that is sometimes used to color pasta or pasta sauces or **risotto**. Unless very tiny, squid must be cleaned before cooking.

SWEET ITALIAN SAUSAGE in northern Italy is a fresh link sausage made from pork seasoned with black pepper. In southern Italy, it is seasoned with fennel and garlic, and a hot version includes red chili pepper in the mixture. Italian sausage is available in Italian shops and well-stocked food stores or butcher shops. See also *sausage.*

SWISS CHARD (silverbeet) is called *bietola* in Italy. The stalks of Swiss chard are served in many ways—with a sauce, with butter and cheese, boiled and dressed with oil, and so on. The leaves are used in pasta sauces, fillings and in savory **tortas**. Red Swiss chard may be used as well.

TAGLIATELLE see *fresh pasta.*

TAGLIOLINI see *fresh pasta.*

TARRAGON, called *dragoncello* in Italian, is a popular herb in Siena but it is not commonly used elsewhere in Italy. It appears in soups and sauces, and, more recently, with pasta such as **lasagne**.

THYME is a fragrant, small-leaved herb called *timo* in Italian. Unlike many other fresh herbs, thyme still retains much flavor when dried.

TOMATOES, available in summer, vary in size from the large salad tomato to the small cherry tomato. At other times **plum (Roma) tomatoes** are best for sauces. While tomatoes are often associated with Italian cooking, they are in fact a relative newcomer to the country, having crossed the ocean from the New World in the seventeenth century. The Italian name for tomato—*pomodoro*—means "golden apple," a result of the yellow color of the original tomatoes.

To peel fresh tomatoes, cut the core from the stem end. Make a shallow X in skin at base. Submerge for about 20 seconds in boiling water. Remove and dip in cold water. Starting at X, peel skin with fingertips or a knife.

TOMATO PURÉE is available canned in most markets. To make fresh tomato purée, peel and seed ripe tomatoes, then purée in a blender or in a food processor fitted with the metal blade, or seed tomatoes and pass through a food mill.

TORTA is a broadly used term for sweet and savory baked dishes. Sometimes the dish includes a crust and sometimes it is more cakelike.

TORTINO is similar to a **frittata**. It differs from the frittata, however, in that it is sometimes cooked in the oven or, if over direct heat, on one side only, until the eggs are almost set but still very moist on top.

TUNA is available fresh and canned. Canned tunas from Italy are packed in olive oil, which give the fish a more complex flavor. American brands of tuna are generally packed in water or vegetable oil.

VERMICELLI see *dried pasta.*

VIN SANTO is a Tuscan dessert wine produced from Trebbiano and Malvasia grapes. Pleasantly sweet and smooth, this brilliant amber wine is traditionally served with hard **biscotti** for dipping. It can be found in better wine shops.

ZUCCHINI FLOWERS are called *fiori di zucca* and are plentiful in Italy when zucchini begin to grow. Usually the male flower—not the female, which goes on to produce the vegetable—is used for cooking. It is recognized by its thinner stem. Zucchini flowers must be picked and eaten while they are still firmly closed.

ZUPPA is a soup, typically of vegetables or seafood. It is often poured over slices of bread that have been browned in the oven or fried in olive oil.

Illustration Guide

OLIVES. Ripe olives and gray-green leaves grow from the branch of an olive tree. The fruit is consumed throughout Italy, primarily in the form of olive oil (*olio d'oliva*). Extra-virgin olive oil comes from the first pressing. The fruit is also cured and eaten out of

hand or used as an ingredient in numerous sauces, toppings and stuffings. The importance of the olive is reflected in the worldwide use of the olive branch as a symbol of peace and goodwill.

GRAPES. Red grapes, ripe and luscious, will be pressed into juice for one of the hundreds of excellent wines made on the Italian peninsula and its islands. Like olives, grapes— in the form of wine—were a foundation of the ancient Mediterranean diet. Today, grapes (*uva*) are also cultivated as a table fruit or dried as raisins (*uvetta*). They are eaten in numerous dishes, from salads to breads to desserts.

FISH. With some 1,860 miles (3,000 km) of coastline and a vast network of inland rivers, streams, lakes and canals, Italy is a paradise for fish lovers. Fish are cooked in fairly simple ways so as not to disguise the flavor of the waters from which they were

caught. Whether in a mixed grill from Amalfi, a *brodetto* (fish soup) from a busy port or a pasta sauce from Sicily, the soul of the dish is the fish itself.

ROSEMARY. Just one of the many fresh herbs whose flavor and fragrance enhance Italian dishes, *rosmarino* is particularly popular with lamb, pork and chicken. The slightly resinous spiky leaves are stripped from their woody stems and chopped or strewn whole into the dish. Or the entire stem can be used as a basting brush for grilled foods, imparting its piny flavor with each stroke.

ARTICHOKES. Purple-tinged artichokes (*carciofi*) are native to the Mediterranean and play a justifiably important role in the Italian vegetable table. Young, tender artichokes are completely edible (the choke has not fully developed) and are often sliced and served raw in salads. In Rome, they are deep-fried or braised and paired with mint. Elsewhere artichokes may be boiled and served with mayonnaise; stuffed and baked; or served in pasta sauces or risotto.

FIGS. In the recent past, a fig tree in a garden in Palermo, Sicily, was reputed to be the oldest one in the world. The first fig tree probably grew in Asia Minor, and figs are mentioned in the Bible. Today, fig trees grow throughout Italy and the fruit is eaten

with passion—drenched with honey and baked for dessert, draped with prosciutto and served as an antipasto, dried and stuffed into pastries, or for the luckiest, plucked straight from the tree and eaten *al naturale*.

RADICCHIO DI TREVISO. This elongated, red-streaked chicory is one of the prized radicchio varieties grown in the Veneto. It has crisp leaves and a bitter flavor that offer pungency in a salad but that melt into sweetness when cooked. A traditional presentation calls for encircling the radicchio with pancetta and grilling it until the bacon crisps and the leaves wilt.

Acknowledgments

For their delicious and inspired contributions to the recipes in this book, LORENZA DE' MEDICI wishes to extend whole-hearted appreciation to: Emanuela Stucchi Prinetti; Maria Luisa de' Banfield; Graziella Brandolini d'Adda; Nanni Guiso; and Carlo Abbagnano.

FRED PLOTKIN acknowledges the love and support of his mother, Bernice, of his agent, David Black, and of his friend, Carol Field. The essays in this book are dedicated to the memory of his adored father, Edward, who died during the writing of this book and who loved Italy so.

STEPHEN ROTHFELD wishes to thank Hannah Rahill and Tori Ritchie for sending him on this magnificent Italian journey. He is grateful to the Consorzio Parmigiano Reggiano for arranging a visit with one of their cheesemakers, Dania and Umberto Lucherini of *La Chuisa* in Montefollonico for graciously opening the doors of their extraordinary kitchen and Angelo Lancellotti for showing him his bucolic garden in Soliera.

JANICE BAKER and PETER JOHNSON thank the following for providing props for the studio photography in Sydney: John Normyle, Paddington; Accoutrement, Mosman; Bay Tree, Woollahra; Hale Imports for Pillivuyt, Brookvale; The Art of Food and Wine, Woollahra; Fred Pazzotti, Woollahra; Liz Nolan, Karen Cotton and Chez Bunting.

WELDON OWEN wishes to thank the following people for their kindness and generosity in helping with arrangements for on-location photographs: In Vicenza, to Brita Dorst Gemmo and Iréne Gemmo for their time, patience and hospitality, and to Giuseppe Michelazzo for the use of his wonderful home and gardens. In Pedeguarda, to Graziella Brandolini d'Adda for her incredible hospitality and generosity in the use of the *Castelletto* kitchen and environs, and access to the *Osteria al Castelletto*. In Tuscany, to Jennifer Grillo for her unflagging spirit, delicious food and last-minute machinations; to Nico Grillo for the wine tips; to John Spratt for inspiration and translation; to John Meis for open-handed hospitality and the use of his home and property; and to Marcello Lago for the use of his farmhouse and kitchen. In Conca dei Marini, to Carlo Abbagnano for his kindness and generosity for the use of his wonderful property and kitchen.

Thanks to the entire staff and crew at Weldon Owen for helping put this book together, especially Tarji Mickelson, Jennifer Dalton and Katherine Cobbs. And special thanks to Meesha Halm.